Equity in Education

Equity in Education

Edited by
Walter G. Secada

The Falmer Press
(A member of the Taylor & Francis Group)
New York . Philadelphia . London

UK The Falmer Press, Falmer House, Barcombe, Lewes, East Sussex, BN8 5DL

USA The Falmer Press, Taylor & Francis Inc., 242 Cherry Street, Philadelphia, PA 19106–1906

First published 1989

British Library Cataloguing in Publication Data

Equity in education
1. Education. Equality of opportunity
I. Secada, Walter G.
370.19

ISBN 1-85000-404-8
ISBN 1-85000-405-6 Pbk

Typeset in 11/13 Bembo by
Alresford Typesetting & Design, New Farm Road, Alresford, Hants.

Printed in Great Britain by
Taylor & Francis (Printers) Ltd, Rankine Road, Basingstoke, Hants.

Contents

List of Contributors

Michael W. Apple is Professor of Curriculum and Instruction and Eductional Policy Studies at the University of Wisconsin–Madison. A former president of a teachers' union, he has been an elementary and secondary school teacher and has lectured widely in Europe, Latin America, and Asia. Among his many books are *Ideology and Curriculum, Education and Power*, and *Teachers and Texts.*

Patricia B. Campbell is Director of Campbell-Kibler Associates in Groton, Massachusetts. Campbell-Kibler is an educational consulting firm specializing in educational research and evaluation, and sex and race equity. She is the author of more than seventy articles, book chapters and books, and has developed eighteen multi-media packages.

Kerry Freedman is Assistant Professor at the University of Minnesota, Minneapolis. Her research is mainly focused upon the uses and representations of art in school. Her publications include articles in the *Journal of Curriculum Studies, Studies in Art Education and Visual Arts Research,* and in Popkewitz (Editor) *The Formation of School Subjects: The Struggle for Creating an American Institution* (Falmer Press).

Elizabeth Fennema is Professor of Curriculum and Instruction at the University of Wisconsin–Madison, also Associate Director of the National Center for Research in Mathematical Sciences Education. She has written and published extensively in the field of mathematics achievement and gender differences.

Carl A. Grant is Professor of Education in the Department of Curriculum and Instruction at the University of Wisconsin–Madison. He is author (with Christine Sleeter) of *After the School Bell Rings* (Falmer Press) and General Editor of the *Wisconsin Series of Teacher Education* (Falmer Press).

Glen Harvey is Associate Director at The Regional Laboratory for Educational Improvement of the Northeast and Islands, which is one of nine federally funded research and development laboratories throughout the United States. Dr. Harvey has previously served as the director of planning and policy development at The Network, Inc., co-director of WGH Associates, and acting senior associate at the National Institute of Education. She is the author of a number of articles on educational equity, restructuring education, and school improvement and reform.

Susan S. Klein is Senior Research Associate at the US Department of Education in the Office of Educational Research and Improvement Information Services. She has written extensively on the role and status of women and educational equity. In 1986 she received the Willystine Goodsell Award from the AERA Committee on the Role and Status of Women, Special Interest Group Research on Women and Education, and Women Educators.

Margaret R. Meyer is Visiting Assistant Professor in Mathematics Education in the Department of Curriculum and Instruction at the University of Wisconsin–Madison. Her particular research interests are in the area of mathematics achievement with reference to gender differences.

Jo Sanders is Director of the Sex Equity in Education Program of the Women's Action Alliance, New York City. She is author of *The Nuts and Bolts of NTU: How to Help Women Enter Non-traditional Occupations* (Carecrow Press) and (with Antonia Stone) *The Neuter Computer: Computers for Girls and Boys* (Neal-Schuman).

Walter G. Secada is Assistant Professor of Curriculum and Instruction at the University of Wisconsin–Madison. Since 1983 he has been Director of the Upper Great Lakes Resource Center which provides training and technical assistance to programs of bilingual education in the four-state region of the US. He has worked extensively in the area of mathematics education. Since 1988 he has been associate editor of the *Journal for Research in Mathematics Education.*

Steven Selden is Associate Professor of Education at the University of Maryland, College Park. His primary area of interest is in general curriculum theory and development where he focuses specifically upon the history of the Popular Eugenics Movement and its impact upon early twentieth century American Education. His book, *The Capturing of Science: Race Betterment, Eugenics and Education, 1900–1940*, is forthcoming.

Equity in Education: An Introduction

Walter G. Secada

The purpose of this book is dual. Our first goal is to help bring equity back into the fore of discourse within educational debates; our second is to move that debate forward by providing new insights into the nature of equity which build upon prior work in the area. In the recent past, within both the United States and Great Britain there has been a shift away from concern for those for whom certain social arrangements have resulted in an unequal distribution of goods — wealth as well as education — towards a concern for more efficient production in terms of economic, military and educational systems.

In the United States, that shift began with an effort by the Reagan administration to dismantle the Department of Education and to remove the federal government from education. Failing at that, federal policy towards education was articulated in a reorganized Department of Education, which took a deregulatory stance; in which standards of 'excellence' replaced those of equity; ability and selectivity replaced needs and access; social and welfare concerns were ignored as economic productivity took the fore; parental choice and private education replaced the neighborhood public school; state and local autonomy overshadowed federal interventions (Clark and Astuto, 1986). By refusing to go along with many of the administration's most extreme positions, and by tempering others, the Congress served a moderating influence in that process.

Adding to this climate were concerns about the quality of American education in the face of increasing economic competition from abroad. The specter of a 'rising tide of mediocrity' haunted *A Nation at Risk* (National Commission on Excellence in Education, 1983). In mathematics, American students — even the most able — were found to lag seriously behind their peers in most other industrialized nations, especially Japan (McKnight *et al.*, 1987).

Not surprisingly, calls for educational reform within the United States, pointed to the need for greater numbers of better educated students who will become a technologically literate work force and military and who will enable the United States to meet increased competition, economically and militarily. (National Alliance of Business, 1986; National Science Board Commission on Precollege Education in Mathematics, Science and Technology, 1983; Task Force on Education for Economic Growth, 1983). The rhetoric of these calls followed the rhetoric of production: schools were judged excellent based on their producing the desired kind of students, and students were expected to engage in work, even if it was termed academic (Tomlinson and Walberg, 1986).

Within that discourse, previous efforts for obtaining equity and/or equality of educational opportunity were faulted for the decline in educational standards. Tomlinson (1986) asked the rhetorically loaded question, 'Which way lies equity: making schools easy by routing students around academic courses, especially hard ones, or insisting that all children encounter the academic core even if some of them have a difficult time of it?' (p. 16), thereby linking efforts at equity with the threatened tide of mediocrity. It is hardly a wonder that the AERA Committee on the Role and Status of Women in Educational Research and Development (1983) likened the context of its equity concerns to being 'in a cold climate'.

Equity was not totally lost; rather, it was transformed by the rhetoric of 'excellence'. In this transformation, the very real disparities between men vs. women; Whites vs. Blacks, Hispanics and Native American Indians; and among socioeconomic groups which can be found along various educational indicators — school completion/dropping out, course taking, and academic achievement being the major ones — were used to help legitimate reform couched in terms of excellence, and for the *overall* populace. In this transformation, the original concern for the education of women, minorities and individuals from lower socioeconomic backgrounds was submerged to a concern for improving education for 'everyone'.

For example, there has been ongoing concern about the mathematics and science achievement and careers comparing men and women, minorities and whites (Cole and Griffin, 1987; Dix, 1987; National Science Foundation, 1986). Differences have also been found on various indicators used to compare the mathematics education for students from this country versus those from other countries (especially, Japan) (McKnight *et al.*, 1987). In response to these parallel sets of disparities, recent reports have provided detailed prescriptions for the mathematics which *everyone* should learn (Commission on Standards for School Mathematics, 1987; Romberg, 1983); yet, these reports fail to provide needed assurance that everyone – including women and minorities – will, in fact, learn that mathematics. This failure to attend to the specific educational requirements of women and minorities results in the default position, as articulated by Tomlinson (1986) of 'insisting that *all* children encounter the academic core (in this case, the reformed mathematics curriculum) even if some of them have a difficult time of it' (p. 16). Without steps to address those difficult times, equity has become little more than 'trickle down excellence'.

No one denies the existence of disparities; nor would anyone deny the real concern about the need to address them. The issue has been, and continues to be, how to interpret those disparities and what sorts of responses, in social and educational terms, should be made. This book is an effort to articulate one such interpretation – one based on equity in education – and to outline some responses which might flow from such a view. Equity, as a position, argues that these disparities represent an injustice in the educational system's distribution of its goods and that affirmative steps should be taken to remedy those injustices.

There *have* been efforts at keeping equity – unreconstructed, but certainly cognizant of the changes in current thinking – alive and in the scholarly, if not public, eye. Strike (1985) argued that *A Nation at Risk* represented 'a triumph of our nation's economic goals over its political goals, of economic efficiency over democratic participation' (p. 416). The American Educational Research Association has kept its committees on the role and status of (a) women and (b) minorities in educational research and development active (AERA Committee on the Role and Status of Minorities in Educational Research and Development, 1986; AERA Committee on the Role and Status of Women in Educational Research and Development 1983; *Educational Researcher*, 1986; Frary *et al.*, 1985; Tittle, 1985). AERA has also criticized the downplaying of equity within the current administration (Committee on the Role and Status of Women in Educational Research and Development, 1983) and it sponsored publication of a *Handbook for Achieving Sex Equity Through Education* (Klein, 1985). Similar efforts can be found elsewhere; for example, a special issue of the *British Journal of Sociology of Education* asked the question: 'Whatever happened to inequality?'

At its 1987 meeting, in Washington, DC, the American Educational Research Association sponsored a symposium entitled 'What is equity in education?' Intended 'to provide a critical analysis of the construct of equity as it is applied in education' (Secada, 1986), it included papers by Maxine Greene, Patricia Campbell, and Walter Secada. Discussants were John Ogbu and Steven Selden. We were pleasantly surprised by the interest in that session, in terms of audience size and subsequent requests for reprints. It convinced us and Malcolm Clarkson, Managing Director of Falmer Press, that there would be a real interest in an edited collection of original papers revolving around the topic *Equity in Education*. This book is the result of that effort.

This book can be read in different ways. The separate chapters represent a variety of views on equity in education. From Apple's analysis of the dynamics underlying the redefinitions of equity and equality, to Sanders' report from the field, one can see varying notions about what would constitute equity. In and of themselves, such variations represent robustness of thought and action. If, as Apple notes, the conservative restoration can accommodate a diversity of views — even some which are contradictory — so can the opposition.

Also, one can find common themes among the chapters. While Campbell argues for research paradigms that are broad enough to incorporate the views of all the groups which are involved in educational equity, Harvey and Klein propose a rather comprehensive framework for organizing that research. They suggest that this framework is general enough to be applied across different equity groups.

Secada's chapter argues that equity, while related to equality, should be viewed as a different construct, and that we need to articulate where equity and equality overlap as well as where they don't. Grant's chapter builds upon that distinction by looking for non-overlapping examples of equity and equality in the classroom through student-teacher interactions and the curriculum.

Both Freedman and Selden pose problems in how curriculum — within domains as seemingly disparate as art and science — has been used to legitimate unequal social arrangements of power, status, wealth and education. Taken together with Apple's chapter, all three provide insights into how equity is reconstructed by dominant groups in order to advance their interests without really addressing those arrangements which gave rise to equity concerns in the first place.

Fennema and Meyer look at equity in mathematics, following what might be considered the classic categories of equality of education — as do Harvey and Klein. Together with Sanders, Fennema and Meyer locate equity at the outcomes of education, and both remind us that, in Yates' (1986) words, 'education (is) a field of practice, not just . . . critique' (p. 130). Fennema and Meyer pose issues in terms of where our efforts should be directed: inputs, outcomes, processes. Sanders documents a rich array of researchable, as well as practical, problems in attempts to manipulate the educational processes in order to achieve equal outcomes.

Readers are also invited to look at these chapters to see if among them can be found conceptual stresses, problems and even contradictions which need to be addressed and thought through a bit more carefully. Recall that ours is an effort to restart and to move a debate forward, one which is couched in terms of equity and which is focused on how one should interpret existing disparities. To succeed, that debate needs to clarify its concepts, to take account of new thinking, to take account of (in Apple's words) what is true in the ideologies of the new right, and to articulate a vision for education that can provide alternative answers to the vision proposed by the right.

There are other themes which could be alluded to and other ways of seeing the interplay of ideas, theory, policy and practice within this book. Our hope is that they engage others — researchers, policy makers and practitioners — in thinking about and working towards equity in education. As others join in the hoped-for discussion, we might develop a stronger consensus on our goals, and move closer to answering — in reality as well as in theory — the question posed in the symposium from which this book developed: 'What is equity in education?'

References

AERA COMMITTEE ON THE ROLE AND STATUS OF MINORITIES IN EDUCATIONAL RESEARCH AND DEVELOPMENT (1986) 'Minority participation in the 1984 AERA annual meeting', *Educational Researcher,* **15**(3), pp. 12–16.

AERA COMMITTEE ON THE ROLE AND STATUS OF WOMEN IN EDUCATIONAL RESEARCH AND DEVELOPMENT (1983) 'Equity in a cold climate: New challenges for women and AERA', *Educational Researcher,* **12**(3), pp. 14–17.

BRITISH JOURNAL OF SOCIOLOGY OF EDUCATION (1986) Special issue: 'Whatever happened to inequality?' **7**(2).

CLARK, D. L. and ASTUTO, T. A. (1986) 'The significance and permanence of changes in federal education policy', *Educational Researcher,* **15**(8), pp. 4–13.

COLE, M. and GRIFFIN, P. (Eds) (1987) *Contextual Factors in Education: Improving Science and Mathematics Education for Minorities and Women,* Madison, WI: Wisconsin Center for Education Research, University of Wisconsin.

COMMISSION ON STANDARDS FOR SCHOOL MATHEMATICS (1987) *Curriculum and Evaluation Standards for School Mathematics: Working Draft,* Reston, VA: National Council of Teachers of Mathematics.

DIX, L. S. (Ed.) (1987) *Minorities: Their Underrepresentation and Career Differentials in Science and Engineering* (Proceedings of a workshop), Washington, DC: National Academy Press.

EDUCATIONAL RESEARCHER (1986) Special issue: 'The new scholarship on women', **15**(6) June/July.

FRARY, R. B., MCBEE, J. K., and WEBER, L. J. (1985) 'AERA opinions on women's equity issues', *Educational Researcher,* **14**(2), pp. 12–17.

KLEIN, S. (Ed.) (1985) *Handbook for Achieving Sex Equity Through Education,* Baltimore: Johns Hopkins.

McKnight, C. C. *et al.*, (1987) *The Underachieving Curriculum: Assessing US School Mathematics from an International Perspective,* Champaign, IL: Stipes.

National Alliance of Business (1986) *Youth 2000: A Call to Action* (Report on a national leadership meeting held 10 June 1986, Washington, DC). Washington, DC: Author.

National Commission on Excellence in Education (1983) *A Nation at Risk,* Washington, DC: US Department of Education.

National science board commission on precollege education in mathematics, science and technology (1983) *Educating Americans for the 21st Century,* Washington, DC: Author.

National science foundation (1986) *Women and Minorities in Science and Engineering,* Washington, DC: Author.

Romberg, T. A. (1983) 'Background discussion paper for the conference', in Romberg, T. A. and Stewart, D. M. (Eds) (1985) *School Mathematics: Options for the 1990s* (Proceedings of a Conference) (pp. 1–10), Washington, DC: Government Printing Office.

Secada, W. G. (1986) *What is equity in education?* Symposium proposal submitted to the American Educational Research Association for its 1987 meeting.

Strike, K. A. (1985) 'Is there a conflict between excellence and equity?' *Educational Evaluation and Policy Analysis,* **7**(4), pp. 409–16.

Task force on education for economic growth (1983) *Action for Excellence: A Comprehensive Plan to Improve our Nation's Schools,* Denver, CO: Education Commission of the States.

Tittle, C. K. (1985) 'Research agenda on sex equity in education: An agenda for divisions, SIGs, and AERA', *Educational Researcher,* **14**(9), pp. 10–18.

Tomlinson, T. M. (1986) *A Nation at Risk: Background for a Working Paper,* in Tomlinson, T. M. and Walberg, H. J. (Eds), *Academic Work and Educational Excellence: Raising Student Productivity,* Berkeley, CA: McCutchan. pp. 3–28.

Tomlinson, T. W. and Walberg, H. J. (Eds) (1986) *Academic Work and Educational Excellence: Raising Student Productivity,* Berkeley, CA: McCutchan.

Yates, L. (1986) 'Theorizing inequality today', *British Journal of Sociology of Education,* **7**(2), pp. 119–134.

How Equality has been Redefined in the Conservative Restoration

Michael W. Apple

Introduction

Concepts do not remain still very long. They have wings, so to speak, and can be induced to fly from place to place. It is this context that defines their meaning. As Wittgenstein so nicely reminded us, one should look for the meaning of language in its specific contextual use. This is especially important in understanding political and educational concepts, since they are part of a larger social context, a context that is constantly shifting and is subject to severe ideological conflicts. Education itself is an arena in which these ideological conflicts work themselves out. It is one of the major sites in which different groups with distinct political, economic, and cultural visions attempt to define what the socially legitimate means and ends of a society are to be.

In this chapter, I want to situate the concern with 'equality' in education within these larger conflicts. I shall place its shifting meanings both within the breakdown of the largely liberal consensus that guided much educational and social policy since World War 2 and within the growth of the new right and conservative movements over the past two decades that have had a good deal of success in redefining what education is *for* and in shifting the ideological texture of the society profoundly to the right (Apple, 1986 b; Giroux, 1984). In the process, I want to document how new social movements gain the ability to redefine—often, though not always, in retrogressive ways—the terms of debate in education, social welfare, and other areas of the common good. At root, my claim will be that it is impossible to fully comprehend the shifting fortunes of the assemblage of concepts surrounding equality (equality of opportunity, equity, etc.) unless we have a much clearer picture of the society's already unequal cultural, economic, and political dynamics that provide the center of gravity around which education functions.

As I have argued at considerably greater length elsewhere, what we are witnessing today is nothing less than the recurrent conflict between *property rights* and *person rights* that has been a central tension in our economy (Apple, 1982; 1986 a; 1986 b). Gintis (1980) defines the differences between property rights and person rights in the following way.

> A *property right* vests in individuals the power to enter into social relationships on the basis and extent of their property. This may include economic rights of unrestricted use, free contract, and voluntary exchange; political rights of participation and influence; and cultural rights of access to the social means for the transmission of knowledge and the reproduction and transformation of consciousness. A *person right* vests in individuals the power to enter into these social relationships on the basis of simple membership in the social collectivity. Thus, person rights involve equal treatment of citizens, freedom of expression and movement, equal access to participation in decision-making in social institutions, and reciprocity in relations of power and authority. (p. 193)

While there is some sense in which a concern for earlier uses of the concept of equity is visible in the struggle for person rights, on the whole rather than trying to guarantee that specific applications of a set of principles are just in an individual case (see Secada's interesting discussion of this in this volume) the extension of person rights is tied to a collective dynamic which over time changes the *basic* rules of the game, so to speak. It argues that, in general, all institutions from the paid workplace to the home, government, school and elsewhere are to be organized around a system of rules and human relationships in which democratic principles guide the interaction. Thus, it lies closer to a concern for establishing social practices which sponsor equality not only of access, but of outcome and, as well, *of maximizing participation in creating the rules which govern these social practices*. Its ultimate grounding resides in a faith both in extending democracy, often in radical ways, and in the desirability of such an extension's social effects on the core values and institutions of the society: on what Levine (1984) calls freedom, justice, equality, welfare and efficiency, and democracy and rights. A concern for the expansion of person rights, therefore, combines elements of both equity and equality, but leans more heavily towards issues of a more extensive restructuring of social life.

For my purposes in this chapter, however, I shall construe both equity and equality as part of a broader and more general constellation of concepts and historic tendencies dealing with increasing the range of institutions and people that are covered by formally democratic mechanisms (see also Bowles and Gintis, 1986).

It is not surprising that in our society dominant groups 'have fairly consistently defended the prerogatives of property', while subordinate groups on the whole have sought to advance 'the prerogatives of persons' (Gintis, 1980, p. 194). In times of severe upheaval, these conflicts become even more intense and, given the current balance of power in society, advocates of property rights have once again been able to advance their claims for the restoration and expansion of their prerogatives not only in education but in all of our social institutions.

The United States economy is in the midst of one of the most powerful structural crises it has experienced since the depression. In order to solve it on terms acceptable to dominant interests, as many aspects of the society as possible need to be pressured into conforming with the requirements of international competition, reindustrialization, and (in the words of the National Commission on Excellence in Education) 'rearmament'. The gains made by women and men in employment, health and safety, welfare programs, affirmative action, legal rights, and education must be rescinded since 'they are too expensive' both economically and ideologically.

Both of these latter words are important. Not only are fiscal resources scarce (in part because current policies transfer them to the military), but people must be convinced that their belief that person rights come first is simply wrong or outmoded given current 'realities'. Thus, intense pressure must be brought to bear through legislation, persuasion, administrative rules, and ideological maneuvering to create the conditions right wing groups believe are necessary to meet these requirements (Apple, 1986 b).

In the process, not just in the United States, but in Britain and Australia as well, the emphasis of public policy has materially changed from issues of employing the state to overcome disadvantage. Equality, no matter how limited or broadly conceived, has become redefined. No longer is it seen as linked to past *group* oppression and disadvantagement. It is simply now a case of guaranteeing *individual choice* under the conditions of a 'free market' (Anderson, 1985, pp. 6–8). Thus, the current emphasis on 'excellence' (a word with multiple meanings and social uses) has shifted educational discourse so that underachievement is once again increasingly seen as largely the fault of the student. Student failure, which was at least partly interpreted as the fault of severely deficient educational policies and practices, is now being seen as the result of what might be called the biological and economic marketplace. This is evidenced in the growth of forms of Social Darwinist thinking in education and in public policy in general (Bastian, Fruchter, Gittell, Greer, and Haskins, 1986, p. 14). In a similar way, behind a good deal of the rhetorical artifice of concern about the achievement levels in, say, inner city schools, notions of choice have begun to evolve in which deep seated school problems will be solved by establishing free competition over students. These assume that by expanding the capitalist marketplace to schools, we will somehow compensate for the decades of economic and educational neglect experienced by the communities in which these schools are found.[1] Finally, there are concerted attacks on teachers (and curricula) based on a profound mistrust of their quality and commitments.

All of this has led to an array of educational conflicts that have been instrumental in shifting the debates over education profoundly to the right. The effects of this shift can be seen in a number of educational policies and proposals now gaining momentum throughout the country:

1 proposals for voucher plans and tax credits to make schools more like the idealized free market economy;
2 the movement in state legislatures and state departments of education to 'raise standards' and mandate both teacher and student 'competencies' and basic curricular goals and knowledge, thereby centralizing even more at a state level the control of teaching and curricula;
3 the increasingly effective assaults on the school curriculum for its supposedly anti-family and anti-free enterprise bias, its 'secular humanism', and its lack of patriotism; and
4 the growing pressure to make the needs of business and industry into the primary goals of the educational system (Apple, 1986 a).

These are major alterations, ones that have taken years to show their effects. Though I shall paint in rather broad strokes here, an outline of the social and ideological dynamics of how this has occurred should be visible.

The Restoration Politics of Authoritarian Populism

The first thing to ask about an ideology is not what is false about it, but what is true. What are its connections to lived experience? Ideologies, properly conceived, do not dupe people. To be effective they must connect to real problems, real experiences (Apple, 1979; Larrain, 1983). As I shall document, the movement away from social democratic principles and an acceptance of more right wing positions in social and educational policy occur precisely because conservative groups have been able to work on popular sentiments, to reorganize genuine feelings, and in the process to win adherents.

Important ideological shifts take place not only by powerful groups 'substituting one, whole, new conception of the world for another'. Often, these shifts occur through the presentation of novel combinations of old and new elements (Hall, 1985, p. 122). Let us take the positions of the Reagan administration as a case in point, for as Clark and Astuto have demonstrated in education and Piven and Cloward (1982) and Raskin (1986) have shown in the larger areas of social policy, significant and enduring alterations have occurred in the ways policies are carried out and in the content of those policies.[2]

The success of the policies of the Reagan administration, like that of Thatcherism in Britain, should not simply be evaluated in electoral terms. They need to be judged by their success as well in disorganizing other more progressive groups, in shifting the terms of political, economic and cultural debate onto the terrain favored by capital and the right (Hall and Jacques 1983, p. 13). In these terms, there can be no doubt that the current right wing resurgence has accomplished no small amount in its attempt to construct the conditions that will put it in a hegemonic position.

The right in the United States and Britain has thoroughly renovated and reformed itself. It has developed strategies based upon what might best be called an *authoritarian populism* (Hall, 1980, pp. 160–61). As Hall has defined this, such a policy is based on an increasingly close relationship between government and the capitalist economy, a radical decline in the institutions and power of political democracy, and attempts at curtailing 'liberties' that have been gained in the past. This is coupled with attempts to build a consensus, one that is widespread, in support of these actions (Hall, 1980, p. 161). The new right's 'authoritarian populism'[3] has exceptionally long roots in the history of the United States. The political culture here has always been influenced by the values of the dissenting Protestantism of the seventeenth century. Such roots become even more evident in periods of intense social change and crisis (Omi and Winant, 1986, p. 214). As Burnham (1983) has put it:

> Whenever and wherever the pressures of 'modernization' – secularity, urbanization, the growing importance of science – have become unusually intense, episodes of revivalism and culture-issue politics have swept over the social landscape. In all such cases since at least the end of the Civil War, such movements have been more or less explicitly reactionary, and have frequently

> been linked with other kinds of reaction in explicitly political ways. (p. 125)

The new right works on these roots in creative ways, modernizing them and creating a new synthesis of their varied elements by linking them to current fears. In so doing, the right has been able to rearticulate traditional political and cultural themes and because of this has effectively mobilized a large amount of mass support.

As I noted, part of the strategy has been the attempted dismantling of the welfare state and of the benefits that working people, people of color, and women (these categories are obviously not exclusive) have won over decades of hard work. This has been done under the guise of anti-statism, of keeping government 'off the backs of the people', and of 'free enterprise'. Yet, at the same time, in many valuative, political, and economic areas the current government is extremely state-centrist both in its outlook, and very importantly in its day to day operations (Hall 1985, p. 117).

One of the major aims of a rightist restoration politics is to struggle in not one but many different arenas at the same time, not only in the economic sphere but in education and elsewhere as well. This aim is grounded in the realization that economic dominance must be coupled to 'political, moral, and intellectual leadership' if a group is to be truly dominant and if it wants to genuinely restructure a social formation. Thus, as both Reaganism and Thatcherism recognize so clearly, to win in the state you must also win in civil society (Hall 1985, p. 119). As the noted Italian political theorist Antonio Gramsci would put it, what we are seeing is a war of position. 'It takes place where the whole relation of the state to civil society, to "the people" and to popular struggles, to the individual and to the economic life of society has been thoroughly reorganized, where "all the elements change" ' (Hall 1980, p. 166).

In this restructuring, Reaganism and Thatcherism did not create some sort of false consciousness, creating ways of seeing that had little connection with reality. Rather, they 'operated directly on the real and manifestly contradictory experiences' of a large portion of the population. They did connect with the perceived needs, fears, and hopes of groups of people who felt threatened by the range of problems associated with the crises in authority relations, in the economy, and in politics (Hall, 1983).

What has been accomplished has been a successful translation of an economic doctrine into the language of experience, moral imperative, and common sense. The free market ethic has been combined with a populist politics. This has meant the blending together of a 'rich mix' of themes that have had a long history — nation, family, duty, authority, standards, and traditionalism — with other thematic elements that have also struck a resonant chord during a time of crisis. These latter themes include self interest, competitive individualism (what I have elsewhere called the possessive individual) (Apple, 1982), and anti-statism. In this way, a reactionary common sense is partly created (Hall, 1983, pp. 29–30).

The sphere of education has been one of the most successful areas in which the right has been ascendant. The social democratic goal of expanding equality of opportunity (itself a rather limited reform) has lost much of its political potency and its ability to mobilize people. The 'panic' over falling standards and illiteracy, the fears of violence in schools, the concern with the destruction of family values and religiosity, all have had an effect. These fears are exacerbated, and used, by dominant groups within politics and the economy who have been able to move the debate on education (and all things social) onto their own terrain, the terrain of standardization, productivity and industrial needs (Hall, 1983, pp. 36–7).[4] Since so many parents *are* justifiably concerned about the economic futures of their children — in an economy that is increasingly conditioned by lowered wages, unemployment, capital flight, and insecurity (Apple, 1986 b) — rightist discourse connects with the experiences of many working class and lower middle class people.

However, while this conservative conceptual and ideological apparatus does appear to be rapidly gaining ground, one of the most critical issues remains to be answered. How *is* such an ideological vision legitimated and accepted? How was this done? (Jessop, Bonnett, Bromley and Ling, 1984, p. 49).

Understanding the Crisis

The right wing resurgence is not simply a reflection of the current crisis as described above and by Hall (1983). Rather, it is itself a response to that crisis (Hall, 1983, p. 21). Beginning in the immediate post World War 2 years, the political culture of the United States was increasingly characterized by American imperial might, economic affluence, and cultural optimism. This period lasted for more than two decades. Socially and politically, it was a time of what has been called the *social democratic accord*, in which government increasingly became an arena for a focus on the conditions required for equality of opportunity. Commodity driven prosperity, the extension of rights and liberties to new groups, and the expansion of welfare provisions provided the conditions for this compromise both between capital and labor and with historically more dispossessed groups such as Blacks and women. This accord has become mired in crisis since the late 1960s and early 1970s (Hunter, 1987, pp. 1–3).

Allen Hunter (1987) gives an excellent sense of this in his own description of this accord.

> From the end of World War 2 until the early 1970s world capitalism experienced the longest period of sustained economic growth in its history. In the United States a new 'social structure of accumulation' — 'the specific institutional environment within which the capitalist accumulation process is organized' — was articulated around several prominent features: the broadly shared goal of sustained economic growth, Keynesianism, elite pluralist democracy, an imperial America prosecuting a cold war, anti-communism at home and abroad, stability or incremental change in race relations and a stable home life in a buoyant, commodity-driven consumer culture. Together these crystallized a basic consensus and a set of social and political institutions which was hegemonic for two decades. (p. 9)

At the very center of this hegemonic accord was a compromise reached between capital and labor in which labor accepted what might be called 'the logic of profitability and markets as the guiding principles of resource allocation'. In return they received 'an assurance that minimal living standards, trade union rights and liberal democratic rights would be protected' (Bowles, 1982, p. 51). These democratic rights were further extended to the poor, women, and people of color as these groups expanded their own struggles to overcome racially and sexually discriminatory practices (Hunter, 1987, p. 12). Yet, this extension of (limited) rights could not last, given the economic and ideological crises that soon beset American society, a set of crises that challenged the very core of the social democratic accord.

The dislocations of the 1960s and 1970s — the struggle for racial and sexual equality, military adventures such as Vietnam, Watergate, the resilience of the economic crisis — produced both shock and fear. 'Mainstream culture' was shaken to its very roots in many ways. Widely shared notions of family, community, and nation were dramatically altered. Just as importantly, no new principle of cohesion emerged that was sufficiently compelling to recreate a cultural center. As economic, political, and valuative stability (and military supremacy) seemed to disappear, the polity was itself 'balkanized'. Social movements based on difference — regional, racial, sexual, religious — became more visible (Omi and Winant, 1986, pp. 214–15). The sense of what Marcus Raskin

(1986) has called 'the common good' was fractured.

Traditional social democratic 'statist' solutions which in education, welfare, health and other similar areas took the form of large scale attempts at federal intervention to increase opportunities or to provide a minimal level of support were seen as being part of the problem not as part of the solution. Traditional conservative positions were more easily dismissed as well. After all, the society on which they were based was clearly being altered. The cultural center could be *built* (and it had to be built by well funded and well organized political and cultural action) around the principles of the new right. The new right confronts the 'moral, existential, [and economic] chaos of the preceding decades' with a network of exceedingly well organized and financially secure organizations incorporating 'an aggressive political style, on outspoken religious and cultural traditionalism and a clear populist commitment' (Omi and Winant, 1986, pp. 215–16; Hunter, 1984).

In different words, the project was aimed at constructing a 'new majority' that would 'dismantle the welfare state, legislate a return to traditional morality, and stem the tide of political and cultural dislocation which the 1960s and 1970s represented'. Using a populist political strategy (now in combination with an aggressive executive branch of the government), it marshalled an assault on 'liberalism and secular humanism' and linked that assault to what some observers have argued was 'an obsession with individual guilt and responsibility where social questions are concerned (crime, sex, education, poverty)' with strong beliefs against government intervention (Omi and Winant, 1986, p. 220).[5]

The class, racial, and sexual specificities here are significant. The movement to create a conservative cultural consensus in part builds on the hostilities of the working and lower middle classes toward those above and below them and is fueled as well by a very real sense of antagonism against the new middle class. State bureaucrats and administrators, educators, journalists, planners, and so on, all share part of the blame for the social dislocations these groups have experienced (Omi and Winant, 1986, p. 221).[6] Race, gender, and class themes abound here, a point to which I shall return in the next section of my analysis.

This movement is of course enhanced within academic and government circles by a group of policy oriented neo-conservatives who have become the organic intellectuals for much of the rightist resurgence. A society based on individualism, market-based opportunities, and the drastic reduction of both state intervention and state support, these currents run deep in their work (Omi and Winant, 1986, p. 227). They provide a counterpart to the new right and are themselves part of the inherently unstable alliance that has been formed.

Building the New Accord

Almost all of the reform minded social movements — including the feminist, gay and lesbian, student and other movements of the 1960s — drew upon the struggle by Blacks 'as a central organizational fact or as a defining political metaphor and inspiration' (Omi and Winant, 1986, p. 164). These social movements infused new social meanings into politics, economics, and culture. These are not separate spheres. All three of these levels exist simultaneously. New social meanings about the importance of person rights infused individual identity, family, and community, and penetrated state institutions and market relationships. These emerging social movements expanded the concerns of politics to all aspects of the 'terrain of everyday life'. Person rights took on ever more importance in nearly all of our institutions, as evidenced in aggressive affirmative action programs, widespread welfare and educational activist programs, and so on (Omi and Winant, 1986, p. 164; see also Bowles and Gintis, 1986).[7] In education this was very clear in the growth of bilingual programs and in the development of women's, black, hispanic, and Native American studies in high schools and colleges.

There are a number of reasons the state was the chief target of these earlier social movements for gaining person rights. First, the state was the 'factor of cohesion in society' and had historically maintained and organized practices and policies that embodied the tension between property rights and person rights (Apple, 1982; 1986 a; 1986 b). As such a factor of cohesion, it was natural to focus on it. Second, 'the state was traversed by the same antagonisms which penetrated the larger society, antagonisms that were themselves the results of past cycles of [social] struggle'. Openings in the state could be gained because of this. Footholds in state institutions dealing with education and social services could be deepened (Omi and Winant, 1986, pp. 177–8).

Yet even with these gains, the earlier coalitions began to disintegrate. In the minority communities, class polarization deepened. The majority of barrio and ghetto residents 'remained locked in poverty', while a relatively small portion of the black and brown population were able to take advantage of educational opportunities and new jobs (the latter being largely within the state itself) (Omi and Winant, 1986, pp. 177–8). With the emerging crisis in the economy, something of a zero-sum game developed in which progressive social movements had to fight over a limited share of resources and power. Antagonistic rather than complementary relationships developed among groups. Minority groups, for example, and the largely white and middle class women's movement had difficulty integrating their programs, goals, and strategies.

This was exacerbated by the fact that, unfortunately, given the construction of a zero-sum game by dominant groups, the gains made by women sometimes came at the expense of Blacks and Browns. Furthermore, leaders of many of these movements had been absorbed into state sponsored programs which – while the adoption of such programs *was* in part a victory – had the latent affect of cutting off leaders from their grass roots constituency and lessened the militancy at this level. This often resulted in what has been called the 'ghettoization' of movements within state institutions as movement demands were partly adopted in their most moderate forms into programs sponsored by the state. Militancy was transformed into constituency (Omi and Winant, 1986, p. 180).

The splits in these movements occurred as well because of strategic divisions, divisions that were paradoxically the results of the movements' own successes. Thus, for example, those women who aimed their work within existing political/economic channels *could* point to gains in employment within the state and in the economic sphere. Other, more radical, members saw such 'progress' as 'too little, too late'.

Nowhere is this more apparent than in the black movement in the United States. It is worth quoting one of the best analyses of the history of these divisions at length.

> The movement's limits also arose from the strategic divisions that befell it as a result of its own successes. Here the black movement's fate is illustrative. Only in the South, while fighting against a backward political structure and overt cultural oppression, had the black movement been able to maintain a *de*-centered unity, even when internal debates were fierce. Once it moved north, the black movement began to split, because competing political projects, linked to different segments of the community, sought either integration in the (reformed) mainstream, or more radical transformation of the dominant racial order.
>
> After initial victories against segregation were won, one sector of the movement was thus reconstituted as an interest-group, seeking an end to racism understood as discrimination and prejudice, and turning its back on the oppositional 'politics of identity'. Once the organized black movement became a mere constituency, though, it found itself locked in a bear hug with the state institutions whose programs it had itself demanded, while simultaneously isolated from the core institutions of the modern state (Omi and Winant, 1986, p. 190).

In the process, those sectors of the movement that were the most radical were marginalized or, and this must not be forgotten, were simply repressed by the state (Omi and Winant, 1986, p. 190).

Even though there were major gains, the movements' integration into the state latently created conditions that were disastrous in the fight for equality. A mass based militant grass roots movement was defused into a constituency, dependent on the state itself. *And very importantly, when the neo-conservative and right wing movements evolved with their decidedly anti-statist themes, the gains that were made in the state come increasingly under attack and the ability to recreate a large scale grass roots movement to defend these gains was weakened considerably* (Omi and Winant, 1986, p. 190). Thus, when there are right wing attacks on the more progressive national and local educational policies and practices that have benefitted people of color, it becomes increasingly difficult to develop broad based coalitions to counter these offensives.

In their failure to consolidate a new 'radical' democratic politics, one with majoritarian aspirations, the new social movements of the 1960s and 1970s 'provided the political space in which right wing reaction could incubate and develop its political agenda' (Omi and Winant, 1986, p. 252). Thus, state reforms won by, say, minority movements in the 1960s in the United States, and the new definitions of person rights embodied in these reforms, 'provided a formidable range of targets for the "counter-reformers" of the 1970s'. Neo-conservatives and the new right carried on their own political 'project'. They were able to rearticulate particular ideological themes and to restructure them around a political movement once again (Omi and Winant, 1986, p. 155). And these items *were* linked to the dreams, hopes, and fears of many individuals.

Let us examine this in somewhat more detail. Behind the conservative restoration is a clear sense of loss: of control, of economic and personal security, of the knowledge and values that should be passed on to children, of visions of what counts as sacred texts and authority. The binary opposition of we/they becomes very important here. 'We' are law abiding, 'hard working, decent, virtuous, and homogeneous'. The 'theys' are very different. They are 'lazy, immoral, permissive, heterogenous' (Hunter, 1987, p. 23). These binary oppositions distance most people of color, women, gays, and others from the community of worthy individuals. The subjects of discrimination are now no longer those groups who have been historically oppressed, but are instead the 'real Americans' who embody the idealized virtues of a romanticized past. The 'theys' are undeserving. They are getting something for nothing. Policies supporting them are 'sapping our way of life', most of our economic resources, and creating government control of our lives (Hunter, 1987, p. 30).

These processes of ideological distancing make it possible for anti-black and anti-feminist sentiments to seem no longer racist and sexist because they link so closely with other issues. Once again, Allen Hunter (1987) is helpful.

> Racial rhetoric links with anti-welfare state sentiments, fits with the push for economic individualism; thus many voters who say they are not prejudiced (and may not be by some accounts) oppose welfare spending as unjust. Anti-feminist rhetoric ... is articulated around defense of the family, traditional morality, and religious fundamentalism. (p. 33)

All of these elements can be integrated through the formation of ideological coalitions that enable many Americans who themselves feel under threat to turn against groups of people who are even less powerful than themselves. At the very same time, it enables them to 'attack domination by liberal, statist elites' (Hunter, 1987, p. 34).

This ability to identify a range of 'others' as enemies, as the source of the problems, is very significant. One of the major elements in this ideological formation has indeed been a belief that liberal elites within the state 'were intruding themselves into home life, trying to impose their values'. This was having serious negative effects on moral values and on traditional families. Much of the conservative criticism of textbooks and curricula rests on these feelings, for example. While this position certainly exaggerated the impact of the 'liberal elite', and while it certainly misrecognized the power of capital and of other dominant classes (Hunter, 1987, p. 21), there was enough of an element of truth in it for the right to use it in its attempts to dismantle the previous accord and build its own.

A new hegemonic accord is reached, then. It combines dominant economic and political elites intent on 'modernizing' the economy, white working class and middle class groups concerned with security, the family, and traditional knowledge and values, and economic conservatives (Hunter, 1987, p. 37). It also includes a fraction of the new middle class whose own advancement depends on the expanded use of accountability, efficiency, and management procedures which are their own cultural capital (see Apple, 1986 a; 1986 b). This coalition has partly succeeded in altering the very meaning of what it means to have a social goal of equality. The citizen as 'free' consumer has replaced the previously emerging citizen as situated in structurally generated relations of domination. Thus, the common good is now to be regulated exclusively by the laws of the market, free competition, private ownership, and profitability. In essence, the definitions of freedom and equality are no longer democratic, but *commercial* (Hall, 1986, pp. 35–36). This is particularly evident in the proposals for voucher plans as 'solutions' to massive and historically rooted relations of economic and cultural inequality.

Will the Right Succeed?

So far I have broadly traced out many of the political, economic, and ideological reasons that the social democratic consensus that led to the limited extension of person rights in education, politics, and the economy slowly disintegrated. At the same time, I have documented how a new 'hegemonic bloc' is being formed, coalescing around new right tactics and principles. The question remains: Will this accord be long lasting? Will it be able to inscribe its principles into the very heart of the American polity?

There are very real obstacles to the total consolidation within the state of the new right political agenda. First, there has been something of a 'great transformation' in, say, racial identities. Omi and Winant (1986) describe it thusly:

> The forging of new collective racial identities during the 1950s and 1960s has been the enduring legacy of the racial minority movements. Today, as gains won in the past are rolled back and most organizations prove unable to rally a mass constituency in racial minority communities, the persistence of the new racial identities developed during this period stands out as the single truly formidable obstacle to the consolidation of a newly repressive racial order. (p. 165)

Thus, even when social movements and political coalitions are fractured, when their leaders are coopted, repressed, and sometimes killed, the racial subjectivity and self-awareness that were developed by these movements has taken permanent hold. 'No amount of repression or cooptation [can] change that.' In Omi and Winant's words, the genie is out of the bottle (Omi and Winant, 1986, p. 166). This is the case because, in essence, a new kind of person has been created within minority communities.[8] A new, and much more self-conscious, *collective* identity has been forged. Thus, for instance, in the struggles over the past three decades by people of color to have more control of education and to have it respond more directly to their own culture and collective histories, these people themselves were transformed in major ways (see, also, Hogan, 1982). Thus:

> Social movements create collective identity by offering their adherents a different view of themselves and their world; different,

> that is, from the world view and self-concepts offered by the established social order. They do this by the process of *rearticulation*, which produces new subjectivity by making use of information and knowledge already present in the subject's mind. They take elements and themes of her/his culture and traditions and infuse them with new meaning. (Omi and Winant, 1986, p. 166)

These meanings will make it exceedingly difficult for the right to incorporate the perspectives of people of color under its ideological umbrella and will continually create oppositional tendencies within the black and brown communities. The slow, but steady, growth in the power of people of color at a local level in these communities will serve as a countervailing force to the solidification of the new conservative accord.

Added to this is the fact that even within the new hegemonic bloc, even within the conservative restoration coalition, there are ideological strains that may have serious repercussions on its ability to be dominant for an extended period. These tensions are partly generated because of the class dynamics within the coalition. Fragile compromises may come apart because of the sometimes directly contradictory beliefs held by many of the partners in the new accord.

This can be seen in the example of two of the groups now involved in supporting the accord. There are both what can be called 'residual' and 'emergent' ideological systems or codes at work here. The residual culture and ideologies of the old middle class and of an upwardly mobile portion of the working class and lower middle class – stressing control, individual achievement, 'morality', etc. – has been merged with the emergent code of a portion of the new middle class – getting ahead, technique, efficiency, bureaucratic advancement, and so on (Apple, 1986 a).

These codes are in an inherently unstable relationship. The stress on new right morality does not necessarily sit well with an amoral emphasis on careerism and economic norms. The merging of these codes can only last as long as paths to mobility are not blocked. The economy must pay off in jobs and mobility for the new middle class or the coalition is threatened. There is no guarantee, given the unstable nature of the economy and the kinds of jobs being created, that this pay off will occur (Apple, 1986 b; Carnoy, Shearer and Rumberger, 1984).

This tension can be seen in another way which shows again that, in the long run, the prospects for such a lasting ideological coalition are not necessarily good. Under the new, more conservative accord, the conditions for capital accumulation and profit must be enhanced by state activity as much as possible. Thus, the 'free market' must be set loose.

As many areas of public and private life as possible need to be brought into line with such privatized market principles, including the schools, health care, welfare, housing, and so on. Yet, in order to create profit, capitalism by and large also requires that traditional values are subverted. Commodity purchasing and market relations become the norm and older values of community, 'sacred knowledge', and morality will need to be cast aside. This dynamic sets in motion the seeds of possible conflicts in the future between the economic modernizers and the new right cultural traditionalists who make up a significant part of the coalition that has been built (Apple, 1986 a). Furthermore, the competitive individualism now being so heavily promoted in educational reform movements in the United States may not respond well to traditional working class and poor groups somewhat more collective senses.

Finally, there are counter-hegemonic movements now being built within education itself. The older social democratic accord included many educators, union leaders, minority group members, and others. There are signs that the fracturing of this coalition may only be temporary. Take teachers, for instance. Even though salaries have been on the rise throughout the country, this has been countered by a rapid increase in the external control of teachers' work, the rationalization and deskilling of their jobs, and the growing blame of teachers and education in general for most of the major social ills that beset the economy (Apple, 1982; 1986 b). Many teachers have organized around these issues, in a manner reminiscent of the earlier work of the Boston Women's Teachers' Group (Freedman, Jackson and Boles, 1982). Furthermore, there are signs throughout the country of multi-racial coalitions being built among elementary and secondary school teachers, university based educators and community members to collectively act on the conditions under which teachers work and to support the democratization of curriculum and teaching and a rededication to the equalization of access and outcomes in schooling. The Public Education Information Network based in St Louis and the Rethinking Schools group based in Milwaukee provide but a few of these examples (Apple, 1986 b; see also Bastian, Fruchter, Gittell, Greer and Haskins, 1986; and Livingstone, 1987).

Even given these emerging tensions within the conservative restoration and the increase once again of alliances to counter its attempted reconstruction of the politics and ethics of the common good, this does not mean we should be at all sanguine. It is possible that, because of these tensions and counter movements, the right's economic program will fail. Yet its ultimate success may be in shifting the balance of class forces considerably to the right and in changing the very ways we consider the common good (Hall, 1983, p. 120; Raskin, 1986). Privitization, profit, and greed may still substitute for any serious collective commitment.

We are, in fact, in danger both of forgetting the decades of hard work it took to put even a limited vision of equality on the social and educational agenda and of forgetting the reality of the oppressive conditions that exist for so many of our fellow Americans. The task of keeping alive in the minds of the people the collective memory of the struggle for equality, for person rights in *all* of the institutions of our society, is one of the most significant tasks educators can perform. In a time of conservative restoration, we cannot afford to ignore this task. This requires renewed attention to important curricular questions. Whose knowledge is taught? Why is it taught in this particular way to this particular group? How do we enable the histories and cultures of the majority of working people, of women, of people of color (these groups again are obviously not mutually exclusive) to be taught in responsible and responsive ways in schools? Given the fact that the collective memory that *now* is preserved in our educational institutions is more heavily influenced by dominant groups in society (Apple, 1979), the continuing efforts to promote more democratic curricula and teaching are more important now than ever. For it should be clear that the movement toward an authoritarian populism will become even more legitimate if only the values embodied in the conservative restoration are made available in our public institutions. The widespread recognition that there were, are, and can be more equal modes of economic, political, and cultural life can only be accomplished by organized efforts to teach and expand this sense of difference. Clearly, there is educational work to be done.

Notes

1 I wish to thank Walter Secada for his comments on this point.

2 Clark and Astuto (1986) point out that during the current Reagan term, the following initiatives have characterized their educational policies: reducing the federal role in education, stimulating competition among schools with the aim of 'breaking the monopoly of the public school', fostering individual competition so that 'excellence' is gained, increasing the reliance on performance standards for students and teachers, an emphasis on the 'basics' in content, increasing parental choice 'over what, where, and how their children learn', strengthening the teaching of 'traditional values' in schools, and expanding the policy of transferring educational authority to the state and local levels (p. 8).

3 I realize that there is a debate over the adequacy of this term. See Hall (1985) and Jessop, Bonnett, Bromley and Ling (1984).

4 For an illuminating picture of how these issues are manipulated by powerful groups, see Hunter (1984).

5 For a more complete discussion of how this has affected educational policy in particular, see Clark and Astuto (1986) and Apple (1986 b).
6 I have claimed elsewhere, however, that some members of the new middle class – namely efficiency experts, evaluators, testers, and many of those with technical and management expertise – will form part of the alliance with the new right. This is simply because their own jobs and mobility depend on it. See Apple (1986 b).
7 The discussion in Bowles and Gintis (1986) of the 'transportability' of struggles over person rights from, say, politics to the economy is very useful here. I have extended and criticized some of their claims in Apple (1988).
8 I say 'new' here, but the continuity of, say, black struggles for freedom and equality also needs to be stressed. See the powerful treatment of the history of such struggles in Harding (1981).

References

ANDERSON, M. (1985) Teachers Unions and Industrial Politics. Unpublished doctoral thesis, School of Behavioral Sciences, Macquarie University, Sydney.
APPLE, M.W. (1979) *Ideology and Curriculum*, Boston: Routledge and Kegan Paul.
APPLE, M.W. (1982) *Education and Power*, Boston: Routledge and Kegan Paul.
APPLE, M.W. (1986 a). 'National reports and the construction of inequality', *British Journal of Sociology of Education,* **7**, 2, pp. 171–90.
APPLE, M.W. (1986 b) *Teachers and Texts: A Political Economy of Class and Gender Relations in Education*, New York: Routledge and Kegan Paul.
APPLE, M.W. (1988). 'Facing the complexity of power: For a parallelist position in critical educational studies', in COLE, M. (Ed.) *Bowles and Gintis Revisited*, Philadelphia: Falmer Press, pp. 112–30.
BASTIAN, A., FRUCHTER, N., GITTELL, M., GREER, C. and HASKINS, K. (1986) *Choosing Equality: The Case for Democratic Schooling*, Philadelphia: Temple University Press.
BOWLES, S. (1982) 'The post-keynesian capital labor stalemate', *Socialist Review*, **12,** 5, pp. 45–72.
BOWLES, S. and GINTIS, H. (1986) *Democracy and Capitalism*, New York: Basic Books.
BURNHAM, W. (1983) 'Post-conservative America', *Socialist Review*, **13,** 6, pp. 123–32.
CARNOY, M., SHEARER, D. and RUMBERGER, R. (1983) *A New Social Contract*, New York: Harper and Row.
CLARK, D. and ASTUTO, T. (1986) 'The significance and permanence of changes in federal education policy', *Educational Researcher,* **15,** 8, pp. 4–13.
FREEDMAN, S., JACKSON, J. and BOLES, K. (1982) *The Effects of the Institutional Structure of Schools on Teachers*, Somerville, MA: Boston Women's Teachers' Group.
GINTIS, H. (1980) 'Communication and politics', *Socialist Review,* **10,** 2/3, pp. 189–232.
GIROUX, H. (1984) 'Public philosophy and the crisis in education', *Harvard Educational Review,* **54,** pp. 186–94.

Hall, S. (1980) 'Popular-democratic vs. authoritarian populism: Two ways of taking democracy seriously', in Hunt, A. (Ed.) *Marxism and Democracy*, London: Lawrence and Wishart, pp. 157–85.
Hall, S. (1983) 'The great moving right show', in Hall, S. and Jacques, M. (Ed.) *The Politics of Thatcherism*, London: Lawrence and Wishart, pp. 19–39.
Hall, S. (1985) 'Authoritarian populism: A reply', *New Left Review*, **151,** pp. 115–24.
Hall, S. (1986) 'Popular culture and the state', in Bennett, T., Mercer, C. and Woollacott, J . (Eds). *Popular Culture and Social Relations*, London: Open University Press, pp. 22–49.
Hall, S. and Jacques, M. (1983) 'Introduction', in Hall, S. and Jacques, M. (Ed.) *The Politics of Thatcherism*, London: Lawrence and Wishart, pp. 9–16.
Harding,, V. (1981) *There is a River: The Black Struggle for Freedom in the United States,* New York: Vintage Books.
Hogan, D. (1982) 'Education and class formation', in Apple, M. (Ed.) *Cultural and Economic Reproduction in Education*, Boston: Routledge and Kegan Paul, pp. 32–78.
Hunter, A. (1984) Virtue With a Vengeance: The Pro-Family Politics of the New Right. Unpublished doctoral dissertation, Department of Sociology, Brandeis University, Waltham.
Hunter, A. (1987). The politics of resentment and the construction of middle america. Unpublished paper, American Institutions Program, Department of History, University of Wisconsin, Madison.
Jessop, B., Bonnett, K., Bromley, S. and Ling, T. (1984) 'Authoritarian populism, two nations, and Thatcherism', *New Left Review,* **147,** pp. 33–60.
Larrain, J. (1983) *Marxism and Ideology*, Atlantic Highlands: Humanities Press.
Levine, (1984) *Arguing for Socialism*, Boston: Routledge and Kegan Paul.
Livingstone, D. (Ed.) (1987) *Critical Pedagogy and Cultural Power*, South Hadley: Bergin and Garvey.
Omi, M. and Winant, H. (1986) *Racial Formation in the United States*, New York: Routledge and Kegan Paul.
Piven, F. and Cloward, R. (1982) *The New Class War*, New York: Pantheon Books.
Raskin, M. (1986) *The Common Good*, New York: Routledge and Kegan Paul.

Educational Equity and Research Paradigms

Patricia B. Campbell

In her classic children's book, *A Wrinkle In Time*, author Madeline L'Engle (1963) has her hero, Meg Murray, exclaim, at the book's climax, that 'like and equal are two entirely different things,' (p. 178). Meg's revelation that similarity does not necessarily mean equal and that difference does not have to mean unequal has been reflected in educational research as well. Educational researchers are questioning if equality and equity may also be entirely different things and what this means for educational equity and associated research paradigms. At least some of these implications can be summarized as a series of stages adapted from Kelly's (1976) model of women's history.

> *Stage I*: A examination of the female [minority] experience from a framework that originated in a masculine [white] consciousness. A documentation of sexism [racism] and efforts to remedy it.
>
> *Stage II*: A critique of the narrowness of the perspective of conventional modes of establishing social knowledge and a placing of women [minorities] at the center of the inquiry.
>
> *Stage III*: A questioning of the knowledge base itself, finding it neither relevant to the female [minority] experience nor adequate for explaining female [minority] behavior and a resulting reconceptualization of the disciplines.

Kelly's work related specifically to women and sexism, however a replacement of the terms 'female, masculine and sexism' with minority, white and racism, as has been done in the brackets, indicates that the model has the potential to be used for minorities and racism as well. This chapter seeks to investigate the degree to which Kelly's stages can be found in research focusing on issues of sex, race or ethnicity.

The Recognition of Bias in Research Methods and Attempts to Remedy it

With increased awareness of the impact of race and sex bias on society came an examination of the possible effects of bias on the areas of social science and social science research. Through this examination came the awareness that bias had a negative effect on all aspects of research from the selection of topics to be studied through the generation, and generalization, of conclusions. As early as 1899 DuBois charged that research on Blacks reflected the racism of its white authors rather than the reality of black lives. Through the 1960s and 1970s book such as *Racism and Psychiatry* (Thomas and Sillen, 1972) documented how research on Blacks emphasized pathology, showing, as Thomas and Sillen (1972) concluded, the black man as victim, 'a patient, a parolee, a petitioner for aid, rarely a rounded human being' (p. 27).

A 1973 analysis of studies of Blacks found that most researchers (82 per cent) 'blamed the victim', concluding that any Black/White comparisons, in which Blacks were found to 'score lower' or 'do less', were due not to racism, not to socioeconomic differences, not to anything other than individual shortcomings (Caplan and Nelson, 1973). These critiques concluded that Blacks were over represented when the pathological, the negative aspects of society were studied, and ignored when the 'human condition', the normal every day aspects of life and decision-making were studied. In addition when research compared Blacks to Whites, it was directed toward measuring and describing the deviation of Blacks from the normative characteristics of the white middle class (Hendricks and Caesar, 1985; Thomas and Sillen, 1972).

Important variables such as socioeconomic status and educational level were ignored rather than controlled and, in studies comparing Blacks and Whites, few even bothered to define, genetically, biologically or socially, what it meant to be Black or to be White. For example Jensen (1969) concluded that there was a genetic basis for Black/White differences in intelligence test scores but did not define what to be Black or to be White meant in genetic terms.

Even the conclusions of so many of these studies supported the stereotypes rather than the results (Campbell, 1988). One of the most famous examples can be found in the Moynihan report (1965) where his conclusions on the relative economic positions of black women and men were based on stereotypes not on his own data.

The assumption of equivalence between Blacks and Whites along research lines has received scrutiny as well. The equivalence of constructs, when applied across racial groups is of critical concern for conducting comparative analysis. Issues of construct validity have been found to arise not only in terms of whether the concept is applicable to what is being studied but also with respect to whether the conceptual definitions have equivalent, though not necessarily identical, meanings across racial groups (Hendricks and Caesar, 1985; Castenell, 1984).

Among those paying close attention to the work examining the effects of racism on social science research methods were women working on research issues related to sex. By the mid 1970s critiques of the effects of sexism on research and research methods appeared following the model used in criticizing racism (Ehrenreich and English, 1979; Parlee, 1975).

These critiques found that almost all studies done over men were generalized to women, while studies done over women tended not to be generalized to men. They also found that when women and girls were studied it was generally in terms of how they reflected (or did not reflect) the white male norm. And while socioeconomic status tended to be ignored in racial comparisons, women were studied in terms of their fathers' or husbands' socioeconomic status rather than their own. The tests and measures used were also found to be biased, measuring males and females skills, feelings and perceptions differently (Campbell, 1988). For example instruments measuring stress included masculine oriented stress experiences such as being drafted, but not feminine oriented stress experiences such as rape or abortion (Belle, 1980).

In a variety of areas including achievement motivation, moral development and stress, either male only or predominantly male populations, such as prisoners of war, football players or industrial employees, were studied (Belle, 1980). Conclusions were often found to reflect stereotypes to the possible exclusion of reality, such as the 'classic' study of infant behavior that concluded that boys try to solve a problem while girls give up; not mentioning other, equally plausible conclusions such as that the boys and girls tried to solve the problem in different ways (Goldberg and Lewis, 1969).

For those studying the effects of racism in research and those studying the effects of sexism in research, the question arose of how much of research was 'true' and how much was the result of researcher 'likes, aversions, hopes and fears'.

Based on the similarities of the effects of racism and sexism on research, it would not be unreasonable to assume similar findings in the area of national origin or language minority research. Such biased research does occur. For example in his 1987 monograph on research on bilingual Hispanic children, Dunn concluded that since Asian students are doing well in schools and Hispanic children are not, a great part of the problem is with the Hispanic children. He reminds the readers that many Mexicans and brown-skinned and Puerto Ricans are dark-skinned and then, concludes, without evidence, 'that about half the IQ difference between Puerto Rican or Mexican school children and Anglos is due to genes that influence scholastic aptitude' (Dunn, 1987, p. 64).

More subtle bias occurs as well, such as the exclusion of language minority subjects from the research. For example, a recent study from the Center for Educational Statistics on home computer use reported that 'persons in households without English speaking adults' were excluded while the results were generalized to young people in general (Ancarrow, 1987, p. 2). A 1986 study of sex differences in GRE performance excluded students whose first language was other than English 'in order to avoid confounding effects' (Ethington and Wolfe, 1986, p. 6). Similarly research has been done using Hispanics who were defined as such because they were 'Spanish surnamed'. Thus the children of Hispanic fathers were included while the children of Hispanic mothers and nonHispanic fathers tended not to be.

Yet little or no published criticism has been developed focusing on bias in research in terms of language minority populations. When, for example, Willig (1985) critiqued language minority research, she discussed such issues as inadequate research design and inappropriate comparison groups but did not mention any issues related to bias in the research methods, such as biases in the tests, definitions of who is an Hispanic or the types of questions being asked.

The analysis of the effects of racism and sexism on social science research used similar models and found a number of similarities including the over-generalization of results to groups not studied, the view of women and Blacks as 'other', and the interpretation of the results to fit existing stereotypes. There were differences found as well. For example unlike the work done on racism, criticisms of the effects of sexism went far beyond social science research to include diverse fields such as home economics, history, biology, literature, anthropology and even physics. And again while the critiques of racism focused primarily on quantitative methods, the critiques of sexism included a much broader number of methodologies including historiography, literary inquiry, ethnological research and even the traditional scientific method (Rosaldo, 1980; Schwager, 1986).

Underlying most of these critiques of the effects of bias on research, was a premise that even though the influences of racism and sexism were causing the methodologies to be incorrectly or inappropriately applied, the methodologies themselves were appropriate. In spite of the acknowledged biases and concerns about oversimplified designs as well as the misuse of results, the value of bicultural or cross cultural perspectives for the study of black populations remained recognized as did the value of studies of sex differences (Hendricks and Caesar, 1985; Castenell, 1984; Richardson and Wirtenberg, 1983).

With the documentation of the effects of race and sex bias on research methods and results came pressure to 'do something' to correct for these biases. In the social sciences the obvious 'next step' was the development of guidelines to reduce the effects of bias in research. Yet in spite of the earlier start of criticisms of the effects of racism, the great deal of research being done on race and the serious effects of racism on research results; most guidelines, including those developed for the American Psychological Association (McHugh, Koeske and Frieze, 1981), the American Sociological Association (Committee on the Status of Women in Sociology, 1980) and the Public Health Service (Hamilton, 1986), dealt only with issues related to sex and sexism. The American Educational Research Association's Guidelines for Eliminating Race and Sex Bias in Educational Research (AERA, 1985) were an exception, dealing with both race and sex issues.

To supplement their guidelines and to take the next step, in 1986, the *American Psychologist* published suggestions for Sex-Fair Research with no reference to race or ethnic background, although most of the issues raised would apply equally well to areas of race (McHugh, Koeske and Frieze, 1986). Similarly the *Educational Researcher* published a research agenda for gender issues that did not reflect race (Tittle, 1985).

For many social science organizations, sex bias in research has become an issue of concern to be addressed and rectified, but race bias has not.

The Criticism of Research Methods Expands

While racism and sexism can effect research methods, they also may be in part of the methods themselves. There is beginning to be some acknowledgement that while the traditional research methodology itself has value, some of the components of that methodology do not. Even the appropriate use of these components can bias against women (versus men) and minorities (versus Whites).

The most basic component of research methodology to be questioned is the 'difference based model' that is the basis of most research designs and analyses. Most research is based on the search for differences. Whether programs, people or even fertilizer are being studied, we consider groups in terms of how they differ from one another, and draw conclusions and design programs based on those differences. While this may not be a problem in terms of fertilizer, it is in terms of people, skewing our knowledge base and how we view people. 'Sex differences' and 'race differences' are fields of study — research is done, books and articles are written and conclusions are drawn based on differences. Sex similarities and race similarities are not studied; even the terms sound a little strange. Thus we tend not to examine or even acknowledge the commonalities that bring together and focus instead of the differences that divide.

Since this difference based model emphasizes 'who's better, who's worse', its use in research on equity is of necessity limited. If, or when, this model is used in researching females and males, minorities and Whites, a definition of equity is assumed that holds for example, that women and men are opposites. Simone De Beauvoir (1970) described it, in *The Second Sex*, as viewing woman as 'other'. As Broverman *et al.*, (1970) discovered in their classic study, even mental health professionals tended to describe women and men as opposite ends of the continuum; men are strong, women are weak; men are independent, women are dependent. Interestingly the professionals rated healthy adults and healthy men in similar ways, while their ratings of healthy women did not reflect those same qualities of healthy adults.

Traditional quantitative research, its design and statistics are for the most part based on a search for differences. Nowhere is this more obvious than in the null hypothesis, the basis of statistical testing. The null hypothesis is used to determine if real differences or real relationships exist. If the null hypothesis is rejected then differences are said to be statistically significant. This means that the differences are large enough that the probability that one is correct in concluding there are real differences between groups is 95 per cent or 99 per cent, or whatever level of significance has been chosen.

The alternative to rejecting the null hypothesis is not to accept it, but rather is to fail to reject it. Failing to reject the null hypothesis does not mean that there are no differences, that the groups are the same. It means that the probability that any differences found are due to error or to chance is too high to be acceptable (generally a more than 5 per cent chance of error) (Edwards, 1967). Thus if you find differences you have got something, if you don't find differences, you don't.

Any assumption that no significant differences 'really' means that there are no differences between groups is incorrect. No significant differences means that there is too high a risk of being wrong if differences are concluded. A 10 per cent or even a 50 per cent chance of being wrong when one concludes there are differences does not mean one can conclude similarities.

Research designs and statistics are slanted toward the search for differences and thus so are researchers and reviewers. Studies with significant difference findings are more apt to be submitted for publication and are more apt to be published. These studies are even more apt to be finished! Researchers have been found to be more than four times as apt to give up on a study if preliminary work reveals no significant differences (Smith, 1980; Greenwald, 1975). It is important to note that some statisticians are beginning to look at similarities as well as differences, (Besag and Besag, 1985) but this has not yet been worked into standard research designs.

Concerns about race and sex bias can be raised about measurement as well. Test formats — multiple choice, fill-in-the-blank, essay — and the context in which test items are set have been found to influence the test performance of females and males (Donlon, 1971). Females have a tendency to score better on essay items and on test items written in a context that includes stereotypically feminine activities. Thus 'sex differences' can be created or eliminated through the selection of items to be included in a test (Dwyer, 1976).

Race differences too can be expanded or contracted according to the items selected. Items with a high cultural loading — those that would be more familiar to people from one culture than from another — or that use language and syntax unfamiliar to some of those taking the test can cause a test to favor or not favor a specific group (Campbell, 1988). This increases the difficulty of determining when sex and race differences actually exist versus when they are measurement artifacts. Indeed, we might ask why not start with the assumption that females and males are equal in mathematics and design a test, based on that assumption, that will find females and males equal in mathematical abilities.

The assumption of female and male equality was made in the development of group IQ tests, and proposed (or at least implied) in recent articles and conferences on sex differences in the math Scholastic Aptitude Tests (Fair Test, 1987). While tests have been attacked as being unfair to minorities there has been no move to assume equality between Blacks and Whites, and to design tests based on that assumption.

When it was discovered that research methods had been used to do research that is biased, guidelines were developed on how to use research methods in less biased ways. Yet, as indicated earlier, an analysis of the methods themselves found that some of the methodologies themselves contribute to bias. To reduce this type of bias one must go beyond guidelines to begin to question the knowledge base itself and expand how that base is developed.

Reconceptualization of a Discipline: The New Scholarship on Women

The Nature of the New Scholarship on Women

Attacks have been made, both in terms of racism and sexism, on research methods and their application. Researchers of issues related to females and males, have gone beyond these attacks to begin to develop a new methodology.

This new methodology is in part a reaction to the presumption that science, by its very nature, is inherently masculine and that women can apprehend it only by an extreme effort of overcoming their own nature, which is inherently contradictory to science. This view of science, both social science and the so called 'hard' sciences, tends to follow Bacon's belief that nature is to be bound to men's service and made his slave, that she [Nature] is commanded by being obeyed, revealed by being 'enslaved, hounded and vexed' (Keller, 1985, p. 37).

Other reasons for the development of this new methodology include a realization that the extent to which the dominant group's view (men's) is imposed on nonmembers (women), the potential for breakthrough conceptualizations is decreased and creative tension between experimental perspectives is lost (McHugh, Koeske and Frieze, 1986). Too, at least in education, there has been a realization that older research methodologies have not been very successful in providing appropriate, usable, good guidance to educators or to expanding the knowledge base. As Gage (1978, p. 21) concluded: 'A healthy progressive research tradition should have come up with more significant results than this one has'.

To come up with 'more significant results', the new scholarship on women, or feminist research, moves away from an emphasis on the 'fight', on the distancing of subject and researcher and on the distrust of individual self reported experiences. Rather the researcher tends 'to extend affection and esteem toward her subject . . . to assume that women are sincere, not chatty fibbers of legend, but reliable witnesses of their own experience' (Stimpson, 1980, p. 5). Rather than separating the researcher and the subject, in this methodology, researcher and subject work in different ways to explore a truth they mutually create and define. Validating the experiences of individual women, these new methods look to embedded phenomena in context, putting women in the center of the inquiry.

These methods involve a shortening of the distance between the observer and the object being studied and a consideration of the complex interaction between an organism and its environment. From the 1970s cry 'the personal is political' the new scholarship on women has developed 'the personal is valuable and contributes to our knowledge of the human condition'.

Implications of the New Scholarship on Women

The implications of the new scholarship on women are beginning to be felt in and out of research. In biology, female primatologists, such as Jane Godall, reduce the distance between themselves and the primates and 'learn more about primate behavior in ten years than in the previous ten centuries' (Eckholm, 1984). In botany, rather than using traditional methodologies Barbara McClintock reported that she 'asked' the maize plant to solve specific problems and then, in the maize's time and setting, sat and watched its responses, and won a Nobel prize (Keller, 1983). In education, participant observation and qualitative research on such topics as women teachers' lives have brought out new information about education (Biklen, 1986). In both education and psychology, with the assistance of Gilligan (1982), we have begun to rethink what is meant by moral development and the roles cooperation rather than competition can play.

With the valuing of women and 'women's ways' comes, for example, the expansion of one organization's (the North East Coalition of Educational Leaders) mandate from 'empowering women to understand and function in the male-based reality of school administration,' to include 'empowering men and women to understand and employ the strengths of female-based reality for school administration' (Regan, 1987, p. 1).

With the new scholarship on women comes a series of methodologies, and a way of thinking that can be combined with objective application of rules to produce better research; research that can provide insight into the complexity of women's lives and that can be used to help us better understand the human condition. By looking at women, we learn about women and we also learn about men.

The new scholarship on women has generated an awareness and has received a degree of acceptance not just from feminist researchers but from more mainstream publications such as the *Kappan* (Shakeshaft, 1986) and the *Educational Researcher* (Biklen and Dwyer, 1986), both of which have had special issues on the new scholarship. Yet comparable development, attention and acceptance has not occurred for minorities and research focusing on minorities.

Why have researchers of women and of issues related to sex, unlike those working in other equity areas, gone on to form a new method of research? One answer to this question can be found in numbers. Forty per cent of educational researchers are female while 12.3 per cent are minority women and minority men (7.6 per cent black, 2.3 per cent Hispanic, 1.9 per cent Asian/Pacific Islander and 0.4 per cent American Indian) (Campbell and Brown, 1982). Absolute numbers can make a difference. While change is a process made first by individuals and then by institutions, a number of individuals must change before the institutions do. It was not until a substantial number of women were active in the humanities and social sciences that the feminist perspective was felt and transformations in those disciplines occurred (MacIntosh, 1983).

Power is also an answer. Women, in research communities, appear to have greater political power than do minorities. Thirty-six per cent of the White male educational researchers had positions at the highest levels (for example directors, principal investigators) compared to 16 per cent of the white females and 3 per cent of black researchers of either sex (Campbell and Brown, 1982). This is true in the professional organizations as well. For example the 1985–86, 1987–88 and 1988–89 presidents of the American Educational Research Association (AERA) are white women while there has never been a minority president of AERA of either sex.

Another aspect of power can be found in who is doing the research on women and on minorities. Those in higher salary levels have been found to be more apt to do research on issues related to sex than were others and those who did research on issues related to sex regularly spent more time doing research than did others (Campbell, 1982). In addition while most of those who report doing research on issues related to sex are women, most of those who report doing research on minority issues are White. Yet those who criticize the methodologies, who address the theoretical, methodological and practical problems associated with research on, for example, black populations, tend to be black (Hendricks and Caesar, 1985).

In addition women are both part of the mainstream power structure and, at the same time, not of it. The contradiction of women belonging and not belonging, of being immersed in and yet estranged from our own particular discipline and western intellectual tradition, develops a personal tension that informs critical dialogue (Weskott, 1979). This combination of being both on the inside and on the outside may help in terms of the development and, perhaps more importantly, the acceptance of new methodologies.

There does appear to be a greater willingness on the part of those in power to accept and acknowledge issues related to women and to sex. As mentioned earlier, with the exception of AERA, social science organizations have worked on and adopted guidelines to reduce sex, not race, bias in research. A 1985 survey of AERA members found that 74 per cent of the men and 79 per cent of the women indicated support of the statement that 'There is a strong need for support and promotion of research on women's equity issues in education' (Frary, McBee and Weber, 1985).

Agencies within the US Department of Education, private foundations and even some state education departments are funding efforts to integrate the results of the new scholarship on women in such diverse colleges and universities as the University of Arizona, Colgate, Duke, Memphis State, Spellman and Wheaton. The relationship between sex roles and science is being explored at over forty universities and even at Yale, long a bastion of male supremacy, over 750 students take women's studies courses (Davis, 1986).

This willingness to accept the new scholarship on women may also be related to a role that the new scholarship on women may play in supporting sex role stereotypes. Stereotypically women are seen as 'more connected', 'more subjective', and more involved with relationships than are men. The new scholarship on women emphasizes precisely these areas and deemphasizes the objective or scientific approach to the world which Keller (1985), as well as others, have said to be synonymous with a masculine world view. Its reinforcement of stereotypes may be a major part of its acceptance.

Its greater acceptance may also be related to a greater belief in basic or biological sex differences than in race differences. Not only are we more apt to accept sex differences, than race differences, we actively work to reject race differences. Thus with the belief that women and men have fundamentally different ways of constructing/experiencing the world can come a greater willingness to acknowledge a 'women's' style of research (Horst, 1987).

The New Scholarship on Women and Other Alternative Methodologies

Others accept and even welcome the types of methodologies brought up by the new scholarship on women but question the definition of these methods as women's scholarship on women or as feminist science. Soltis

(1984, p. 5), in his work on the nature of educational research, concludes that 'Good social and political theory [and pedagogy] must at one and the same time be empirical (objective), interpretive (deal with human intersubjective and subjective meaning) and normative-critical (bring operative ideologies to conscious awareness and make action-value decisions)'.

Similarly Stake (1986) in his examination of social service evaluation, shortened the distance between researcher and study, by the researcher becoming, at least in a small way, part of that being studied and focusing more on the context and the complex interaction of reform, education and public interest.

In physics, Ching-Wu Chu's successful work on superconductors has been credited to his 'intuitive feelings'. Theoretical physicist Marvin Cohen explained that Chu 'has an intimate relationship with his materials. It's different from the cold analytical machine-like style of some people in our field' (Gleick, 1987, p. 55).

These researchers see a less distancing research, as an alternative mode, not masculine, not feminine, but different. Naturalist Stephen Gould (1981) agrees, concluding that 'The rejection of dualism, the focus on interaction rather than dominance, the abandonment of reductionism for a holistic vision [is something that] naturalists (most of them men) have been urging for centuries'.

Gould, who examined the effects of bias, particularly race bias on research on intelligence, is an exception. When most mainstream researchers and philosophers discuss objectivity (or the lack of objectivity) in research; references to race and sex as issues related to objectivity aren't made (Soltis, 1984; Garrison and Macmillan, 1984; Kuhn, 1962; Nagel, 1961).

It may be that issues related to race and sex are not included because if they are, then those dealing with the issues tend to be seen as advocates rather than researchers or philosophers. It may also be that some feel that by labelling a research method 'feminist' or 'women's' research, alternative methods will never reach the mainstream. And of course, these new methodologies may be another example of the overlapping insights that have been achieved by others who travelled to a similar endpoint along alternate roads.

The Old and the New: A Possible Synthesis

There are those who see feminist science as a step in the process of defining a research method that is more inclusive and accurate as well as more complex. For example Gilligan (ND, p. 56) theorizes that 'If the exclusion of women in the past obscured our understanding of the psychology of care, perhaps the inclusion of men and women in future studies will help reveal its complexity for both sexes, thus presenting a new base for theory construction'. In her work she found that what was missing when women were not considered was 'a representation of what we have termed the morality of response and care and the connected self which call attention to the reality of interdependence in the lives of all human beings'. As Gilligan explains, 'when we bring in women, the models change' (p. 57).

Thompson (1986) feels that the models need to do more than change and that divisions into masculine and feminist research are both counter productive and inaccurate. She suggests 'an alternative to gender-bound lenses because both "masculinist" and feminist lenses are too limited to focus adequately on the new knowledge' (p. 278). She questions whether 'we are exchanging (or reversing) the premises of a male ground analytic lens for a new one ground by feminists?' (p. 278).

Instead Thompson (1986) suggests two spheres, Hermean and Hestian, which exist in dialectic relation—interdependent, interconnected and interactive. While she feels that males predominate in an Hermean sphere which is public and visible, and females predominate in the Hestian or private sphere, she does not see them as masculine or feminine. Neither does she see them as mirror images, rather 'they exist in relation . . . are more amenable to systems thinking than linear thinking. They interface . . . Transactions (inputs and outputs) take place across their boundaries' (p. 278).

Keller after analyzing issues related to sex and science in the 'hard' sciences, also feels that one must go beyond feminist science. While she feels that 'our traditional definition of science carries nonscientific assumptions that reflect basic attitudes about gender and therefore a certain parochialism . . . My goal is to make room for other visions of science and for an alternative philosophy of science that recognizes the value of empathy and engagement with, not just power over the world around us' (Bromwell, 1985, p. 13).

Yet once again the issue of race must be raised. Why aren't questions being raised about effects of basic attitudes about race on science being asked? Questions such as 'What are the consequences of the exclusion of women?' and 'What would it mean if women were included and truly shared in the making of a culture with men?' (Bromwell, 1985, p. 44) are being asked about women and men. Similar questions can, and must be asked about race, about women and men of color. While 'the awareness of what it's like to be confined to the margins of culture has linked some feminists with the situation of other "outsiders" minorities in the United

States' (Bromwell, 1985, p. 54); too often 'white women theorists ... step up there and do exactly what white men have done. So few white feminists really deal with the way racism not just sexism enters into the theory' (Bromwell, 1985, p. 54).

Throughout the analysis of educational equity and research paradigms it has been clear that, for a variety of reasons, issues related to sexism in research and scholarship on women have received more attention and acceptance than have comparable issues on race. The infusion of some of the insights of the new scholarship on women has improved research. The insights of other 'outsiders' are needed to further improve research.

Equitable research paradigms demand alternative methodologies that can bring out new ways of examining realities. If we can develop enough alternatives and integrate them such that the problem and the population studied define the methodology we just might get it right.

There is a frequent charge that there is good research or bad research but there is no such thing as feminist or anti-racist research. Yet to quote a recent best selling thriller (Follett, 1986, p. 250) 'there was no such thing as Christian mathematics but still it took a heretic such as Galileo to prove that the earth goes around the sun'.

References

AMERICAN EDUCATIONAL RESEARCH ASSOCIATION (1985) 'AERA Guidelines for eliminating race and sex bias in educational research and evaluation', *Educational Researcher,* **14**, 6, pp. 16–17.

ANCARROW, J. (1987) *Use of Computers in Home Study,* Washington, DC: Center for Educational Statistics.

BELLE, D. (1980) Studying the context of women's lives. Paper presented to the Conference on Attitudinal and Behavioral Measurement in Social Processes/Women's Research (NIE), Washington, DC.

BESAG, F. and BESAG, P. (1985) *Statistics for the Helping Professions,* Beverly Hills: Sage.

BIKLEN, S. (1986) 'I have always worked: Elementary school teaching as a career', *Phi Delta Kappan,* **67,** 7, pp. 504–8.

BIKLEN, S. and DWYER, C. (1986) 'The new scholarship on women in education', (Special issue) *Educational Researcher,* **15,** 6.

BROVERMAN, I., ROSENKRANTZ, P., BROVERMAN, D. and VOGEL, S. (1971) 'Sex role stereotypes and clinical judgments of mental health', *Journal of Clinical Psychology,* **32,** pp. 1–7.

BROMWELL, N. (1985) 'Feminist perspectives', *The Boston Globe Magazine*, 13 January, pp. 12–15, 44–45, 53–57.

CAMPBELL, P.B. (1982) Researchers of women in education: Who are we? Paper presented to the Eighth Annual AERA SIG:RWE Midyear Conference on Research on Women in Education, Philadelphia.

CAMPBELL, P.B. and BROWN, M.V. (1982) *Survey on the Status of Educational Researchers*, Washington, DC: US Department of Education.

CAMPBELL, P.B. (1988) *The Hidden Discriminator*, Newton, MA: Educational Development Centre, pp. 199–221.

CAPLAN, N. and NELSON, S. (1973) 'On being useful: The nature and consequences of psychological research of social problems', *American Psychologist,* **28,** pp. 119–211.

CASTENELL, L. (1984) 'A cross cultural look at achievement motivation research', *Journal of Negro Education,* **53,** pp. 435–43.

Committee on the Status of Women in Sociology (1980) 'Sexist biases in sociological research: problems and issues', *ASA Footnotes*, pp. 6–7, 9.

DAVIS, L.V. (1986) 'A feminist approach to social work research', *Affila,* **1,** 1, pp. 32–46.

DEBEAUVOIR, S. (1970) *The Second Sex*, New York: Bantam Books.

DONLON, T. (1971) Content factors in sex differences on test questions. Paper presented to the annual meeting of the American Educational Research Association, Boston, MA.

DUNN, L.M. (1987) Bilingual Hispanic children on the US mainland: A review of research on their cognitive, linguistic and scholastic development. Circle Plains, MN: American Guidance Service.

DWYER, C. (1976) 'Test content and sex differences in reading', *Reading Teacher,* **29,** pp. 753–7.

EHRENREICH, B. and ENGLISH, D. (1979) *For Her Own Good*, Garden City, NY: Anchor Books.

EDWARDS, A.L. (1967) *Statistical Methods*, New York: Holt, Rinehart and Winston, Inc.

ETHINGTON, C.A. and WOLFLE, L.M. (1986) *Sex Differences in Quantitative and Analytic GRE Performance: An Exploratory Study.* Paper presented at the annual meeting of the American Educational Research Association, San Francisco, April.

FAIR TEST (1987) 'SAT: Why are women losing out?' *Fair Test Examiner*, 2–3.

FOLLETT, K. (1986) *Lie Down With Lions*, New York: Signet.

FRARY, R.B., MCBEE, J.K. and WEBER, L.J. (1985) 'AERA opinions on women's equity issues', *Educational Researcher,* **14,** 2, pp. 12–17.

GAGE, N.L. (1978) *The Scientific Basis of the Art of Teaching*, New York: Teachers College Press.

GARRISON, J.W. and MACMILLAN, C. (1984) 'A philosophical critique of process-product research on teaching', *Educational Theory,* **34,** pp. 255–74.

GLEICK, J. (1987) 'In the trenches of science', *New York Times Magazine*, 16 August, pp. 28–30, 55, 74, 77.

GILLIGAN, C. (1982) *In a Different Voice: Psychological Theory and Women's Development*, Cambridge: Harvard University Press.

GILLIGAN, C. (ND). The contribution of women's thought to developmental theory: The elimination of sex bias in moral development research and education. Washington, DC: NIE Final report.

GOLDBERG, S. and LEWIS, M. (1969) 'Play behavior in the year-old infant: Early sex differences', *Child Development,* **40,** pp. 21–31.

GOULD, S. (1981) *The Mismeasure of Man*, New York: W.W. Norton and Company.

GOULD, S.J. (1984, August 12) *New York Times Book Review,* p. 7.

GREENWALD, A.G. (1975) 'Consequences of prejudice against the null hypothesis', *Psychological Bulletin,* **82,** pp. 1-20.

HAMILTON, J.A. (1986) *Guidelines for Avoiding Methodological and Policy-Making Biases in Gender Related Health Research.* Commissioned Paper: Public Health Service: Washington, DC.

HENDRICKS, L. and CAESAR, P. (1985) *Racial and Comparative Research: Program Narrative,* Washington, DC: Howard University.

HORST, L. (1987). Personal communication.

EČKHOLM, E. (1984) 'New view of female primates assails stereotypes' *New York Times,* 18 September, Cl.

JENSEN, A.R. (1969) 'How much can be boost IQ and scholastic achievement?' *Harvard Educational Review,* **39,** pp. 1–139.

KELLER, E. (1985) *Reflections on Gender and Science,* New Haven: Yale University Press.

KELLER, E. (1983) *A Feeling for the Organism: The Life and Work of Barbara McClintock,* New York: W.H. Freeman and Co.

KELLY, J. (1976) 'The social relations of the sexes: Methodological implications of women's history'. *Signs,* **1,** pp. 809–23.

KUHN, T. (1962) *The Structure of Scientific Revolutions,* Chicago: University of Chicago Press.

L'ENGLE, M. (1963) *A Wrinkle in Time,* New York: Farra, Straus and Giroux.

MACINTOSH, P. (1983) Interactive phases of curricular re-vision: A feminist perspective. Working Paper No. 124, Wellesley College, Center for Research on Women.

MCHUGH, M.C., KOESKE, R. and FRIEZE, I. (1981) Guidelines for nonsexist research. Division 35, American Psychological Association.

MCHUGH, M.C., KOESKE, R. and FRIEZE, I. (1986) 'Issues to consider in considering nonsexist psychological research', *American Psychologist,* **41,** 8, pp. 879–90.

MOYNIHAN, D.P. (1965) *'The Negro Family: The Case for National Action,* Washington, DC: US Department of Labor.

NAGEL, E. (1961) *The Structure of Science,* New York: Harcourt, Brace and World.

PARLEE, M. (1975) 'Psychology', *SIGNS: A Journal of Women in Culture and Society,* **1,** pp. 119–38.

REGAN, H.B. (1987) 'Future directions: A feminist perspective on educational leadership', *NEXUS (NorthEast Coalition of Educational Leaders),* **8,** 2, pp. 1, 3.

RICHARDSON, B. and WIRTENBERG, J. (1983) *Sex Role Research: Measuring Social Change,* New York: Praeger.

ROSALDO, M.V. (1980) 'The use and abuse of anthropology: Reflections on feminism and cross cultural understanding', *SIGNS: A Journal of Women in Culture and Society,* **5,** 3, pp. 389–93.

SCHWAGER, S. (1986) *American History: The Female Experience,* A report to the National Endowment for the Humanities.

SHAKESHAFT, C. (1986) 'A gender at risk', *Phi Delta Kappan,* **67,** 7, pp. 499–526.

SMITH, M.L. (1980) 'Publication bias and meta-analysis', *Evaluation in Education,* **4,** pp. 22–4.

SOLTIS, J.F. (1984) 'On the nature of educational research', *Educational Researcher,* **13,** 10, pp. 5–10.

STAKE, R.E. (1986) *Quieting Reform: Social Science and Social Action in an Urban*

Youth Program, University of Illinois Press: Urbana.

STIMPSON, C. (1980) 'The new scholarship about women: The state of the art', *Annnals of Scholarship,* **1,** pp. 2–14.

THOMAS, A. and SILLEN, S. (1972) *Racism and Psychiatry*, New York: Brunner/Mazel.

THOMPSON, P.J. (1986) 'Beyond gender: Equity issues for home economics education', *Theory Into Practice,* **25,** 4, pp. 276–83.

TITTLE, C. (1985) 'Research on sex equity in education: An agenda for the divisions, SIGs, and AERA', *Educational Researcher,* **14,** 9, pp. 10–18.

WESKOTT, M. (1979) 'Feminist criticism of social science', *Harvard Educational Review,* **49,** 4, pp. 422–30.

WILLIG, A.C. (1985) 'A meta analysis of selected studies on the effectiveness of bilingual education', *Review of Educational Research,* **55,** 3, pp. 269–318.

Understanding and Measuring Equity in Education: A Conceptual Framework[1]

Glen Harvey
Susan Shurberg Klein[2]

Since the 1954 *Brown* decision that found that separate educational facilities are inherently unequal, interest in educational equity as a field of intellectual inquiry has been growing. Evaluators, researchers, and scholars have assembled an extensive and diverse body of knowledge pertaining to equity-related issues. However, during the more than thirty years since the *Brown* decision, problems of measurement have persisted. How to validly determine whether equity has been achieved – or progress is being made – remains extremely problematic. Even reaching agreement about the meaning of 'equity' itself presents substantial conceptual problems.

This article describes a conceptual framework for measuring educational equity, designed to address some of the measurement problems inherent to this relatively new but crucial area of inquiry. Like others, researchers and evaluators in the field of educational equity must make hard choices about what to investigate and how to examine the relationships they measure. As in other social science fields, investigators in the area of equity sometimes make choices that do not adequately capture the reality of the complex situations they are studying. The framework described below is intended to facilitate more consistent and comprehensive thinking about educational equity. It is also intended to help researchers and educators make more informed and rational choices about what to measure. To accomplish this, the framework is designed to first, focus attention on frequently omitted but potentially important variables and relationships and, secondly, clarify assumptions about the nature and relationship of these variables so that readers of research and evaluation reports will have a more accurate understanding of the perspectives and values implicit to such research reports.

The application of this conceptual framework to research and evaluation activities in the equity field should (i) improve the overall quality, consistency, and utility of both descriptive and prescriptive work; (ii) provide investigators and other users of research and evaluation with a mechanism to facilitate efforts to critically examine and synthesize many related equity investigations; and (iii) make it easier for investigators who had not initially intended to focus on equity variables to increase the validity and value of their research in other areas by including appropriate equity dimensions.

Overview of the Framework for Measuring Equity in Education

The impetus for the approach to measuring equity presented here developed from previous efforts to apply conceptual frameworks in the equity field (Bornstein, 1981; Campbell and Klein, 1982; Harvey, 1980, 1982) to sex equity-related research and evaluation issues and studies. This resulted in a conceptual framework for examining issues relevant to the achievement of sex equity in and through education that was used to guide the authors of the American Educational Research Association-sponsored *Handbook for Achieving Sex Equity Through Education* (Klein, Russo, Campbell and Harvey, 1985).

We have now designed a framework that cuts across equity-related research and evaluation activities regardless of equity group focus. The framework is intended to be widely applicable across the domains of research, policy, evaluation, and practice and is designed to be essentially value neutral both with respect to differing conceptions of equity and to the equity groups whose claims and issues it has been developed to address.

By 'equity group focus' we mean the social groups between or among whom equity is being measured. As Weale (1978) has pointed out, 'equity arguments are normally used in a context where one social group is being benefited relative to another' (p. 28). Equity groups most commonly identified and compared in research and evaluation activities include groups characterized by race, ethnicity, gender, economic status, handicapping condition, primary language, and age. We view the bodies of work focusing on these and similar equity groups as having shared concepts, methodologies, and assumptions that can be molded into an emerging equity paradigm, one manifestation of which would be an educational equity measurement framework.

One purpose of the measurement framework, then, is to develop a strong, coherent equity paradigm by identifying and articulating methodological and conceptual commonalities in equity research and evaluation, regardless of the particular equity group(s)[3] being studied. To do this, we focus on three distinct but related aspects of measuring educational equity: (i) general learner focused research and evaluation measurement dimensions, independent of equity considerations; (ii) equity group-based measurement dimensions, differentiated according to discrimination and stereotyping; and (iii) goal-oriented educational equity-based measurement dimensions, reflecting distinctions among alternative predictions and conceptions of how to achieve equity.

Each of these sets of measurement dimensions is discussed below in detail and is portrayed in a separate segment (Figures 1–3). Figure 1 represents the bottom segment or simplest version of the measurement framework and is based on variables and relationships used in many educational research or evaluation models. The second illustration (Figure 2) describes the additional considerations that are included as a result of an equity group focus. The third figure describes alternative equity-related goals based on philosophical, historical, and scientific assumptions about attaining equity. Together these three figures form the overall educational equity measurement framework depicted in Figure 4.

All four figures are designed to indicate general categorical measurement considerations. It is anticipated that Figures 2, 3, and 4 can be adapted for use with specific equity groups as well as for diverse types of research and evaluation activities. Means for such adaption will become apparent as each of the figures is discussed.

Educational Research and Evaluation Measurement Dimensions

The set of measurement dimensions depicted in Figure 1 represents the basic core of the model, reflecting key elements that are common to educational research and evaluation. It is designed to focus on the individual learner or groups of learners who receive identifiable educational treatments.

Frameworks used in social science research and evaluation that deal with treatments or interventions commonly focus on *input, process,* and *outcomes*. Input or 'antecedents' include 'any condition existing prior to teaching and learning that may relate to outcomes such as student aptitude,

Figure 1: Individual learner-focused educational research and evaluation measurement dimension

1. *Initial Input*	2. *Educational Process as It Involves the Learner*	3. *Learner Outcomes or Claims of Actual Results*	4. *Goals and Objectives*
1.1 *Learner Attributes*	2.1 *Learner Access*	3.1 *Learner Outcomes*	4.1 *Goals/Objectives*
A. Described nonmalleable, ascribed learner characteristics or attributes that may be relevant to the treatment or outcome, e.g., race, sex, ethinicity, age, disability. B. Describe learner characteristics and attributes that may/may not be alterable and that may be relevant to the treatment of outcome, e.g., intelligence, level of motivation, aptitude. C. Describe previous salient socialization experiences that may be relevant to treatment or outcome, e.g., SES, family influence, prior educational treatments. D. Describe initial (pre-treatment) scores on likely malleable outcome measures or covariables that are related measures known to correlate consistently with the outcome measures.	A. In describing access to treatments experienced by the learner, note: • Policies that influence the learner's participation in educational treatments. • Roles of teachers, other key personnel, learner peers, and investigators that influence the learner's participation in educational treatments. • Practices and products that influence the learner's participation in educational treatments.	A. Identify nonbehavioral measures such as: attitudes, expectations, self-assessments. B. Identify short-term behavioral indicators in: (1) cognitive area (achievement tests, assessment of critical thinking skills); (2) affective area (indicators of anxiety, cooperation, aggression, etc.); (3) psychomotor area (physical skills assessments); and (4) experimental area (course enrollment decisions, participation in classroom interactions). C. Identify summative, cumulative behavioral indicators relating to long-term effects. (Achievement re: SAT, cumulative grades, educational attainment, employment status and income levels, and other productivity measures.)	A. Identify predetermined, desired processes or outcomes. (See Columns 2 and 3 for categories.)
1.2 *External Preprocess Influences*	2.2 *Learner Treatment*	3.2 *Related Outcomes*	
A. Describe the relevant institutional input that may differentially influence learners, e.g.: • per pupil expenditures • educational facilities • relevant personnel ratios • expectations for learners • attitudes toward learners B Describe other aspects of the larger institutional/community context if they can be expected to influence the educational process as it involves the learner.	A. In describing the actual treatment as experienced by the learner, note: • Content of treatment (cognitive, affective, psychomotor, etc.). • Roles of teachers, other key personnel, learner peers, and investigator(s) in the treatment process. • Role of intended and unintended educational products or practices such as instructional materials.	A. These outcomes need not be comprised of results from a learner, e.g.: • Have educators changed their attitudes toward and expectations of the learner? • Has teacher effectiveness increased or decreased? • Have school test scores changed?	

previous experience or entry behaviors' (Worthen and Sanders, 1973, p. 112). 'Transaction' is another common term for process or treatment and suggests dynamic interactions of students and teachers, students and students, students and instructional materials, and so on. Outcomes are actual results or claims about the influence of the process on the learner. They may be measured nonbehaviorally or behaviorally and include short-term results of the transactions or summative results such as achievement over the life span.

Evaluation frameworks also frequently include the concepts of *goals* or *objectives* for the predetermined desired results or outcomes. The value of the educational process is then judged by analyzing the relation between the actual outcomes and the goals, objectives, or performance standards (Worthen and Sanders, 1973). Recently, educational researchers and evaluators have recognized the value of assessing discrepancies between actual and expected processes as well as outcomes.

Learner Input

Four ways to measure antecedent learner variables are described in Figure 1, ranging from ascribed nonmalleable learner attributes such as skin color to pretest scores on a career awareness instrument. Researchers' choices of the various types of learner inputs, as well as their own and others' views about the extent to which a treatment can alter such inputs can significantly influence the entire research or evaluation design. Although most attention will be focused on learner attributes (Figure 1, section 1.1), external preprocess influences that may affect the learning environment are included in section 1.2 of Figure 1.

Educational Process as It Involves the Learner

During the last twenty years, educational researchers and evaluators have focused increasing attention on identifying what is actually happening to the learner. In describing the process experienced by the learner, we suggest that access and treatment categories be used. Access includes policies and practices that influence learners' opportunities to participate in educational treatments. The treatments consist of content; teacher, learner, peer, and investigator roles and activities; and instructional practices or materials as they influence the learner. We also suggest that, to the extent possible, the investigator should specify the amount of treatment received by the learner in terms of duration, intensity, salience, and relationships to the other concurrent treatments. Researchers and evaluators are using these categories to clarify many key dimensions of the instructional process.

Learner and Related Outcomes

Learner outcomes may be categorized in multiple ways. However, in Figure 1, we suggest that they be grouped into the categories of long- and short-term nonbehavioral and behavioral psychosocial indicators of learner success. The nonbehavioral measures include learner attitudes, expectations or self-assessments, and other psychological variables that are difficult to observe.

The short-term behavioral or observable indicators range from cognitive outcomes (e.g., critical thinking skills) to experiential outcomes (e.g., classroom interaction patterns). It should be noted that some of these experiential outcomes, such as the decision to enroll in a course, may be difficult to separate from the learner's contribution to the educational process. The behavioral indicators of long-term effects range from cumulative achievement measures to educational attainment levels.

Related nonlearner outcomes such as changes in teachers' attitudes and expectations, cost of treatment, ease in using the instructional process, and satisfaction of school personnel with the materials or results are included in column 3.2 of Figure 1.

Goals or Objectives

Unlike the column describing outcomes, goals or objectives refer to the predetermined desired results. They can be measured using the same process and outcome categories as previously discussed. Objectives are commonly described as subcategories under goals and are often referred to as behavioral objectives or performance standards by educational researchers and evaluators (Worthen and Sanders, 1973). Given the generic nature of the educational equity measurement framework and its component parts (Figures 1–3), we will focus on goals at a relatively general level of specificity.

Other Measurement Concerns

Instruments used to measure the types of variables described in Figure 1 will vary greatly. However, we remind researchers that they should select and use instruments that are reliable and valid for the group(s) studied. In the process column in particular, we further urge that the investigators specify whether the instrument used to collect this information was based on high levels of inference such as observer appraisals of learners or low levels of inference such as three second observer codings of specific categories of classroom interactions.

Equity Group-Based Measurement Dimensions

In dealing with equity concerns, researchers and evaluators generally examine group patterns. In so doing, they look for similarities and differences between or among groups and for patterns that may lead to stereotyping about groups. This set of dimensions is organized according to the same input, process, outcome, and goal categories discussed in the previous section. Within each column in Figure 2, categories similar to those in Figure 1 are used to explicate dimensions that require investigation as a result of a particular equity group focus rather than the individual learner focus indicated in Figure 1. The column on goals is omitted because they will be the focus of Figure 3.

The pattern is repeated twice in Figure 2. The top half of Figure 2 depicts considerations pertaining to *discrimination*. As such, it is designed to help investigators focus on comparisons to identify similarities and differences between or among groups, such as females and males; black, Hispanic, Asian, and white students; English and limited English proficient students. The bottom half of Figure 2 focuses exclusively on *stereotyping*, either by members of that group or outsiders.

It is possible to merge the dimensions relating to these two interrelated concepts of discrimination and stereotyping because one may contribute to the other. However, given that such a merger would have made it difficult to clarify important measurement distinctions, we will differentiate between the two concepts and discuss them separately.

Comparisons by Equity Group

Initial learner group input characteristics

It is general practice to provide input population characteristics when describing research and evaluation studies, but it is rare for an investigator to describe what happens to each population group during or after treatment even when such information is required by funding agencies (Klein, 1986, 1987 b; Larson, 1980).

Figure 2: Equity group-based measurement dimensions in education:

1. *Initial Input*		2. *Educational Process as it Involves Groups of Learners*		3. *Group Outcomes or Claims of Actual Results*	
		Discrimination Comparisions by Equity Group			
1.0 *Initial Learner Group Characteristics*	1.1 *External Preprocess Influences on Groups of Learners*	2.0 *Group Access*	2.1 *Group Treatment*	3.0 *Group Outcomes*	3.1 *Related Outcomes*
A. Describe learners according to their biological sex and race and other nonmalleable ascribed characteristics relevant to the study. State any assumptions about controversial genetically based nonmalleable differences. B. Describe learners according to characteristics (e.g., intelligence, aptitude) that may/may not be alterable and that may be relevant to the study. State assumptions about the relative malleability of these characteristics. C. Describe prior and current socialization differences as related to the treatment or outcome. These may be experiences known to have been specific for the learner or general experiences likely to have influenced one equity group of learners (e.g., female, minority) differently from another (e.g., male, majority).	A. Describe institutional attributes; student and staff equity group population characteristics; comparison with schools serving other equity groups related to school resources and facilities. B. Describe expectations and attitudes toward equity groups. Are differences in the group's behavior anticipated by the community, family, and school?	A. Do educational policies for different groups such as the handicapped differ in influencing their participation in educational teatments? Are there different enrollment standards for different groups of students? B. Are there different practices for different groups that may influence their participation in educational treatments, e.g., are students from economically disadvantaged families more likely to be encouraged not to take qualifying tests such as the SAT because it may decrease the school average than learners from affluent families?	A. Content — Are cognitive, affective, and psychomotor activities taught differently according to equity group? Do these differences occur in segregated or integrated settings? B. Do teachers or other key personnel, peers, or investigators interact differentially with students according to their equity group? Does the equity group or the teacher, peer, etc. make a difference? Are students tokens for their sex, race, etc.? C. Are the same or equivalent instructional materials used by students of different equity groups with the same or equivalent intensity and perceived similarly?	A. Examples of variables on which groups of learners might differ: • Nonbehavioral: attitudes, expecations, motivations, aspirations, self-assessments, moral development, cognitive achievement. • Short-term behavioral: anxiety, empathy, sociability, nurturance, cooperation, level of activity, aggression, dependency, competitive behavior, enrollment in courses. • Summative behavioral: educational attainment, income, success in parenting, nurturing, career choices, civic activities.	A. Outcomes may be the by-products of the equity process and not a direct result of group outcomes, e.g.: • Have educators changed their expectations about the performance of group members? • Has the community's perception of the school changed as its equity group composition changed? • Are certain instructional procedures seen as being more appropriate for one equity group over another?

Discrimination Comparisions by Equity Group

1.0 *Initial Learner Group Characteristics*	1.1 *External Preprocess Influences on Group of Learners*	2.0 *Group Access*	2.1 *Group Treatment*	3.0 *Group Outcomes*	3.1 *Related Outcomes*
D. By equity group, describe initial (pre-treatment) scores on outcome measures or related measures known to correlate consistently for equity groups with these outcome measures. (See Column 3 for a sample list of measures relevant to discrimination.)					

Stereotyping as it Pertains to Equity Groups

1.2. *Initial Learner Group Stereotypes*	2.2 *Educational Process as it Involves Groups of Learners*	3.2 *Group Outcomes or Claims of Actual Results*
A Are there ascribed, nonmalleable stereotypes for equity groups that are accurate for most members of these groups (e.g., greater male physical strength due to larger general size)? B. Are there assumptions that some characteristics are nonmalleable for one equity group and not the other? C. Prior to the treatment, were members of different equity groups socialized to be different from each other according to stereotypes and equity group-based roles? D. Describe initial pre-treatment ''scores'' on outcome measures. For each category of outcome measure, describe those that measure stereotyping specifically. Focus on learners' internalized stereotyped views or self-perceptions particularly as they are perceived in relation to members of different equity group(s).	A. Is the Content: • biased or stereotyped? • about stereotyping in society and equity laws? B. Are teachers, peers, and others teaching stereotyping or the elimination of same by their actions relating to direct instruction such as assignment of stereotyped tasks or by modeling stereotyped behaviors. C. Are the instructional materials biased, fair, or affirmative?	A. Identify nonbehavioral measures, attitudes, and expectations towards stereotyping. B. Identify short-term behavioral indicators, e.g. • Knowledge of equal rights, contributions of different equity groups, awareness of inaccurate stereotypes. • Social process measures such as information on segregation patterns, sexual harassment or racism, and sexism in language. • Experiential measures of non-traditional career choice, compliance with legal protections (e.g., Title VII and IX, P.L. 94-142). C. Identify summative behavioral indicators, e.g.: • selection of non-traditional careers • assumption of multiple roles

As in the Learner Input category of Figure 1, investigators should note any ascribed nonmalleable learner characteristics that may be relevant to their study. Because Figure 2 focuses on 'equity group dimensions', it is necessary to describe the learners by their membership in the particular equity group(s) being studied. To the extent possible, multiple membership in equity groups should also be specified; for instance, if a research study focused on racial comparisons, it is also useful to indicate sex, ethnicity, age, permanent disability status, and so forth.

There is debate about whether some learner characteristics such as intelligence and aptitude are malleable or not. If these characteristics are measured for the study, assumptions about whether each is malleable for learners should be presented and justified (Campbell and Klein, 1982).

Researchers have pointed out that a characteristic such as sex is a stimulus variable — that people will treat females or males in distinctly different ways if they know their sex, even if they know little else about the person (O'Leary and Wallston, 1981). Therefore, information on salient socialization experiences that occurred prior to or independent of the educational process being studied should be provided separately for learners according to their equity group.

Initial pretreatment data on outcomes or related measures should also be provided separately for learners according to equity group. In selecting related measures, priority should be given to using those that are known to correlate consistently with the outcomes measures. Columns 3.1 and 3.2 in Figure 2 contain a sample list of outcomes. If these initial differences or similarities are considered to be nonmalleable, reasons for such assumptions should be stated.

Educational process as it involves groups of learners

Again, the major process categories include access and treatment columns that parallel Figure 1. With respect to content, it is important to learn whether the same cognitive, affective, and psychomotor items are taught to all groups of learners; for example, are boys taught advanced science and girls shorthand? It is also important to determine whether the content was presented in a segregated or integrated setting; for instance, are minority students placed in vocational educational courses and majority students in college prep?

Similarly, interactions between and among groups of students and staff must be carefully documented. Research suggests, for example, that teachers, other personnel, peers, and sometimes even investigators may interact differentially with students by sex and by race (Scott-Jones and Clark, 1986; Genova and Walberg, 1980; Harvey, 1986; Lockheed,

1985 a; Morrison and Gurin, 1979; Wirtenberg, Klein, Richardson and Thomas, 1981). In investigating equity group differences in interpersonal situations, it is important to note subtle as well as overt differences that may arise when the learners are token representatives of their sex, race, and so forth.

Information pertaining to instructional materials is often — though certainly not always — fairly straightforward. Are the same or equivalent[4] instructional materials used by diverse populations of students in the same or equivalent ways, with the same intensity, and perceived to be similarly important? For example, recent findings suggest that most economically disadvantaged elementary school students are using computers for remedial instruction in subject areas, rather than for learning about computers (Campbell, 1983; Klein, 1984; Lockheed, 1985 b; Shubert, 1986).

Group outcomes

The major categories suggested here are the same as in the parallel section of Figure 1. In choosing outcomes that may differ by equity group, efforts should be made to identify outcomes where the less dominant equity group excels (e.g., bilingual students' facility with other languages; females' caretaking skills and cumulative grades) as well as the more typical outcomes where the dominant group generally excels, such as educational attainment, earned incomes, and leadership positions. This consideration is particularly important in the selection of achievement test instruments (Klein, 1987 a). Where possible, additional neutral long-term outcomes should also be selected and related outcomes examined.

Stereotyping as it Pertains to Equity Groups

The bottom half of Figure 2, although organized like the top half, focuses on stereotyping — attributing abilities, motivations, behaviors, values, and roles to a person or group solely because of their membership in a particular group. The dimensions in the top half of Figure 2 address differences that may or may not have been stereotyped; for example, black and white students may have different school attendance patterns but neither they nor their significant others may possess stereotyped expectations that would have contributed to this difference.

The dimensions in the bottom half of Figure 2, unlike those in the top half, assume that stereotyping, much like mathematics or human relation skills, is learned and performed by members within as well as by those outside the equity groups. It also assumes that some stereotypes are fairly accurate predictors for most members of a group but that many more stereotypes are misleading and thus, undesirable. It is important to distinguish between knowledge about group characteristics and views about what these characteristics should be, as has been done in the development of separate instruments to measure career knowledge and career attitudes.

Initial group stereotypes

Investigators should indicate their assumptions about ascribed, nonmalleable stereotypes for all learners according to their equity group. For example, overall greater male physical strength may be attributed to the fact that most males are larger than females in size. Assumptions, if any, that some learner characteristics may be malleable or learnable for one equity group and nonmalleable for another should also be specified.

The relevant ways in which members of appropriate equity groups are socialized into stereotyping — often by being taught that they must behave in particular ways and sometimes even segregating themselves — are frequently referred to as internal barriers. Both they and externally imposed stereotypes or external barriers should be specified. Results from pretreatment outcome measures assessing existing stereotyping should also be included.

Educational process as it involves learner groups

It is fairly easy to distinguish stereotypes in the educational process from the simple differential processes described in the top half of this column of Figure 2. To identify stereotyping in content, ask if the same or equivalent information is presented to all students in the same or equivalent ways, or if it is biased or stereotyped. Stereotyping in content generally may be identified according to some or all of the following flaws: members of the less dominant equity group(s) are frequently omitted or 'invisible'; individuals are generally portrayed in traditional roles, and overgeneralizations are made about what they can do based solely on a characteristic or characteristics stereotypically associated with their membership in a particular equity group; errors are made in assigning stereotypes; and members of less dominant equity group(s) and their activities are often devalued or described in derogatory roles as compared with the dominant group(s).

If the above types of stereotypes are avoided, the content is probably fair. However, content may also be affirmative and help students understand the nature of bias and equity laws so that they will be in a position to resist harmful stereotyping.

To identify stereotyping in interpersonal interactions, investigators should note whether or not the teachers and students are teaching each other to adopt traditional roles and to segregate themselves, or whether they are teaching, modeling, and facilitating nonstereotyped responsibilities and behaviors and cross-equity group interactions. For example, are teachers assigning tasks such as running the movie projector to boys and watering the plants to girls? Are physically handicapped students assigned more individualized tasks than non-handicapped students? Are white children from wealthy families treated as though they had more academic ability than black students from poor families? Are all bilingual students grouped together when teams and groups are selected?

As in dealing with stereotyping in content, investigators should describe whether the instructional materials being used are biased, fair, or affirmative. (For additional information on this distinction see Scott and Schau, 1985.)

Learner outcomes

Indicators of stereotyping, such as social distance measures, could be included in the examples for column 3 in the top half of Figure 2, which is focused on comparing scores by equity group. However, we have singled out many of these indicators for special attention in the bottom half of column 3, which focuses exclusively on stereotyping.

As was the case in measuring learner outcomes with respect to discrimination, we included nonbehavioral as well as short-term and summative behavioral indicators of stereotyping. Examples of non-behavioral measures of stereotypes include attitude, perceptions, and expectations toward stereotyping.

Examples of short-term behavioral measures that focus on role indicators include cognitive knowledge outcome measures such as knowledge of equal rights, contributions to all equity groups, and awareness of inappropriate stereotyping in society. Social process measures of short-term stereotyping behaviors may include sociometric instruments designed to describe segregation patterns, observations of sexual harassment patterns, and analyses of racist, sexist, or otherwise biased language and speech patterns in classroom oral communications. Experiential outcome measures of stereotyping may document nontraditional or educational career choices, awards for increasing equity, or measures of instructional racism and sexism.

Summative behavioral indicators of decreased stereotyping may include the selection of nontraditional careers or the assumption of multiple roles. We urge caution in selecting indicators on stereotyping as their design may have been based on stereotyped assumptions. For example, masculinity/feminity scales are based on sex stereotypes that are difficult to validate in a nontautological way.

Goal-Oriented Educational Equity Based Measurement Dimensions

The equity dimensions of our measurement framework are designed to address alternative process and outcome goals within the context of contrasting interpretations of the meaning of 'equity'. The third figure of our model represents an often overlooked aspect of equity-related work – predictive conceptual distinctions that underlie definitions of equity.

Discussions of equity often involve substantial controversy and disagreement. This is at least in part because people differ in the meaning that they attach to the concept of equity and because knowledge of equity-related cause and effect relationships is frequently limited. Even where research has been informative, the outcomes from specified equitable or inequitable treatments are frequently not predictable because other aspects of the situation are different or change (Klein, 1984, 1986, 1987 b).

Historically, equity tends to be associated with fairness or justice, as distinct from equality, which tends to be associated with sameness (Harvey, 1980, 1982). However, there is no one empirically or philosophically correct definition of equity. Meanings reflect the values and priorities of the person supplying the definition and their understanding of how the implementation of their values will affect the results for the target group. Hence, it is hardly surprising that confusion and disagreements about the meaning of the concept commonly occur and that assumptions about seemingly shared, unstated definitions generally turn out to be unfounded.

Analyses of the various meanings assigned to equity indicate that although definitions of equity may vary, our circular 'input, process, and outcome' continuum is useful in defining equity goals. The understandings and assumptions about initial inputs frequently influence choices of equity process and outcome goals. There is, for example, debate about whether society has responsibility for ensuring the same outcomes if differential outcomes can be shown to be the result of nonmalleable characteristics or personal (internal) factors (see, for example, Ennis 1978; and Harvey, 1978). However, these input assumptions will be ommited from Figure 3 where emphasis will be on process and outcome goals as they relate to eliminating discrimination or decreasing stereotyping.

Like Figure 2, the top half of Figure 3 addresses differences between or among equity groups. The general goal is to eliminate these differences — or to eliminate discrimination. However, this goal model will show that some goals involved in eliminating discrimination actually end up advocating differential treatments.

Goals to Eliminate Discrimination

Goals to decrease discrimination in *access* to educational treatments between or among equity groups reflect positions that emphasize either providing the *same* access or *differential* access. Same access equity goals focus on the necessity of providing equal (same) access to everyone. Whether an individual has the necessary background or ability to take advantage of the available access is not the issue; that depends on individual effort, capability, and motivation. Open competition for entrance to postsecondary educational institutions exemplifies this position.

Differential access goals, on the other hand, are based on the belief that individual differences and needs affect an individual's ability to take advantage of routes of access, as do past and existing inequities, barriers, privileges, restrictions, and so on. These positions emphasize the need to provide appropriate routes of access that allow everyone to avail themselves of existing educational treatments and benefits. This will often require providing different routes of access to different individuals or groups of individuals, justified on the basis of need and merit. Assumptions about initial learner group characteristics help determine the need or merit for the process goals. Programs and policies reflecting a differential access position are often oriented toward outreach activities and are designed to provide access to individuals who tend to be unserved or underserved by the educational system. Efforts to recruit minorities and women to postsecondary educational programs exemplify this approach.

Equity *treatment* goals focus on what needs to be made accessible, done, or given to an individual or equity group to achieve the desired outcome goals. Many equity discussions focus on external preprocess factors or inputs on the part of an organization, institution, or program, such as per-pupil expenditures, libraries, quality of teachers, teacher

Figure 3: Goal-oriented educational equity dimensions

1. *Goal Foci*	2. *Process Goals*	3. *Outcome Goals*
	Discrimination-Related Goals	
1.1 *Discrimination Goal*	2.1 Access/Treatment Goals	3.1 *Outcome Goals*
A. Eliminate discrimination (between or among equity groups)	A. Describe process goals in terms of *Access* or *Treatments** *Access* • Provide the same access to X† to everyone regardless of previous inequities, e.g., open competition for admission to higher education with no out-reach activities. — within the same context — in a separate, segregated but equal context • Provide differential access on the basis of: — need, e.g., recruitment activities to encourage females/minorities to enroll in advanced math programs — merit, e.g., recruitment activities to encourage students with high test scores to enrol in advanced math programs — need and merit, e.g., recruitment activities to encourage females/minorities with high test scores to enroll in advanced math *Treatment* • Provide the same treatment to everyone — within the same context (random or fixed pattern) — in a separate, segregated but equal context • Provide differential treatment on the basis of: — need, e.g., financial assistance to low SES students — merit, e.g., financial assistance to students with the highest test scores and grades — need and merit, e.g., financial assistance to low SES students with the highest test scores and grades	A. Describe outcome goals in terms of *educational* and *long-range societal outcomes* with respect to the applicable category *Educational Outcomes* • Same outcomes (all possess the same skills, know the same facts, etc.) — select outcomes most valued by diverse groups — select outcomes most valued by dominant groups • Same minimum outcomes for all, e.g., minimum competency standards for desired outcomes • Same progress for all (same rates of progress given different starting points) • Proportionate results (according to representation in the population) • Equivalent results (comparable achievement given unique abilities) *Long-Range Societal Outcomes* • Same outcomes (all possess the same skills, know the same facts, etc.) — select outcomes most valued by diverse groups — select outcomes most valued by dominant groups • Same minimum outcomes for all • Same progress for all • Proportionate results • Equivalent results B. Outcome goals should be identified within the three categories indicated in Column 3, Figures 1 and 2 (nonbehavioral, short-term behavioral, summative behavioral).
	Stereotyping-Related Goals	
1.2 *Stereotyping Goal*	2.2 Access/Treatment Goals	3.2 *Outcome Goals*
AA. Decrease stereotyping (within and about equity groups)	AA. Describe process goals to decease stereotyping, e.g.: • Decrease groups' expectations and behaviors that limit the opportunities of its members to maximize their individual talents. • Increase knowledge and use of equitable (fair and affirmative) processes by examining and counteracting stereotyping in society.	AA. Describe outcome goals to decrease stereotyping, e.g., • Fewer jobs, roles, activities,and expectations become differentiated by equity group membership. • There is decreased use of stereotypes in decision-making by and about individuals. • Segregation in education and society caused by stereotyping is reduced.

*Describe process goals in terms of *Access* or *Treatment* with respect to: (a) whether they are the same or differential; (b) if differential, explain the differences; (c) justification for differential access/treatment. (Include in this description a discussion of the content, role of teacher(s) and others, and role of intended/unintended educational products and practices, as they relate to access or treatment process goals).
†indicates some particular access or treatment activity.

morale, equipment, attendance regulations, and so forth. However, the focus of our framework is on treatments that affect the learner more directly, such as the educational activities, materials, or opportunities provided to the student. Although treatment goals can be assigned a variety of specific definitions, the more general notions of *same* and *differential* treatment can be identified in a manner similar to that discussed in connection with access interpretations.

Some equity treatment goals emphasize treating all learners in the same manner. They tend to focus on the provision of educational activities and programs to learners who take advantage of access to those activities. Goals of this type are relatively straightforward due to the emphasis placed on providing every learner with the same treatments. Some of these goals include the notion of 'color blindness' or that it is undesirable to notice differences among individuals or equity groups.

Program and policy goals reflecting the notion of differential treatment are far more complex and can take many forms. Some emphasize the importance of providing different but equivalent treatments, based on individual needs, interests, background, and so on. Some multicultural and bilingual programs exemplify this approach. Others emphasize the importance of providing supplementary or compensatory treatments to individuals who have traditionally been unserved or underserved by the educational system, thus enabling students to take advantage of available educational opportunities that would otherwise be unaccessible to them. Chapter 1 of the Education Consolidation and Improvement Act of 1981 exemplifies this position.

Differences are not necessarily a sign of an inequitable activity or situation nor is 'sameness' necessarily a sign of an equitable activity or situation. Differential access, for example, has been used as a means to remedy inequitable situations, such as outreach activities to increase the participation of minorities and women in mathematics and science careers.

Both of the above described differential treatment approaches are based on an assumption that some individuals have educational needs justifying that they be treated differently at least in the short term. A somewhat similar *merit*-based argument also can be made in defense of differential treatment. Students with high achievement scores, for example, 'merit' academic scholarships and placement in classes designed for the academically gifted.

Equity *outcome* goals focus on educational and societal output or results and represent a somewhat different approach to equity than access and treatment process goals. Access and treatment interpretations focus on the provision of routes of access or particular treatments; outcome interpretations focus on addressing either an existing inequity or the success or failure of particular treatments or access designed to promote equity. Within the context of education, outcome interpretations often focus on some type of cognitive achievement results. Societal outcome goals are frequently more long-range and general performance-oriented.

Unlike access and treatment goals to eliminate discrimination, most equity advocates agree that the long-term outcome goals should focus on decreasing differences between or among equity groups on key commonly valued outcomes such as literacy. Reaching agreement on what constitutes these commonly held values is often difficult, however. The different ways that people tend to measure these increased similarities are listed under the outcome goals section of Figure 3 and range from minimum achievement to the same rates of progress assuming different starting points. Common equity outcome goals include: (i) having both or all groups achieve minimum levels of competencies; (ii) having the less dominant group(s) achieve parity with the more dominant group(s); and (iii) decreasing differences by making the groups more similar to each other at least in the possession of desirable outcomes, for example, 'English speakers should learn Spanish while Spanish speakers learn English; females and males should learn leadership skills with a caring dimension' (Campbell and Klein, 1982, p. 584).

Many equity advocates also value diversity of outcomes within equity groups so that the range of acceptable and likely responses is equally broad for all groups. Others believe that it is appropriate to choose where to increase or decrease differences or similarities among groups. Nonequity advocates generally prefer the status quo and believe that educational and societal goals should play no role in decreasing the differences among groups and some argue that goals and strategies should be designed to increase these differences (Campbell and Klein, 1982).

In addition to achievement goals, other outcomes may also be considered important indicators of the success or failure of access or treatment-related activities and policies designed to enhance equity. Examples of outcome measures that may indicate the success or failure of efforts to promote equity in education include the following: the number of members of a particular equity group enrolled in particular academic programs; dropout and graduation rates; university application, acceptance, and graduation rates; and the percentage of equity group members employed in particular professions, such as medicine and law.

Goals to Decrease Stereotyping

In some ways both the process and outcome goals to decrease stereotyping (described in the bottom half of Figure 3) are like the outcome goals to eliminate discrimination because one goal of decreasing stereotyping is to have members of all equity groups perceived as more similar to one another. Thus, the goal would be to have both Blacks and Whites having less stereotyped understanding of their own and each other's histories and capabilities, for example. However, like the goals to eliminate discrimination, goals to decrease stereotyping become complicated, primarily because some stereotypes such as 'the gender gap' are based on real generalizations, whereas others are grounded in inaccurate, discriminatory assumptions, or are subtle and difficult to identify (Wirtenberg *et al.*, 1981). In addition, the goals to decrease stereotyping should be viewed as both internal and external because members of groups are often limited by stereotypes they make about themselves as well as those others make about their group.

Success in attaining outcome goals to decrease stereotyping in education will influence goals in the top half of this figure because they will decrease differences between or among groups. Thus, if goals to decrease stereotyping are attained, there is evidence to suggest that there may be less segregation in the larger society (Eisler, 1987).

In identifying equity goals, the overall goal should be identified, as should the more specific process-related objectives. For example, the overall goal of a particular activity may be to increase access of minorities to professional academic programs, such as medicine and law, that traditionally have been dominated by Whites. The process-related objectives may include increasing the number of minorities enrolled in such programs, altering attitudes toward minority participation in these programs, increasing employment opportunities for minorities in these fields, and so on.

Researchers and evaluators may also want to use mandated equity goals or standards as their point of departure. If they do so, they will realize that these may not have a consistently direct, positive effect on attaining equity outcomes because of a variety of contextual differences (Klein, 1986, 1987 b, 1988).

Educational Equity Measurement Framework: Combined Dimensions

Figure 4 represents the synthesis of three critical components of our measurement framework as depicted separately in Figures 1–3. Imagining the three previous figures as transparent overlays, the completed framework is a reflection of their streamlined combination, the pieces of which have been discussed in detail in prior sections. As were Figures

Figure 4: Educational equity measurement framework

1. *Initial Input*		2. *The Educational Process as it Involves Groups of Learners*	
			Comparisons by
1.0 *Learner Attributes*	1.1 *External Pre-Process Influences*	2.0 *Access*	2.1 *Treatment*
A. Compare equity groups according to their ascribed characteristics such as race, gender, ethnicity, age, handicap as well as any pretreatment experiences or scores on outcome or other measures known to correlate consistently for equity groups with the outcome measures. Discuss assumptions about the causes of any differences between/among equity groups such as whether they are genetic (biochemical) or learned (psychological).	A. Describe the relevant institutional input, e.g., per pupil expenditures, educational facilities, male-female majority-minority personnel ratio, expectations for learners, attitudes toward learners, that may differentially influence equity groups.	A. Describe access to educational treatments (policies and practices that influence learners' opportunities to participate in educational treatments, such as admissions, recruitment, enrollment, and mentoring). B. Note whether access is the same or different for different equity groups. If the same, describe whether it is separate but equal. If different, is it provided on the basis of need, merit, or both? Measurement should consider the importance of and difficulty in obtaining the access.	A. Describe the educational treatments (activities, programs, products, or practices that involve the learner such as courses, materials, and classroom interactions). B. Note whether the treatment is the same or different for different equity groups. If the same, describe whether it is separate but equal. If different, is it provided on the basis of need, merit, or both? C. Include relevant information on the content of instruction, role of educators, and role of educational products and practices as they relate to different equity groups. D. Measurement should consider adequacy and frequency of the activity as it affects the learners.

	Extent of
1.2 *Initial Learner Group Stereotypes*	2.2 *Educational Process as it Involves Groups of Learners*
A. Describe common stereotypes about members of different equity groups and the degree to which learners and educators believe that these stereotypes can be changed. For each category of outcome measured, describe those that measure stereotyping specifically (i.e., attitudes toward desirability of stereotyping). Focus on learners' internalized stereotyped views of self-perceptions particularly as they are perceived in relation to members of different group(s). Where possible describe the interaction of stereotypes under study with pertinent stereotypes of different groups (e.g., racial stereotypes with sex, ethnic, age, disability, etc. stereotypes).	A. Describe the nature and extent of stereotyping in any of the two above categories of the educational process as it involves the learner by answering questions such as: Are the policies or activities: • biased or stereotyped? • about stereotyping in society and equity laws? B. Are teachers, peers, and others teaching stereotyping or the elimination of stereotyping by their actions relating to direct instruction such as assignment of stereotyped tasks or by modeling stereotyped behavior? C. Are the instructional materials biased, fair, or affirmative with respect to the stereotyping of specified equity groups? D. Are group expectations and behavior that limit the opportunities of its members to maximize their individual talent increasing or decreasing?

3. *Outcomes*

4. *Goals*

Equity Group

3.0 *Learner Outcomes*

A. Compare equity groups on variables such as the following:
- Nonbehavioral: attitudes, expectations, motivations, aspirations, self-assessment, moral development, cognitive achievement.
- Short-term behavioral: anxiety, empathy, sociability, nurturance, cooperation, level of activity, aggression, dependency, competitive behavior, enrollment in courses.
- Summative behavioral: educational attainment, income, success in parenting, nurturing, career choices, civic activities.

B. Equity-group based comparisons of the above outcomes may be measured on the basis of whether they are:
- the same (identical)
- proportional
- minimal standards
- same progress (gains)
- equivalent, but not identical

3.1 *Related Educational and Societal Outcomes*

A. These outcomes do not need to be comprised of results from learners and may be by-products of the equity process. Examples include:
- Measures of organizational effectiveness
  - —School attendance rate
  - —school climate
- Increased teacher effectiveness if teachers were not considered the learners.
- Measures of reduced discrimination in society.
- Cost of the equity process
  - —Cost in time, money, effort for educators
  - —Feasibility for educators in terms of ease of use, conflicts with other activities
  - —Satisfaction of teacher, administrator, or trainer with the equity process

4.0 *Process Goals*

A. Describe process goals in terms of access and/or treatment.
- Provide the same access and/or treatment to everyone regardless of previous inequities.
- Provide differential access and/or treatment on the basis of:
  - —need
  - —merit
  - —need and merit

4.1 *Outcome Goals*

A. Describe outcome goals in terms of educational and long-range societal outcomes with respect to the applicable category:
- Same outcomes
- Same minimum outcomes
- Same progress for all
- Proportionate results
- Equivalent results

Stereotyping

3.2 *Outcomes*

A. Describe common learner outcomes in terms of:
- Nonbehavioral measures, attitudes, and expectations toward stereotyping
- Short-term behavioral indicators:
  - —knowledge of equal rights, contributions of different equity groups, awareness of inaccurate stereotypes
  - —affective measures such as information on sexual harassment or segregation patterns, sexism or racism in language
  - —experiential measures of nontraditional career choice, compliance with legal protections (e.g., Title VII, IX, P.L. 94-142)
- Summative behavioral indicators such as employment in nontraditional jobs, or assuming nonstereotyped roles.

4.2 *Goals*

A. Describe goals in terms of both process and outcomes:
- Process goals:
  - —Decrease stereotyping within equity group
  - —Decrease stereotyping about equity group(s) by other groups
- Outcome goals:
  - —Evidence of less stereotyping in education and society
  - —Evidence of less group segregation or among group differences

2 and 3, the final figure is differentiated according to (i) comparisons by or among equity groups and (ii) extent of stereotyping, reflecting the distinctions we make between these two means of measuring equity in education.

The predictive goal-oriented aspects of Figure 3 have also been incorporated along with the Figure 2 equity variables to help researchers consider similarities and differences as well as some of the subtleties in addressing stereotyping.

The framework is intentionally designed to be both value neutral and general in nature to provide a generic tool for measuring educational equity. It is anticipated that researchers and evaluators will use it as a flexible framework, adapting it to the specifications and needs of their particular individual projects while preserving the generic categorical measurement considerations that we have found to be integral to any analysis of educational equity.

Conclusion

The educational equity measurement framework presented here is only the first step in addressing a multitude of issues involving the measurement of educational equity. It is designed to specify the various generic dimensions that must be considered in such a measurement process, including: general research and evaluation measurement dimensions independent of equity considerations; equity group-based measurement dimensions, differentiated according to discrimination and stereotyping; and educational equity goal-based measurement dimensions, reflecting distinctions among definitions and conceptions of equity. Knowing that these dimensions should be considered in any equity-related research or evaluation efforts does much to improve the quality, reliability, and utility of work in the field of educational equity.

How a researcher or evaluator actually translates these measurement considerations into her or his individual research design raises other issues that must also be addressed. The measurement framework provides an organized, systematic means by which such issues can and should be identified and examined, providing some cohesiveness and uniformity to a field that in the past has tended to be fairly segmented. In so doing, the framework identifies measurement considerations common to all educational equity investigations, whether they focus on education of the handicapped, sex equity, bilingual education, race equity, migrant education, and so on. Thus, it not only moves us one step forward in addressing measurement issues, it also sets in motion the difficult — but much needed – process of developing an educational paradigm that reflects the common concepts and methodologies unique to this broad and complex field of inquiry.

Notes

1 This chapter is a slightly revised version of an article published by the authors in the Summer 1985 issue of *Journal of Educational Equity and Leadership,* **5,** 2, pp. 145–68.
2 This article was written by Dr Klein in her role as a private citizen and does not necessarily reflect the views of her employer, the U.S. Department of Education.
3 It is important to note that the framework for measuring equity described throughout this chapter focuses primarily at the level of the group rather than the individual. This is not intended to preclude its application within the context of individual appeals to equity, however. Nor is it intended to suggest that equity claims at the level of the individual are any less valid or involve any less complex measurement issues.
4 The concept of 'equivalence' is a particularly important consideration in measuring educational equity. Although there is considerable controversy about whether access and/or treatment should be the 'same' or 'differential' to achieve equity, it is important to recognize that individual and/or group differences (in past and existing barriers, restrictions, etc.) can limit the capacity of an individual to take advantage of certain treatments and avenues of access.

References

BORNSTEIN, R. (1981) *Title IX Compliance and Sex Equity: Definitions, Distinctions, Costs and Benefits*, Urban Diversity Series (No. 73) ERIC Clearinghouse on Urban Education. New York: Teachers College, Columbia University. (ERIC Document Reproduction Service No. ED 202 948)

CAMPBELL, P.B. (1983) Computers in education: A question of access. Paper presented at the American Educational Research Association Annual Meeting, Montreal. (ERIC Document Reproduction Service No. ED 233 684)

CAMPBELL, P.C. and KLEIN, S.S. (1982) 'Equity issues in education', in MITZEL, H. *et al.* (Eds) *Encyclopedia of Educational Research* (5th ed.) New York: MacMillan.

EISLER, R. (1987) *The Chalice and the Blade*, New York: Harper and Row.

ENNIS, R.H. (1978) 'Equality of educational opportunity', *Educational Theory,* **26**, 1, pp. 3–8.

GENOVA, W.J. and WALBERG, H.J. (1980) *A Practitioners' Guide for Achieving Student Integration in City High Schools.* Report submitted to the National Institute of Education, Washington, DC. (ERIC Document Reproduction Service No. ED 200 699)

HARVEY, G. (1978) 'Response to Ennis', *Educational Theory*, **28**, 2, pp. 147–51.

HARVEY, G. (1980) *Information Equity in the Field of Education: A Concept Paper*. San Francisco: Far West Laboratory for Educational Research and Development. (ERIC Document Reproduction Service No. ED 188 603)

HARVEY, G. (1982) *Competing Interpretations of Equity*, Washington, DC: National Institute of Education. (Available from G. Harvey, The Regional Laboratory for Educational Improvement of the Northeast and Islands, 290 South Main Street, Andover, MA 01810.)

HARVEY, G. (1986) 'Finding reality among the myths: Why what you thought about sex equity in education isn't so', *Phi Delta Kappan*, **67**, 7, pp. 509–12.

KLEIN, S.S. (1984) *Computer Education: A Catalog of Projects Sponsored by the US Department of Education*, 1983. Washington, DC: National Institute of Education. (ERIC Document Reproduction Service No. ED 244 624; GPO-065-000-00202-7)

KLEIN, S.S. (1986) 'Identifying elements of equity in federal, state, and local educational standards', *Equity and Excellence: The University of Massachusetts, School of Education Quarterly*, **22**, 4–6, pp. 132–8.

KLEIN, S.S. (1987 a) Dealing with sex inequities in standardized testing. Paper presented at Women in Science and Engineering: Changing Vision to Reality Conference, University of Michigan, sponsored by the American Association for the Advancement of Science, Washington, DC and to be published in conference proceedings, 1989.

KLEIN, S.S. (1987 b) 'The role of public policy in the education of girls and women', *Educational Evaluation and Policy Analysis*, **9**, 3, pp. 219–30.

KLEIN, S.S. (1988) 'Using sex equity research to improve education policies', *Theory into Practice*, **27**, 2, pp. 152–60.

KLEIN, S.S., RUSSO, L.N., CAMPBELL, P.C. and HARVEY, G. (1985) 'Introduction: Examining the achievement of sex equity in and through education', in KLEIN, S.S. (Ed.), *Handbook for Achieving Sex Equity Through Education*, Baltimore: Johns Hopkins University Press, pp. 1–11.

LARSON, M. (1980) An exploration of the use of race and sex as variables in federally sponsored education evaluation. Report submitted to the National Institute of Education. Washington, DC, (Contract No. NIEP 800065).

LOCKHEED, M.E. (1985 a) 'Sex equity in classroom organization and climate', in KLEIN, S.S. (Ed.), *Handbook for Achieving Sex Equity Through Education*, Baltimore: Johns Hopkins University Press, pp. 189–217.

LOCKHEED, M.E. (Guest editor) (1985 b) 'Women, girls, and computers', [Special Issue] *Sex Roles*, **13**, 3/4.

MORRISON, B.M. with GURIN, P. (1979) *Two-way Socialization Processes in the Classroom*, Washington, DC: National Institute of Education (ERIC Document Reproduction Service No. ED198194).

O'LEARY, V. and WALLSTON, B.S. (1981) 'Sex makes a difference: The differential perceptions of women and men', in WHEELER, L. (Ed.) *Review of Personality and Social Psychology* (Vol. 2). Beverly Hills, CA: Sage.

SCHUBERT, J.G. (1986) 'Gender equity in computer learning', *Theory into Practice*, **25**, 4, pp. 267–75.

SCOTT, K.P. and SCHAU, C.G. (1985) 'Sex equity and sex bias in instructional material', in KLEIN, S.S. (Ed.) *Handbook for Achieving Sex Equity through Education*, Baltimore: The Johns Hopkins University Press, pp. 218–36.

SCOTT-JONES, D. and CLARK, M.L. (1986) 'The school experiences of black girls: The interaction of gender, race, and socioeconomic status' *Phi Delta Kappan*, **67**, 7, pp. 520–6.

WEALE, A. (1978) *Equality and Social Policy*, London: Routledge and Kegan Paul.

WIRTENBERG, J., KLEIN, S., RICHARDSON, B. and THOMAS, V. (1981) 'Sex equity in American education', *Educational Leadership*, **38,** 4, pp. 311–9.

WORTHEN, B.R., and SANDERS, J.R. (1973) '*Educational Evaluation: Theory and Practice*, Worthington, OH: Charles A. Jones.

Educational Equity Versus Equality of Education: An Alternative Conception[1]

Walter G. Secada

Equity in education seems to be uniquely an American notion. Most writers who write about both equity and equality of education come from the United States. Elsewhere, equality is what is written about; equity is hardly ever mentioned (see, for example, *British Journal of Sociology of Education*, 1986). Equity, in this chapter refers to our judgments about whether or not a given state of affairs is just. Within Western traditions of law, for example, an appeal to equity was — and still is — an appeal to justice that goes beyond a given law's application (McDowell, 1981; Re, 1982). This relationship between equity and justice was first stated by Aristotle, to whom both McDowell and Re trace our notions of equity jurisprudence:

> There are two kinds of right and wrong conduct towards others, one provided for by written ordinances, the other by unwritten . . . The other kind (i.e., the unwritten kind) has itself two varieties . . . (of which the second variety) makes up for the defects in a community's written code of law. This is what we call equity; people regard it as just; it is, in fact, *the sort of justice which goes beyond the written law* [emphasis added] (Aristotle, *Rhetoric*, 1981, pp. 63–4; also, McDowell, 1981, p. 17).

The heart of equity lies in our ability to acknowledge that, even though our actions might be in accord with a set of rules, their results may be unjust. Equity goes beyond following those rules, even if we have agreed that they are intended to achieve justice. Equity gauges the results of actions directly against standards of justice, and it is used to decide whether or not what is being done is just. Educational equity, therefore, should be construed as a check on the justice of specific actions that are carried out within the educational arena and the arrangements that result from those actions.

Equality in education often gets defined in terms of inequality – its opposite. Commonly, groups are defined along some demographic characteristic: social class, race, gender, ethnicity, language background. Aggregate differences among these groups are then explored using some educationally important index. Group differences are interpreted to demonstrate the existence of inequality. Equality, therefore, is defined implicitly as the absence of those differences. In this chapter, equality will be used to describe parity between groups along some agreed upon index. Parity is in the aggregate, e.g., when the distributions of achievement scores in two (or more) groups has the same average.[2]

The purpose of this chapter is to develop and to explore the implications of a simple proposition: the relationship of educational equity to equality of education is problematic. In the first section, that relationship is explored to identify how these terms – equity and equality – have been linked in current usage within the United States. In the second section, I will discuss tensions, if not outright contradictions, between the two concepts when too strong a coupling is made. Hence, this chapter is an argument that there are good reasons for loosening the link between educational equity and equality of education. This chapter ends with some points on how we might reconsider educational equity to develop and to further explore the results of such a conceptual uncoupling.

The Interrelationship Between Equity and Equality of Education

In much of the current literature on educational equity, we can find writers who treat equity and equality as interchangeable. When they do so, it seems likely that they actually mean to use only one of these terms (usually equality) in a technical sense. On the other hand, there are writers who relate equity and equality to each other, and who seem to be using each of these terms in a more or less technical manner. Campbell and Klein (1982), for example, provide a litany of 'examples of educational inequity' (p. 581), which are, in fact, examples of denial of equal educational opportunity to specific groups within our society: compulsory ignorance laws, dual educational systems, denial of higher education to women, and the isolation of handicapped learners. In their examples, the aggrieved parties – Blacks, women and the handicapped – were denied meaningful access to education. Though acceptable at one time, the practices described by Campbell and Klein seem manifestly unjust today. In a more positive vein, efforts to remedy such denials of opportunity and to provide an equal education to these groups were based on, and serve to document, our social commitments to justice in education, i.e., to educational equity.

Education and schools have been described in terms of inputs, processes, and outputs (Good and Brophy, 1986; Harvey and Klein, 1985, this volume; Mosteller and Moynihan, 1972); in terms of access, participation, and outcomes (Brookover and Lezotte, 1981; Winfield, 1986); or in other, yet similar, terms (see, for example, Fennema and Meyer, this volume). At each of these junctures in the educational system, something is construed as being distributed among the students by the schooling system. Schooling inputs, for example, include what a school starts with when educating its students. Those resources—financial (monies), physical (books in a library, science lab equipment) and personnel (its teachers and how qualified they are)—are distributed (i) directly among schools and (ii) indirectly among the students who enroll in those schools. Educational processes include what happens within the school to educate students (how they are treated by teachers, whether or not students are promoted/retained, what courses they take). The distribution of such processes has also been examined by writers interested in equity. Educational outcomes refer to the goals and the results of the educational processes. Outcomes that have been studied include student rate of dropping out—or its converse, rate of completion—academic achievement, and attitudes. Each of these, especially knowledge as measured by academic achievement, can be—and has been—construed as a valued good that the educational system has within its power to distribute among its students. The distribution of those goods can be judged in terms of whether it is just, which usually is interpreted to mean whether the goods in question have been distributed equally among different groups.

The concern for equality of education, therefore, is a concern that the goods of which the educational system can distribute are equally distributed—in the aggregate—among different groups of students. In many ways, the *Coleman Report* (Coleman, 1967; Coleman *et al.*, 1966) typifies this approach. Equality of educational opportunity was defined by the EEOS (Equality of Educational Opportunity Survey) team in terms of three major kinds of inputs and two major kinds of outputs (Coleman, 1967, 1975; Marjoribanks, 1975):

(i) Differences in global input characteristics such as per pupil expenditure, physical facilities, and library resources;
(ii) The social and racial student composition of the school;

(iii) Intangible characteristics of the school such as teachers' expectations of students, teacher morale, and the level of interest of the student body in learning;
(iv) Equality of results given the *same* individual input;
(v) Equality of results given *different* individual inputs (Marjoribanks, 1975, p. 1).

It was assumed, 'implicit in the statute (which funded the study reported in the *Coleman Report*) and explicit within the EEOS research team, . . . that the schools for minority students were grossly inferior. The survey was to establish that once and for all' (Mosteller and Moynihan, 1972, p. 8). In effect, the study was intended to demonstrate that at the input level, specifically at point (i) above, there would be group differences between schools attended by black students and those attended by Whites. To everyone's surprise that was not the finding.

> As these data stand, they suggest that by the time of the EEOS, the nation had, within geographic regions, come close to supplying equal, though largely separate, facilities to Negroes and whites according to the classical notion of traditional physical *inputs* [emphasis added]. Insofar as that is true, the country, having chosen a goal in a social problem, had come close to reaching it (Mosteller and Moynihan, 1972, p. 11).

As Mosteller and Moynihan pointed out, if equality of educational opportunity is defined to be equality—in the aggregate between groups—at the inputs of education, then such equality had been achieved with respect to the educational opportunity provided to Blacks versus that provided to Whites. Rather than to accept such 'a definition of educational opportunity, which, given his findings on input differences, casts the American educational system as rather *equitable*' [emphasis added] (Murphy, 1981, p. 63), Coleman switched his criterion for equality of opportunity from being located at the inputs of schooling to its effects, more specifically, to point (v), above.

More recently, Coleman (1975) has rejected both inputs and outputs as the sole criteria for equality of educational opportunity because 'neither definition, neither inputs nor outputs, is viable when taken at the extreme' (p. 27). Coleman has settled on a definition for equality of educational opportunity that relates inputs to outputs: the *reduction* of inequalities in the outcomes of education arising from students' family characteristics.[3]

Much of the current literature on equality of education traces its roots to the *Coleman Report*. Authors typically raise equity concerns by arguing that there should be an equal distribution of that which is being measured between those groups about whom an inquiry is being made. According to such views, the achievement of equality of that which is being distributed—in the aggregate and between groups—should be pursued at a specific location as a matter of public policy. Brookover and Lezotte (1981) made this link between equity and equality explicit in their discussion:

> A substantial part of the history of federal involvement in education is represented by a series of policies designed to advance the principle of *educational equity*. These policies reflect a governmental response to the belief that all citizens, regardless of sex, race, creed, or economic circumstance should be guaranteed *equality of education* [emphasis added] (p. 65).

Brookover and Lezotte argued that educational equity has been pursued by federal policies that have tried to achieve equality at any one of three junctures: access, participation, and outcomes. After considering whether or not educational equity would be achieved if parity between groups were attained in terms of access to schools or in terms of actual student participation in such schools, and after rejecting both of these standards as inadequate, Brookover and Lezotte settled on 'the outcomes standard (which) is not only hypothetically plausible, but logistically possible. This growing body of research has begun to accumulate evidence that in some cases the assessed educational outcomes for minority and disadvantaged youngsters can be at parity with those for their nonminority, nondisadvantaged counterparts' (p. 67). Moreover, 'the outcomes standard does not state that *all* students perform the same, but that the *aggregate* performance in various *groups* is the same, or nearly so' (p. 69) [emphases added]. Hence, educational equity would be achieved if we could obtain an equal distribution of academic achievement scores—parity—between 'disadvantaged youngsters' and Whites.

There are many who follow distinctions that are similar to Brookover and Lezotte's distinctions among access, participation, and outcomes: Fennema and Meyer (this volume), Harvey and Klein (1985, this volume), Winfield (1986). Their work serves to document the problematic nature of locating equity at just one juncture, as do Brookover and Lezotte. The interrelationships among access, participation, and outcomes vary as a function of subject matter, as well as what group one is considering. Moreover, Fennema and Meyer, as well as Winfield, conclude that, regardless which definition of equality of education one settles on, it does not exist as a function of gender or social class.

Green (1983) is another writer who systematically tried to explore the connection between equity and equality. He maintained that equity and equality are linked, but also, he draws a distinction between those inequalities that are inequitable and those that are not: 'Inequity always implies injustice. Inequality does not' (p. 324). In a more positive vein, Green described the 'ideal of educational equity' as a

> statistically describable social condition within which there is a random distribution of resources, attainment, and educational achievement in respect to variables irrelevant to educational justice together with a predictable distribution in respect to variables relevant to educational justice (p. 324).

Following Green, we could create groups based on a range of demographic variables. Educational equity, in Green's usage, would dictate that some of these variables should be irrelevant (uncorrelated) to the distribution of the aforementioned educational goods: gender, social class, race, or geography (p. 325). On the other hand, there are other demographic variables that *should be relevant* (correlated) to inequalities in that distribution: individual choice, ability, or virtue (p. 324). Moreover, it would seem to be our responsibility to create inequalities of the second kind were they not to exist.

Green provided the example of college attendance by students who were grouped along academic aptitude and socioeconomic status. Green's data show that along both dimensions the distribution of college attendance is unequal across groups. He argued not only that the unequal distribution of college attendance as a function of academic aptitude is equitable[4] but also that an equal distribution of college attendance among students of differing ability groups would, in fact, be inequitable: 'There may be more inequity when inequalities are nonexistent than when they are small' (p. 331). Regarding socioeconomic status, Green concluded that the unequal distribution of college attendance *might* be inequitable, though there are confounding factors, such as student choice, which render this conclusion uncertain.

Hauser and Featherman (1976, p. 100) argued that among the inequities found in the American schooling system are those inequalities that are correlated to social factors: socioeconomic status (father's education and occupation), number of siblings, family structure, location of birth, Hispanicity and race. They provide data to demonstrate that the correlation of these factors to the number of years of schooling individuals from these groups have decreased during the twentieth century. Hence, we are closer to achieving equality of schooling, and, by implication, equity.

In each of these three examples—Brookover and Lezotte (1981), Green (1983), and Hauser and Featherman (1976)—equity is used to identify a specific location within the educational system where the authors argue that between-group parity (for specific groups) should be sought. Given the number of ways in which groups can be defined, the number of locations where between-group parity can be sought, and the large number of indices that can be used for investigating those disparities, there is a need to distinguish the *preferred* grouping variables, locations, and indices from the others. Linking that which is preferred to *equity* conveys, at least implicitly, that by pursuing equality at that particular juncture of the educational system, we also pursue justice.

This characterization can be made more explicit. Assume that we have settled on groups (or characteristics by which to form those groups) for whom there is an agreed upon consensus that educational equity is a concern[5]; moreover, assume that there are agreed upon locations and indices for measuring educational opportunities. Then the search for equity becomes little more than a search for the null hypothesis (see also Campbell, this volume).

If educational equity becomes equality of education, then arguments about justice are in danger of being recast as technical arguments about equality. Such a transformation may limit, severely, our ability to consider other fundamental issues that should fall under the rubric of educational equity. In the following section of this chapter, I would like to return to my original characterization of equity as a qualitative concern for what is just. I will argue, and provide examples in support of that argument, that, even if we succeed in achieving equality of education, equity—based on our ability to say, 'Yes, but is it just?'—will remain a serious issue.

Yes, But Is Equality Just?

Is that which is being distributed worth having?

To ask a question based on equality, without first asking if that along which the equality is being measured is desirable and/or just, is to miss what equity is about. For example, let us assume that a number of school systems have each properly implemented a text reviewed by Selden (this volume), that teachers treated their students in a fair and otherwise desirable manner, and that the distribution of achievement scores shows no group differences based on gender, class, race, ethnicity, or language. It seems unlikely that anyone would want to claim that this result was equitable, since the eugenics-based content of those texts renders them inherently inequitable.

Though there may be equality of outcomes between groups, the curriculum and the knowledge that it distributes among students must first be scrutinized. In discussing equality of education, writers such as Coleman *et al.* (1966), Brookover and Lezotte (1981), and Green (1983) are silent on the content of what is distributed. Yet the questioning of how curriculum content gets legitimated as knowledge would seem to be a critical concern for equity (see Freedman, this volume; Selden, this volume).

I do not argue for an impoverished curriculum, which is how some critics characterize educational equity.[6] Rather, note that there are different visions of what should be in the curriculum—and some of those visions incorporate content that is inherently unjust. Selden's example of eugenics materials being included and discussed within biology texts through the late 1940s provides a paradigmatic example of this point.

Closer to current educational practice, Anyon (1979) showed how history texts are made to serve the interests of dominant groups. Efforts to ensure equal knowledge of such histories—between dominant and nondominant groups—would serve to legitimate those arrangements. The new scholarship on women (e.g., *Educational Researcher*, 1986) explores what has been lost, in both research and educational practice, due to gender-based discrimination in academic scholarship and it seeks a redefinition of scholarship and instructional practice that include those values. Hispanics and other minority language groups argue that educational opportunity should *not* come at the price of losing either their native languages or their cultures (Stein, 1986). Grant and Sleeter (1986 a) argued that educational equity consists of 'education that is multicultural and social reconstructionist' (p. 105). In this view, to be equitable, education must help students address issues of cultural differences; it should help students to understand the dynamics that have led to certain social arrangements, to question those arrangements, and to do so effectively.

The point is this: equality of education explores quantitative differences between groups. It cannot address those qualitative issues related to the curriculum against which that equality is assessed. It is precisely such issues that must be addressed as part of any effort to ensure educational equity. If we fail to ask whether or not the curriculum is just in what it legitimates as knowledge, we may well achieve equality of education, but it seems highly unlikely that that equality will represent a just distribution of knowledge.

Is equality enough?

Another problem in linking educational equity to equality of education is that it limits us to considering internal justifications for schooling. Typically used indices of educational opportunity demonstrate how the equality-of-education discourse is limited to the educational system as an end in itself: the distribution of school resources and finances; school-based knowledge as measured by academic achievement; opportunities to learn school-based knowledge as measured by course taking and completion; successful school completion as measured by rates of dropping out and, conversely, of graduation; and treatment of students within classrooms. Educational equity, as an appeal to what is just, must look beyond such immediate outcomes to schooling's more distantly related external outcomes.

For example, assume that the curriculum itself has been scrutinized and that the concerns outlined above have been addressed. Assume, once again, that equality of education—based on the relevant groups and the relevant indices—has been achieved. Could we claim to have achieved educational equity in *that* case? The answer would depend how one sees the goals of schooling.

If education were viewed as an end in and of itself—as an enclosed system—we might say, Yes. All the statistical tests of whatever empirical distributions one cared to consider would be within chance levels. We would meet Brookover and Lezotte's (1981), Green's (1983) and Hauser and Featherman's (1976) empirically defined criteria for equity. Moreover, my objections based on what is contained in the curriculum would have been, in theory, met.

But schooling has purposes other than the transmission of knowledge from one generation to the next. That schooling is meant to prepare students for later life employment is one of its most important and most readily acknowledged functions. It seems patently unjust for equal levels of schooling and of school knowledge to result in unequal job opportunities in later life.[7] Jencks *et al.* (1972) found that, though educational attainment is correlated to income, group income disparities among different social classes exist, even after controlling for level of education.[8] Though equality of education does not typically address such out-of-school disparities, educational equity, as an appeal to what is just, should be concerned with that state of affairs.

Jencks' results also suggest one method for addressing this out of school inequality within the context of schooling. We could compensate for the unfair effects of social class on later life employment by educating lower SES students to higher educational levels than their middle and upper class peers. Hence, in the name of educational equity, it is possible to argue for *inequality in educational outcomes* in the reverse direction of what has been classically found.

In fact, there is evidence that some groups have adopted a strategy of overachievement in science and mathematics as a means of overcoming unequal employment opportunities. Ogbu and Matute-Bianchi (1986) report that 'a number of Chinese informants have told one of the authors that the disproportionate representation of Chinese students in science and mathematics fields is a kind of insurance against employment discrimination ... even if an Anglo employer is prejudiced against Chinese, the one with the technical skills will be hired' (p. 110). Tsang (1988) provides an historical account for the 'over-representation' of Asian Americans in mathematics and science fields, as has been repeatedly borne out (Dix, 1987; National Science Foundation, 1986). Indeed, Asian Americans are often omitted from discussions of how to increase the participation of women and minorities in mathematics (see, for example, Cole and Griffin, 1987).

This position—that existing inequalities in educational attainment should be reversed—is obviously different from the position that inequality should be eradicated. The latter position is one that most proponents of equity would seem to advocate. In part, this is because educational inequalities are so pervasive and resistant to change that equality seems like a major accomplishment in and of itself. Yet such a view may be too limiting, especially if education is linked to later life employment.

This position is also different from arguments for affirmative action in employment. Affirmative action in employment is a noneducational response to the unequal representation of various groups in the workforce. Affirmative action acknowledges that members from one group might not be as qualified—on the whole—as members from another for some jobs, and that, all too often when two people from different groups are equally qualified, other factors enter into play that bias against the hiring of the non-middle-class, non-white, non-male individual. Hence, affirmative action entails hiring the individual who represents the discriminated-against group, provided that individual has met minimum job requirements. Reversing the direction of educational inequalities in favor of underachieving groups represents an *educational* response to such unequal employment opportunities. In this case, affirmative action becomes superfluous, since the discriminated-against group would be the better qualified group.

Hence, if one accepts that a primary purpose of schooling is to prepare students for later life employment, and if one believes equal school outcomes should lead to equal employment opportunities, then one may end up committed to the position that equality of educational outcomes is not enough. Groups that have been historically discriminated against in employment opportunities may need to attain higher levels of achievement, or to be overrepresented in specific fields, to overcome employment discrimination. Whether it is equitable to seek such an educational outcome cannot be addressed by debates couched only in terms of equality of education; its terms are too restrictive. Yet such an issue should be of critical concern for educational equity.

Can simple groups be constructed and maintained in a just manner?

There has been a broad consensus within American educational policy concerning groups that qualify for considerations under the rubric of equality of education. These include groups based on race, gender, ethnic/language status, and social status. The variables represented by the formation of these groups should be, in Green's (1983) terms, irrelevant or uncorrelated to indices of educational equality. The documentation of such correlations has a long, if depressing, history.

This consensus is based, in part, on the successes of Blacks, Hispanics, women, and other groups in having their educational concerns legitimated by US courts of law and the Congress. For example, courts consider most actions that impact upon the education of Blacks as being 'suspect', which means that, in any legal proceedings, the burden of proof lies in showing that an action is not discriminatory (Abraham, 1982; Hogan, 1984). Federal mandates and assistance to schools for overcoming barriers to equal educational opportunity for these groups has a history dating back to Johnson's Great Society (Elementary and Secondary Education Act, 1965; Equal Educational Opportunities Act, 1976). In spite of the Reagan administration's efforts to dismantle (and failing at that, to change the focus of) these programs (Apple, this volume; Clark and Astuto, 1986), there remains a consensus that education should be seen in terms of how its resources and outcomes get distributed among these groups.

It is not my intent to review that history. What I wish to discuss are four problems in this sorting of individuals into groups. The first is the exclusion of subgroups from groups based on the technical need for homogeneity. Campbell (this volume) discusses biases in research that occur when group membership is restricted to a subset of the larger group, but when research findings subsequently are generalized to the whole group. For example, in their study of gender differences in mathematics as a function of college course taking, Ethington and Wolfle (1986) decided that 'in order to avoid confounding effects of differing student background, the analyses were restricted to United States citizens with English as their first language' (p. 6). The purported confounding effects failed to be specified, so it is not possible to evaluate the validity of their claim. Either their results—that course of mathematics study during college interacts with gender in producing differing GRE scores—apply to the general population, in which case the restriction of their sample is not justified; or it has applicability which is limited to 'United States citizens with English as their first language', in which case its generalizability is open to question and the omitted group is necessary for further study. The technical demands of group-based research—as in the case of equality of education—may result in decisions that limit representation by individuals who are located at the most disadvantaged fringes of our educational system. Such decisions would seem to be, if not inherently inequitable, at least problematic.

A second problem with the formation of groups is that within-group homogeneity disappears when one investigates the actual makeup of the group. Drawing distinctions within the commonly accepted, major demographic classifications—Hispanic, Asian/Pacific Islander, American Indian-Alaskan Native (National Center for Education Statistics, 1985) has become a litany among minority language groups. For example, Hispanics are broken down into Mexican-American, Puerto Rican, Cuban, and other Latin American (National Center for Education Statistics, 1981; Orfield, 1986). Yet even within *each* of these subgroups, further subclassifications seem necessary to understand their educational differences. Matute-Bianchi (1986) identified no fewer than five different subgroups into which Mexican-American students sort themselves, and she tied membership in each of these subgroups to different patterns of beliefs about education and to academic achievement.

This fracturing of groups into smaller and smaller subgroups creates a problem in the search for equality. It may be possible to create aggregate equalities between large groups, or to find inequalities in favor of a minority group (as is the case for Asian students in mathematics). On the other hand, equality between larger groups (for example, Hispanic versus white)—if achieved—is very likely to mask inequalities *within* the groups (i.e., among the subgroups). If disparities among the larger groups indicates inequity (Green, 1983), then it would seem that similar disparities among the smaller subgroups should also. Few researchers involved in equality of education have given serious consideration to this problem.

A third difficulty with the formation of groups is that unidimensional groupings may impoverish our ability to understand and hence to respond to the dynamics that lead to the inequalities being considered. For example, gender and social class cut across race, ethnicity and language. Grant and Sleeter (1986 b) pointed out how attention to just one status group tends to oversimplify much-needed analysis of how students socialize among themselves in desegregated schools as well as in cooperative groups. One response to Grant and Sleeter's analysis has been to create multidimensional grouping schemes (Coldiron *et al.*, 1987).

The responses to each of these three problems—the need for homogeneity in measurement, the internal fracturing of groups into smaller and smaller subgroups, and the crossing of grouping variables—go beyond being technical. Not only has complexity increased, the commitment to equality has become problematic. For example, it might be possible to create parity between Hispanics and Whites as large-scale groups. Such overall parity could be created by increasing the achievement levels of Cubans (who already outperform other Hispanic subgroups, even when socioeconomic status is controlled for, NCES, 1981), while allowing the achievement of other Hispanics to lag behind. Similarly, it may be possible to obtain parity between men and women by increasing the achievement of white and/or of middle and upper class women while ignoring the condition of education for nonwhite and/or lower class women. In each case, the fracturing of the Hispanic category into smaller subcategories and the crossing of gender with social class and race, may represent an evolving, if tacit, position that these options would be considered inequitable. On the other hand, I have not seen anyone make such a commitment explicit. The larger equalities might be acceptable if the creation of subgroups and the crossing of grouping variables were simply technical adjustments within the equality of education paradigm.

A fourth problem in creating groups lies in the increasing number of groups that are claiming legitimacy in terms of educational equity. Campbell and Klein (1982) discussed that list: students with learning disabilities and physical handicaps (over thirty such conditions), those who suffer discrimination because of age, religious preferences, and other conditions. Not included by Campbell and Klein, but certainly a group that has been in the center of recent debates on the right to school attendance, are students who contract AIDS. That list is likely to grow further.

Again, it is not clear if the response to these developments might be technical insofar as groups get added to the list of what Harvey and Klein (this volume) call equity groups. Whether such an addition represents a commitment to achieving equality for them, or whether it entails more modest goals,[9] remains an open question.

The formation of equity groups is clearly nontrivial. The exclusion of individuals because of the technical need to avoid confounding one's results with extraneous factors, the fracturing of groups into smaller and smaller subgroups, the attempt to reintegrate social class with gender with race/ethnicity/language status, and the clamoring by newly forming groups for recognition of their claims to educational equity must be seen as part of an overall pattern of stress that is being placed on how we have interpreted educational equity in terms of equality of education. As long as claims for equity are automatically transformed into claims for equality, the responses will tend to be all or none: we add the group to the equation in some way, or we deny its legitimacy. It is not clear, though, if adding groups into the discourse on equality of education carries with it a commitment to providing them the same status as the larger-scaled groups that have been part of the traditional discourse on equality of education. If we grant that equity can be—must be—other than equality, then the responses can be more fine grained. In either case, deciding the legitimacy of groups and the responses that their claims will receive is a concern of educational equity.

Beyond Equality

Equity attempts to look at the justice of a given state of affairs, a justice that goes beyond acting in agreed upon ways and seeks to look at justice of the arrangements leading up to and resulting from those actions. Note that the actions *do* represent an effort at being just, much as the laws represent our legal and written efforts at justice. However, just as law cannot anticipate all eventualities and moreover, just as our notions of justice are constantly evolving and changing, so too, our actions and social arrangements may be found wanting, in the face of both unforseen occurrences and our evolving notions of what is just. Equity inhabits this ground between our actions on the one hand and our notions of justice on the other.

Our educational system represents a social effort to distribute certain kinds of knowledge—as well as doing other things—from one generation to the next. How that system acts and the results of its actions can be weighed against whether or not they are just. Educational equity is what gauges how well our educational system lives up to our ideals of justice in the face of changing circumstances and of our evolving notions of justice.

The recognition that there are many inequalities in our social and educational systems, on the other hand, has a long history (Tawney, 1964). The labeling of a specific form of inequality as unjust by the US Supreme Court in its *Brown* decisions (1954, 1955) was not based on any laws of that time. Many laws, the Court's own decision in *Plessy v. Ferguson* (1898), and agreed upon ways of doing things, in fact, supported that inequality. Rather, the labeling of 'separate but equal' as unconstitutional was based on an evolving notion of justice that recognized the importance of group-based differences.[10]

Certainly, the recognition that educational inequalities between some groups is unjust should not be lost. Yet not all group differences represent inequities: one need only read some psychology to see the myriad ways in which group differences get interpreted. Only some group differences are inequitable. In American educational scholarship and practice, the identification of those group differences, their location at specific locations within the educational system, and the definition of what indices count, all have been used to define equality of educational opportunity as equity.

On the other hand, equality of education assumes the existence of curriculum within which to seek that equality. As my examples demonstrate, educational equity should be concerned about the curriculum, which is assumed, and it may be invoked in order to seek inequality in the reverse direction of what has been usually found. Moreover, the creation and maintenance of equity groups has become problematic due to a variety of factors. These include the technical need for homogeneity within equity groups (and the subsequent dropping of individuals who do not fit), the fracturing of equity groups into increasingly smaller subgroups, the recognition that certain grouping characteristics cut across one another, and the increasing number of groups that are claiming status under the rubric of equity. Whether our responses to those forces are construed as technical within the equality paradigms, or whether they represent new commitments to how equality should be sought, is by no means clear at present. Yet our responses to those developing circumstances must be considered in light of what we think is just, i.e., in terms of educational equity.

The fundamental difference between equity and equality is that equity is a qualitative property while equality is quantitative. Yet, one of the most powerful constructs at the disposal of equity is equality, and the recognition that group inequalities may be unjust. The two terms, however, are—or at least should be—different. Work in educational equity needs to discriminate when its concerns coincide with those of equality and when they do not.

Equity should also be concerned with the individual, who in fact seems almost totally absent from the current discourse on equality of education. As Maxine Greene (1987) reminded us:

> Of course it is necessary, at times, to think in terms of aggregates—gender, social class, race. So often, however, as

> Michael Ignatieff makes clear, we become abruptly aware of distinctions between 'needs which can be specified in a language of political and social rights and those which cannot'. Rights language . . . can express the claims individuals make against the collectivity, the very claims with which we are most concerned when we speak of equity. But the language turns out to be 'relatively impoverished as a means of expressing individuals . . . needs *for* the collectivity'. On the presumption that everyone has a right to be treated with dignity, Ignatieff makes the point that there is always more to respect in a person than his/her rights . . . We all know, for example, that in our mental hospitals and old peoples' homes and even public schools, administrative good conscience appears to consist in respecting peoples' rights while demeaning them as persons (p. 5).

When we create groups and assign individuals to them, regardless how well intentioned that grouping is, we also have taken steps to marginalize and to dehumanize the members of the other group, the one to which we do not belong. The danger in assigning individuals to groups is that 'we homogenize outsiders; we impose an objective interpretation of group membership in full confidence . . . that our beliefs are well founded, that our ways of sorting people out are good and right' (Greene, 1987, p. 6).

Indeed, until the *Brown I/II* (1954, 1955) decisions, equity in jurisprudence was concerned primarily with individual appeals to justice (McDowell, 1981). Subsequent to *Brown*, the equality of education debate took on the rubric of equity. Hence, discourse on educational equity has focused on groups to the virtual exclusion of individuals. We need to consider both.

My whole discussion has turned on the assumption that there is something that can be called justice. Our notions of equity have changed with changes in our notions of justice. For example, in ancient Greek times, justice was found in the natural order of things. Law was predicated on the discovery of that order and in its reflection within human affairs. In the event of circumstances that could not have been foreseen by the lawgiver, equity was invoked to set aright errors in the application of law. Equity was the human intervention that ensured that the natural order was maintained, lest nature itself intervene and reestablish that order. For another example, the king ruled through divine right at the beginnings of British Common Law. Divine justice was supposed to be reflected in the king's laws. Hence, equity was an appeal to the king's conscience, that he review how his law had been implemented in light of divine justice (see McDowell, 1981, for a more detailed discussion).

How educational equity would fare under different notions of justice and of the purposes for education is an open question. For example, Ogbu (1987) argued that we must take into account folk theories about the nature of equity. He noted the existence of competing paradigms for defining equity within differing national responses to perceived inequities. In India there is affirmative discrimination in education; in Israel, separate norms are used for judging the achievements of Ashkenaz Jews and of Sephardic Jews; in the United States, the ideal is to treat everyone alike. Similarly, Ogbu argued, groups within the United States will have different perceptions of what is just or equitable. For example, minority language groups who have willingly entered the United States adopt theories that one gets ahead in this country by doing well in school. Minorities whose status can be likened to that of a colonized or conquered people have adopted different views related to the efficacy of schooling.[11] For the former group, the link between success in school and later life rewards are real; educational opportunity is precisely that. For the latter group, however, schooling is inherently unjust since, in the groups' historical experiences, such links are nonexistent. According to Ogbu, research and policy that fail to take into account these historical facts, and their translation into folk theories among these groups, cannot hope to address issues of educational equity.

In sum, there are three areas into which scholarship on educational equity might move. First, future work should seek to set equity apart from equality of education, while not losing the valuable insights that have been gained through that discourse.[12] Second, equity needs to concern itself with the individual as well as with the group case. Finally, the link of educational equity to justice needs exploring in terms of how differing notions of justice—at both the folk and the individual level—may give rise to different notions of equity. As Apple notes elsewhere in this volume, 'There is educational work to be done'.

Notes

1 An earlier version of this paper was discussed at the annual meeting of the American Educational Research Association, Washington, DC., April 1987. I would like to acknowledge the helpful discussions I have had with Carl Grant on this topic, and the careful commentary that Tom Popkewitz gave to an earlier working draft.

2 There are writers who discuss equality in terms of egalitarian notions of distributive justice, i.e., that everyone should get an equal amount of all goods within a society. For education, egalitarian views of equality would hold that each student should leave school knowing the same amount as every other student. That notion of equality is not found in most of the American

literature on equity and equality and thus, lies beyond the scope of this chapter.

3 In settling on this definition, Coleman has returned to the US Supreme Court's *Brown I* (1954) decision, which rejected equality of inputs — separate but equal — as a priori unjust, but which did not embrace equality of educational outcomes as its sole criterion for equality, either. Gordon (1972) presented other ways for defining equality of educational opportunity.

4 Whether or not a parallel form of unequal opportunity — tracking of ability groups in secondary school — also would be considered equitable by Green is an open question.

5 In the current discourse on educational equity, there is consensus that groups formed on the basis of race, gender, or national origin (see the Equal Educational Opportunities Act, 1976) should show no differences on measures of educational opportunity. Though a similar consensus seems to have been formed, at one time, with respect to social class, there seems to be an overall pessimism about our ability to achieve equality with respect to this variable. For example, the effective schools literature accepts constraints based on social class since schools are labeled as being effective only as compared to other schools of the *same* socioeconomic status (Good and Brophy, 1986).

6 For example, Tomlinson (1986) asks the rhetorical question: 'Which way lies equity: making school easy by routing students around academic courses, especially hard ones, or insisting that all children encounter the academic core even if some of them have a difficult time of it?' (p. 16).

7 Willis (1986) calls unemployment the final inequality. Equality of education, as it is typically construed in American scholarship, tends not to consider such inequalities.

8 This does not suggest, as Tanner (1973) interpreted Jencks to believe, that schooling does not matter in later life employment. Rather, what Jencks seemed to have actually argued is that schooling does not matter as much as the historically accepted folklore would have us believe (see Gordon, 1972).

9 For example, the education of the handicapped — particularly those with severe handicaps — is problematic. Green (1983) argued that ability — and clearly handicaps constrain ability — is one grouping variable along which we *should* have inequality, provided those inequalities are not too great. Weinberg (1981) poses other, and more fundamental, problems. She ends with the comment 'that it may be difficult to show why severely retarded or disturbed human beings have a right to such things as an education but that nonhuman animals with similar capacities do not' (p. 187).

10 Footnote 11 documents that the Court was aware of social science research on the effects of segregation on black students. The relevance of those studies has since been severely questioned (McDowell, 1981).

11 For a more complete discussion of Ogbu's analysis of the relationship between folk theories of schooling and its outcomes, see Ogbu (1978), Ogbu and Matute-Bianchi (1986). Matute-Bianchi (1986) extended Ogbu's analysis to subgroups within larger groups.

12 See Yates (1986) for a discussion of what was lost when discourse on inequality moved too far from its liberal origins in the Australian and British experiences.

References

ABRAHAM, H.J. (1982) *Freedom and the Court: Civil Rights and Liberties in the United States* (4th ed.), New York: Oxford Press.

ANYON, J. (1979) 'Ideology and United States history textbooks', *Harvard Educational Review,* **49**, pp. 361–86.

APPLE, M. (this volume) 'How equality has been redefined in the conservative restoration'.

ARISTOTLE, (1981) *Rhetoric* (Translated by W. Rhys Roberts). Philadelphia: Franklin. [Reprinted from *The Words of Aristotle.* Oxford University Press]

British Journal of Sociology of Education (1986) **7**, 2. Special number: 'Whatever happened to inequality?'

BROOKOVER, W.B., and LEZOTTE, L. (1981) 'Educational equity: A democratic principle at a crossroads', *The Urban Review,* **13,** 2, pp. 65–71.

CAMPBELL, P.B. (this volume) 'Educational equity and research paradigms'.

CAMPBELL, P., and KLEIN, S. (1982) 'Equity issues in education', in MITZEL, H. (Ed.), *Encyclopedia of Educational Research* (5th ed.), New York: Macmillan, pp. 581–7.

CLARK, D.L., and ASTUTO, T.A. (1986) 'The significance and permanence of changes in federal educational policy', *Educational Researcher,* **15,** 8, pp. 4–13.

COLDIRON, J.R., *et al.* (1987) The influence of race, class and gender on mathematics achievement and self-concept for 5th-, 8th-, and 11th-grade students in Pennsylvania schools. Symposium conducted at the annual meeting of the American Educational Research Association, Washington, DC, April.

COLE, M., and GRIFFIN, P. (1987) *Contextual Factors in Education: Improving Science and Mathematics Education for Minorities and Women*, Madison: Wisconsin Center for Education Research, University of Wisconsin.

COLEMAN, J. (1967) *The Concept of Equality of Educational Opportunity,* Baltimore, MD: Johns Hopkins University. [ERIC Document Reproduction Service No. ED 015 157]

COLEMAN, J. (1975) 'What is meant by an "equal educational opportunity"?' *Oxford Review of Education,* **1,** 1, pp. 27–9.

COLEMAN, J. *et al.* (1966) *Equality of Educational Opportunity*, Washington, DC: US Department of Health, Education and Welfare. [ERIC Document Reproduction Service No. ED 012 275]

DIX, L.S. (1987) *Minorities: Their Underrepresentation and Career Differentials in Science and Engineering* (Proceedings of a workshop). Washington, DC: National Academy Press.

Educational Researcher (1986) **15,** 6. Special issue: The new scholarship on women in education.

ELEMENTARY AND SECONDARY EDUCATION ACT (1965).

EQUAL EDUCATIONAL OPPORTUNITIES ACT (1976) 20 USC 1703–1706.

ETHINGTON, C.A., and WOLFLE, L.M. (1986) Sex Differences in Quantitative and Analytic GRE Performance: An Exploratory Study. Paper presented at the annual meeting of the American Educational Research Association, San Francisco, April.

FENNEMA, E., and MEYER, M.R. (this volume) 'Gender, equity and mathematics'.

FREEDMAN, K. (this volume) 'Dilemmas of equity in art education: Ideologies of individualism and cultural capital'.

GOOD, T.L., and BROPHY, J.E. (1986) 'School effects', in WITTROCK, M. C. (Ed.), *Handbook of Research on Teaching* (3rd ed.), New York: Macmillan, pp. 570–602.

GORDON, E.W. (1972) 'Toward defining equality of educational opportunity', in MOSTELLER, F. and MOYNIHAN, D.P. (Eds), *On Equality of Educational Opportunity*, New York: Vintage Books. pp. 423–434.

GRANT, C.A., and SLEETER, C.E. (1986 a) 'Educational equity: Education that is multicultural and social reconstructionist', *Journal of Educational Equity and Leadership,* **6**, pp. 105–18.

GRANT, C.A., and SLEETER, C.E. (1986 b) 'Race, class and gender effects in education: An argument for integrative analysis', *Review of Educational Research,* **56,** 2, pp. 195–211.

GREEN, T.F. (1983) 'Excellence, equity and equality', in SHULMAN, L.S. and SYKES, G. (Eds), *Handbook of Teaching and Policy,* New York: Longman, pp. 318–41.

GREENE, M. (1987) Educational equity and interpretation theory. Paper presented at the Symposium, *What is equity in education?* annual meeting of the American Educational Research Association, Washington, DC, April.

HARVEY, G., and KLEIN, S.S. (1985) 'Understanding and measuring equity in education: A conceptual model', *Journal of Educational Equity and Leadership,* **5,** 2, pp. 145–68.

HARVEY, G., and KLEIN, S.S. (this volume) 'Understanding and measuring equity in education: A conceptual framework'.

HAUSER, R.M., and FEATHERMAN, D.L. (1976) 'Equality of schooling: Trends and prospects', *Sociology of Education,* **49**, pp. 99–120.

HOGAN, J.C. (1984) *The Schools, the Courts and the Public Interest,* (2nd ed.), Lexington, MA: Lexington Books.

JENCKS, C. *et al.* (1972) *Inequality: A Reassessment of the Effect of Family and Schooling in America,* New York: Basic Books.

McDOWELL, G.L. (1981) *Equity and the Constitution,* Chicago: University of Chicago Press.

MARJORIBANKS, K. (1975) 'Equal educational opportunity: A definition', (Editorial introduction), *Oxford Educational Review,* **1,** 1, pp. 25–6.

MATUTE-BIANCHI, M.E. (1986) 'Ethnic identities and patterns of school success and failure among Mexican-descent and Japanese-American students in a California high school: An ethnographic analysis', *American Journal of Education,* **95,** 1, pp. 233–55.

MOSTELLER, F., and MOYNIHAN, D.P. (1972) 'A pathbreaking report', in MOSTELLER, F., and MOYNIHAN, D.P. (Eds), *On Equality of Educational Opportunity,* New York: Vantage Books, pp. 3–66.

MURPHY, J. (1981) 'Disparity and inequality in education: The crippling legacy of Coleman', *British Journal of Sociology of Education,* **2,** 1, pp. 61–70.

NATIONAL CENTER FOR EDUCATION STATISTICS (1981) *Hispanic Students in American High Schools: Background Characteristics and Achievement* (Contractor Report). Washington, DC: US Government Printing Office.

NATIONAL CENTER FOR EDUCATION STATISTICS (1985) *The Condition of Education,*

(1985 edition), Washington, DC: US Government Printing Office.
NATIONAL SCIENCE FOUNDATION (1986) *Women and Minorities in Science and Engineering* (NSF 86–301). Washington, DC: Author. January.
OGBU, J.U. (1978) *Minority Education and Caste: The American System in Cross-cultural Perspective,* Orlando, FL: Academic Press.
OGBU, J.U.(1987) Comments made at the Symposium, *What is equity in education?* Annual meeting of the American Educational Research Association, Washington, DC. April.
OGBU, J.U., and MATUTE-BIANCHI, M.E. (1986) 'Understanding sociocultural factors: Knowledge, identity, and school adjustment', in CALIFORNIA STATE DEPARTMENT OF EDUCATION, BILINGUAL EDUCATION OFFICE *Beyond language: Social and Cultural Factors in Schooling Language Minority Students.* Los Angeles: Evaluation, Dissemination and Assessment Center, CA State University, pp. 73–142.
ORFIELD, G. (1986) 'Hispanic education: Challenges, research and policies', *American Journal of Education,* **95,** 1, pp. 1–25.
RE, E.D. (1982) *Remedies: Cases and Materials,* (University Casebook Series). Mineola, NY: Foundation Press.
SELDEN, S. (this volume) 'Biology versus equality: The high school biology textbook from 1914 to 1949'.
STEIN, C.B. (1986) *Sink or Swim: The Politics of Bilingual Education,* New York: Praeger.
TANNER, D. (1973) 'Inequality misconstrued?' *Educational Leadership,* **30**, pp. 703–5.
TAWNEY, R.H. (1964) *Equality,* London: Allen and Unwin.
TOMLINSON, T.M. (1986) 'A nation at risk: Background for a working paper', in TOMLINSON, T.M., and WALBERG, H.J. (Eds), *Academic Work and Educational Excellence*, Berkeley, CA: McCutchan, pp. 3–28.
TSANG, S. (1988) 'The mathematics achievement characteristics of Asian-American students', in COCKING, R.R., and MESTRE, J.P. (Eds), *Linguistic and Cultural Influences on Learning Mathematics*, Hillsdale, NJ: Lawrence Erlbaum, pp. 123–36.
US SUPREME COURT (1898) *Plessy v. Ferguson,* 163 US, p. 537.
US SUPREME COURT (1954) *Brown v. Board of Education of Topeka,* 347 US, pp. 483–96.
US SUPREME COURT (1955) *Brown v. Board of Education of Topeka,* 349 US pp. 295–301.
WEINBERG, L.A. (1982) 'The problem of defending equal rights for the handicapped', *Educational Theory,* **31,** 2, pp. 177–87.
WILLIS, P. (1986) 'Unemployment: The final inequality', *British Journal of Sociology of Education,* **7,** 2, pp. 155–69.
WINFIELD, L.F. (1986) 'Do Chapter I programs promote equity? A review and some comments', *Journal of Educational Equity and Leadership,* **6,** 1, pp. 61–71.
YATES, L. (1986) 'Theorising inequality today', *British Journal of Sociology of Education,* **7,** 2, pp. 119–34.

Equity, Equality, Teachers, and Classroom Life[1]

Carl A. Grant

Since *Brown v. Board of Education* (1954), front line educators (principals and teachers) have been so busy dealing with educational inequality at all levels of school life that they may not have considered the difference between equity and equality in schooling. Educators need to understand the difference and how it can impact classroom life. This impact, I will argue, greatly affects the schooling of students of color, white female students, poor students, and students who are differently able.

Explaining the difference between equity and equality is difficult. There is confusion in the educational literature regarding the use and meaning of these terms, and often the two are used interchangeably. For some educators, for example Turner (1986) and Secada (1987), the meaning of equity is tightly connected with concepts of fairness and justice. Secada (1987) explained it as follows: 'Educational equity concerns those areas for which rules and procedures are based on this notion of justice' (p. 1). The common meaning ascribed to equality is 'the quality or state of being equal' (*Webster*, 1977, p. 306). This meaning comes from early American history and rests 'on an inherited philosophy of natural right' that is proclaimed in the US Constitution under the 'All men are created equal' clause. Wilson (1966) regarded equality as meaning or being related to fraternity, liberty, and democracy (p. 18).

Because equity and equality as concepts do have a great deal in common — they are related to egalitarian concepts of liberty, democracy and freedom from bias — they are often used interchangeably, without specific meaning given to each of the terms. The following statement from Brookover and Lezotte (1981) illustrates this point:

> A substantial part of the history of federal involvement is represented by a series of policies designed to advance the principle

> of educational *equity*. These policies reflect a governmental response to the belief that all citizens regardless of race, creed, or economic circumstance should be guaranteed *equality* of education. While few would deny the societal goal of educational *equity*, there is considerable disagreement as to appropriate ways and means of advancing this principle. (p. 65) [emphasis added]

Additionally, some educators define equity and/or equality more broadly or narrowly than others. For example, Brookover and Lezotte (1981) provided three definitions for the concepts. They described them in terms of 'access', 'participation', and 'outcomes' that are evaluated at 'intent' and 'practice' levels. On the other hand, Campbell and Klein (1982) argued that 'most definitions of educational equity focus only on a singular aspect of equity, that is, either equity regarding *access* to schooling, equity regarding the *process of schooling* or equity regarding the *outcome from schooling*' (p. 583).

They defined *access* as 'an equal opportunity to gain entry' (p. 583) and included the use of different admissions or application procedures. The *process* definition of educational equity is 'the elimination of separate but equal treatment and the mainstreaming of diverse groups of students into school and class activities' (p. 583) and 'a state beyond nondiscrimination which is characterized by fair and just, but not identical treatment'. Finally, they pointed out that the *outcome* definition of educational equity 'means that all students are provided educational experiences that ensure the achievement of certain uniform goals and objectives' (p. 583). It is an equitable share of the benefits of schooling, and equity reduces the predictive value of race, sex, and social class in determining educational achievement.

Finally, confusion exists in the educational literature because educationists and sociologists typically write about inequality, not equality (Turner, 1986, p. 17). Inequities and inequalities still existing at an institutional and personal level, both in school and society, are newsworthy or of sufficient academic importance to be reported in educational books or journals. These inequities and inequalities are obvious in the daily reading of most major newspapers and many educational publications: the failure to effectively desegregate public schools (Fine, 1986; Metcalf, 1983), people of color and white women being proportionally underrepresented in the corporate structure (*New York Times*, 4 January 1987; *New York Times*, 14 July 1987), the racism occurring on college campuses (*Time*, 6 April 1987; *Wisconsin Week*, 13 May 1987).

It is not my purpose in this chapter to become an active participant in the debate on the meaning of equity and equality; however, pointing out that confusion exists about the meaning of the terms helps to situate and provide direction for my discussion of equity, equality, teachers, and classroom life. Hurst (1979) reminded us:

> The manner in which a term is defined and measured has clear implications for what we see and choose to focus on. The concepts we use organize our world and determine what we see. Through symbols, people create their own world. If the symbols and concepts we use vary, so do our beliefs about the central contents of society . . . When we define a concept such as stratification or class one way rather than another, the result is that we focus on certain elements in the society rather than others, others that may be crucial for understanding the dynamics of inequality in society. Some conceptualizations may turn our attention from more disturbing aspects of inequality. (pp. 6–7)

For the purpose of this chapter, educational equity means 'fairness' and 'justice'. Providing fairness and justice in classroom life for students of color, poor students, and white female students would require establishing a classroom environment that is not colorblind and teaching in a manner that accepts and affirms learning style differences, based on culture and gender socialization. Equity also includes being sensitive to past injustices suffered by people of color, white females, people with handicaps, and poor students and the residual impact the past has on those students today. Secada (1987) argued:

> Education equity concerns those areas in which rules and procedures are based on notions of justice . . . equity concerns itself with the exception to the rule. It revolves around our ability to say: 'Yes, you are following the rules, but is the result fair?' (pp. 2–4)

I will borrow from Turner's (1986) explanation of four types of equality to frame my meaning of that concept.

> The first type of equality is ontological equality, or the fundamental equality of persons. The second is equality of opportunity to achieve desirable ends. The third is equality of conditions where there is an attempt to make the conditions of life equal for relevant social groups. Fourth, there is equality of outcome or equality of result. (p. 35)

The work of Good and Brophy (1987) and Grant and Sleeter (1986) identified a number of areas of classroom life. Good and Brophy's discussion included student motivation, classroom management, classroom instruction, and teacher expectations. In the ethnography by

Grant and Sleeter, students identified several areas of classroom life that are similar to the ones cited above: teachers, class work (instruction and curriculum), rules and discipline, and extracurricular activities. This chapter is limited to equity and equality in the following areas: students' learning styles, teacher-student interaction, and curriculum.

Equity, Equality, and Learning Styles

There is a growing body of literature that examines learning style variations among cultural groups and how these various styles affect classroom learning. This literature points out that ethnicity and social class are related to the strategies children learn at home for acquiring, organizing, and remembering information (for example, Cole and Bruner, 1971; Hale, 1982; Kagan and Madsen, 1971; Ramirez and Castaneda, 1974). Shade (1982) warned that black studcents have difficulty academically because their learning style tends to be oriented toward cooperation, content about people, discussion and hands-on work, and whole-to-part learning. This conflicts with the independent, task-oriented, reading-oriented, part-to-whole style teachers often employ. Deyhle (1985) discovered that young Navajo students, as a result of family socialization, interpret tests as games. In contrast, white students viewed tests from a more serious stance. While white children learn early to display knowledge publicly for evaluation, Navajo children are taught that serious learning is a private matter and often they do not exert their best effort when tested. Treating the Navajo and black students the same as (equal to) white students would, according to my interpretation of the educational literature discussed above, not be fair to them.

The learning style of girls, particularly as it relates to mathematic instruction, also has relevance to this point. Fox (1976) argued that, when girls who fear math are taught upper-level math by teachers who individualize instruction, support cooperative interaction (help) between the students, and incorporate social content into problems, girls' achievement levels increase.

Equity would demand that teachers change a good deal of what they are doing in the classroom. What does the learning environment look like now? Cuban (1984), Everhart (1983), Goodlad (1984), and Grant and Sleeter (1986) among others have reported strong similarities in the way instruction is delivered. Cuban aptly summarized these similarities.

In elementary school, almost half of the teachers (43 per cent) put up a daily schedule on the blackboard. If it were time for reading, the teachers would work with one group and assign seatwork to the rest of the class. If it were math, social studies, science, or language arts time, generally the teacher would work from a text with the entire class answering questions from it or from dittoed sheets or workbooks (p. 220).

Both Cuban in his study of six school districts and Goodlad (1984) in his study of thirteen elementary, middle, and high school feeder systems found many elementary teachers who deviated from this pattern by individualizing instruction, utilizing learning criteria, and providing small-group instruction. However, both noted that the majority of elementary teachers favored teacher-centered, large-group instruction in which *all* students worked on the same task. Much of the work was from textbooks, dittoed sheets, or workbooks.

Cuban (1984) observed much more uniformity at the secondary level:

> Rows of tablet-arm chairs facing a teacher who is talking, asking, listening to student answers, and supervising the entire class for most of the period — a time that is *occasionally* punctuated by a student report, a panel or a film. (p. 222) [emphasis added]

These rigid patterns of instruction do meet some of Turner's criteria for equality. The teacher may see all students in the class as being equal (ontological equality). Placing the work on the blackboard and using the same materials with each student may be considered meeting Turner's second explanation of equality, providing equal opportunity to achieve desirable ends. Having classroom conditions that are the same for all may meet Turner's third explanation, equality of conditions. And, if students of color, white female students, and poor students score as well on the test as white male students, the teacher would have achieved equality of result or outcome.

Nevertheless, fairness or equity will not exist for students of color, white female students, and poor and differently able students until their learning styles are accepted and instruction is geared to be responsive to them. Phillips' (1982) research with Warm Springs Indians showed that communication patterns that the children learned in their community conflicted with the communication patterns used and expected by the white teachers in school. Phillips argued that teachers of Indian children could be much more successful if they learned to use communication patterns of the local community. Jordan (1985) argued that, if Hawaiian students are allotted a moderate level of peer interaction, they tend to stay on task. DeLain, Pearson, and Anderson (1985) discovered that black students who exhibit competence in oral games, such as sounding, understand the use of figurative language better than white students. They argued that teachers who incorporate black students' verbal skills in language arts instruction will have a definite strength on which to build further achievement. Block (1984) recommended that girls should work apart from boys to help them catch up with male students in mathematics, science, and leadership skills. Separately, girls develop the skills, attitude, and self-confidence necessary to be successful in male domains.

Involving students actively in classroom activities and in classroom decisions, building on students' learning styles, adapting instruction to the students' skill levels, using cooperative learning, and having teachers who understand and accept the learning styles of the students are baseline essentials for providing educational equity in the classroom. However, it is important to be cautious and not overgeneralize about learning styles for any particular group. For example, all black children may not be oriented toward cooperative, whole-to-part learning thus it is the responsibility of the teacher to find out individual students' learning styles.

Equity, Equality and Student-Teacher Interaction

It is a common belief among teachers that students know when the teacher has their best interest at heart. At schools with diverse populations quality student-teacher interactions are paramount; these interactions convey strong messages concerning the characteristics identified in this paper with equity and equality. Observational studies point out that students of color, white female students, and poor and handicapped students have not achieved equality or equity in their interaction with teachers (Buford, 1973; Freijo and Jaeger, 1976; Pugh, 1974; Williams and Whitehead, 1971). Harvey and Slatin (1975) discovered that teachers tend to rate white students as having more academic potential than black students. Teachers who disliked Black English or saw it as unacceptable gave lower reading comprehension scores to a reader who used Black English than to a reader who used Standard English, although there were no significant differences in quality of answers to comprehension questions (McDermott, 1977). Classroom observational studies have found that teachers call on, ask harder questions of, and praise middle-class white male students most; students of color and of lower class are called on less and their responses are accepted, praised, and elaborated on less (Byalick and Bershoff, 1974; Grant, in press; Jackson and Cosca, 1974; Rist, 1970).

Male students of color were the recipients of more negative responses from teachers than any other group; female students of color were often ignored or were praised more for social accomplishments. White female students tended to be rewarded for neatness more than males and for academic accomplishments more than black females (Rist, 1978).

These research findings point out that Turner's (1986) four types of equality (equality of person, equality of opportunity, equality of condition, and equality of outcome) are not being met in teacher-student interactions. Nor is equity present. One might ask, since inequality is so blatant in these research findings, why the fuss over equity and equality. As noted in the previous section, equality in classroom interaction will not be equity in classroom interactions. The following example will be helpful. Good and Brophy (1987) identified seventeen behaviors that teachers use to indicate differential treatment of high and low achievers, for example, waiting less time for lows to answer, criticizing lows more often for failure, seating lows farther away from the teachers, accepting and using lows' ideas less. Teachers who decided to be numerically equal with these behaviors in their student-teacher interactions could argue using the first three of Turner's criteria for equality (and depending on the results, the fourth criterion also), that all students are being treated identically. However, equity would not be present. Wait time for students of color, especially black boys, may need to be longer in grades three and above. According to Kunjufu (1985, 1986) and others, the young black male often sees school as hostile to his welfare, and may see the teacher as a person who is out to get him. The wait time for the black male student needs to explicitly inform him that he is expected to be academically successful. The teacher should provide both verbal and the nonverbal support that encourages his efforts.

Seating arrangements that make students of color feel at home in the classroom let them know that they have full classroom membership. Seating students of color far away from the teacher revives the 'back of the bus' idea, and assigning students of color to seats very close to the teacher may imply that the students are not to be trusted. It is important to use flexible seating patterns that are based on principles of cooperative group instruction (see Johnson and Johnson, 1984; Johnson, Johnson and Maruyama, 1983; Sharan, 1980).

Teacher-student interactions adopting the principles of equity would include teaching in the manner that acknowledges students' cultural background, as discussed previously, and using the concept of curriculum discussed in the following section. Finally, teacher-student interactions should demonstrate to the students that the teacher has a genuine concern for their present and future welfare; the demonstration is made not only through words but through action, for example, taking them on field trips to colleges and places of business so they can see (and begin to eliminate myths about) the real world. Students need to know that teachers are not afraid to be firm and fair and are willing to stand up for them. Furthermore, teachers should be willing to extend their interactions beyond the school, possibly visiting students' homes.

Equity, Equality and Curriculum

Many educators who examine instructional materials would argue that blatant race and gender stereotypes have been eliminated and that people of color and white women are more frequently included in curriculum materials. These educators would further argue that people of color are presently portrayed more positively in instructional materials and women (white women especially) are more represented in nontraditional roles than they were in the not too distant past (1960–1980). *But* equality in curriculum materials has not been achieved (Butterfield *et al.*, 1979; Council on Interracial Books for Children, 1977; Grant and Grant, 1981; Scott, 1981). For example, women of color, Asian Americans, Hispanic Americans, and poor Americans are not shown often in decision-making positions, and handicapped people are shown different from, rather than similar to, other people. Furthermore, Scott (1981) argued that, although the representation of females in basal reading series has increased, and females are more likely to be portrayed in nontraditional than traditional roles, the opposite is true for males. 'Boys', Scott said, 'are stereotyped often in text when seen in primarily traditional roles and expecting aggressiveness and competition as the norm'. She further added, 'Readers, especially boys, could benefit from seeing a wider range of role behavior for males' (p. 140).

Other evidence that equality is not represented in curriculum was reported by a series of NEA Special Study Committees (1987 a, 1987 b, 1987 c, 1987 d). Concerning Asians and Pacific Islanders, (NEA, 1987 b), they noted that 'Asian and Pacific Islanders are either not included or not portrayed correctly in curricula material' (p. 11). Similarly, the Study Committee for the American Indian/Alaska Native Concerns (NEA, 1987 a) reported that 'the Indian history that is taught is most often from a stereotypical and not a historically factual perspective' (p. 15). Additionally, Anaya (1984), a Hispanic novelist, said,

> In most cases, my work, and the work of my contemporaries who are Black, Native Americans, Asian American, or women writers, is still stuck away in specialized courses. Our work is not allowed to enter the mainstream study of literature. (p. 29)

These examples illustrate that curriculum materials do not meet the criteria of equality defined by Turner: equality of persons, equality of conditions, equality of opportunity, and equality of outcome.

Equity (fairness and justice) is also not evident in the instructional materials, according to the reports of the four National Education Association (NEA) Special Study Committees (1987 a, 1987 b, 1987 c,

1987 d). For example, the Study Committee for Black concerns (NEA, 1987 c) argued that multicultural curricula that represents Blacks accurately and adequately and that can help perpetuate positive self-concept and cultural identity on the part of Black students are not in place in most schools (p. 8), and the Study Committee for Asians and Pacific Islanders (NEA, 1987 b) argued that 'many textbooks reflect cultural bias toward the group' (p. 10).

That neither equity nor equality are present in curriculum materials is most disturbing because materials are the aspect of curriculum most closely examined by educators for equity and equality. The quest for equity and equality was begun decades ago, especially around the time of *Brown v. Board of Education* (1954). Observe the following statement from the Michigan textbook reform committee in 1971 (Michigan Department of Education, 1971). Textbooks and other instructional materials need to:

1 Present a pluralistic — rather than a 100 per cent white, Protestant, Anglo-Saxon — view of history and of the current social sciences.
2 Portray minority groups not as 'out groups' strange, different and isolated, but sympathetically and in depth as valuable dynamic, contributing elements in our culture, deal frankly with past and current barriers to full equality in citizenship and constructive intergroup relations, and with ongoing attempts to achieve both civil and human rights for all. (p. 41)

The Michigan textbook reform committee's criteria seems to be consistent with three of Turner's criteria for equality: equality of person, equality of condition, and equality of opportunity.

However, equality in curriculum materials is still mainly concerned with Turner's 'equality of opportunity' criterion. By this I mean curriculum materials are written mainly to show that people of color (particularly Blacks) and women (especially white women) are present — they have achieved 'access'.

Recent ethnographies of classroom life in urban areas have found that most teachers still do not consistently supplement their biased, commercially prepared curriculum materials with other materials that reflect equity and equality, even materials that they may have personally prepared (see, for example, Grant and Sleeter, 1986). Other teachers will accept — and some will even try to locate — instructional materials that do not have race, gender, or handicap biases. They will use integrated stories that show people of color in roles similar to Whites (for example, doctors, lawyers) and will hunt for materials that show people of color proportionally represented in pictures with Whites. However, these teachers rarely attempt to locate and use materials that present information from the perspective of people of color, highlight issues important to people of color and white women, teach social or political empowerment, or describe how to bring about social justice for people of color, white women, and poor people (see, for example, Grant and Sleeter, 1986; Payne, 1985; Sleeter, 1987 a, 1987 b).

In the classroom, the concept of equality for people of color and white women often is manifested as special days or weeks – Black History Week or Mexican American day – or the occasional use of materials that have pictures of people of color in them or show some women in nontraditional roles.

The importance of using curriculum materials that are fair and just to the students is presented in the observation by Parkay (1983) who taught in an inner city school in Chicago:

> I did find it helpful to relate the content of English to the students concerned, on their percepts of life. I could present materials of surprising difficulty to my students if I related it to where they were at the moment. I came to disagree with many of my fellow teachers who felt that their main job was to bring material down to the students' level. More precisely, I felt the art of teaching involved trying to place subject matter within the students' collective frame of reference. (p. 125)

Curriculum materials responsive to equity would include attention to race, class and gender issues in the concepts presented. As often as possible, these materials would relate to the life experiences of the students and include people and ideas familiar to the students. These materials should provide a context for developing social action skills, empowerment skills, and learning how to analyze oppression. They should provide an understanding of history as well as current social issues from the perspectives of different groups in the United States. In sum, the curriculum materials should be written and presented in a manner that prepares all United States citizens to work toward structural equality, equity, and cultural pluralism.

Conclusion

Equity and equality in classroom life are not the same. Attention to equality is not attention to equity. Students of color, white women, poor students, and students with handicaps are often shortchanged in their educational experiences, criticized for not performing as well as white middle class males, and denied full and comprehensive participation in the American dream.

Front line educators need to become more directly involved in the discussions and debates regarding equity and equality, because an understanding of the difference is important to what takes place in the daily curriculum and instructional program. Also, by becoming engaged in this discussion teachers and school administrators may more readily understand that the elimination of curriculum and instructional inequalities that occur in the school only *begins* the work in this area. Too often, educators believe that when they can say 'I am not racist or biased and I treat all my students the same' they have satisfactorily conquered and resolved most of the problems associated with school inequality. From my perspective these educators have a whole set of problems to understand before they can provide equity and equality in education for all students; equity and equality as concepts and actions in the classroom are waiting to be understood. I hope the contributions in this volume will serve to help that understanding become a reality.

Note

1 Discussions with Walter Secada led to the development of this paper. I am particularly grateful to him for his keen insights and intellectual bravado. Thanks, also, to Maureen Gillette for her excellent comments on an earlier draft of the paper.

References

ANAYA, R.A. (1984) 'The light green perspective: An essay concerning multi-cultural American literature', *Melus,* **11**, pp. 27–31.

BLOCK, J.H. (1984) *Sex Role Identity and Ego Development*, San Francisco: Jossey-Bass.

BROOKOVER, W.B. and LEZOTTE, L. (1981) 'Educational equity: A democratic principle at a crossroads', *The Urban Review,* **13,** 2, pp. 65–71.

Brown v. Board of Education (1954) 347 US 483.

BUFORD, B.I. (1973) Teacher expectancy of the culturally different student subgroups in Texas in relation to student achievement. PhD dissertation, Texas A&M University.

BUTTERFIELD, R.A., DEMOS, E.S., GRANT, G.W., MOY, P.S. and PEREZ, A.L. (1979) 'A multi-cultural analysis of a popular basal reading series in the International Year of the Child', *Journal of Negro Education,* **48**.

BYALICK, R. and BERSHOFF, D. (1974) 'Reinforcement practices of black and white teachers in integrated classrooms', *Journal of Educational Psychology,* **66**, pp. 473–80.

CAMPBELL, P.B. (1984) 'The computer revolution: Guess who's left out?' *Interracial Books for Children,* (Bulletin 15, pp. 3–6).

CAMPBELL, P.B. and KLEIN, S. (1982) 'Equity issues in education', in HOWARD, M. (Ed.) *Encyclopedia of Educational Research* (5th ed., pp. 581–587), New York: Free Press, Macmillan.

COLE, M.A. and BRUNER, J.S. (1971) 'Cultural differences and inferences about psychological processes', *American Psychologist,* **26**, pp. 867–76.

COUNCIL ON INTERRACIAL BOOKS FOR CHILDREN (1977) *Stereotypes, Distortions, and Omissions in US History Textbooks,* New York: Racism and Sexism Resource Center for Education.

CUBAN, L. (1984) *How Teachers Taught,* New York: Longman.

DELAIN, M.T., PEARSON, T.D. and ANDERSON, R.C. (1985) 'Reading comprehension and creativity in black language use: You stand to gain by playing the sounding game!' *American Journal of Educational Research,* **22**, pp. 155–74.

DEYHLE, D. (1985) 'Testing among Navajo and Anglo students: Another consideration of cultural bias', *Journal of Educational Equity and Leadership,* **5**, pp. 119–31.

EVERHART, R. (1983) *Reading, Writing and Resistance,* Boston: Routledge and Kegan Paul.

FINE, D. (1986) *When Leadership Fails,* New Brunswick, NJ: Transaction Books.

FOX, L.H. (1976) 'Sex differences in mathematical precocity: Bridging the gap', in KEATING, D.F. (Ed.), *Intellectual Talent: Research and Development,* Baltimore: Johns Hopkins University Press.

FREIJO, T.D. and JAEGER, R.M. (1976) 'Social class and race as concomitants of composite halo in teachers' evaluative ratings of pupils', *American Educational Research Journal,* **13**, pp. 1–14.

GOOD, T.L. and BROPHY, J.E. (1987) *Looking in Classrooms,* New York: Harper and Row.

GOODLAD, J.I. (1984) *A Place Called School,* New York: McGraw-Hill.

GRANT, C.A. and GRANT, G. (1981) 'The multicultural evaluation of some second and third grade textbook readers: A survey analysis', *Journal of Negro Education,* **50**, pp. 63–74.

GRANT, C.A. and SLEETER, C.E. (1986) *After The School Bell Rings,* Lewes, England: Falmer Press.

GRANT, L. (in press) 'Black females' place in desegregated classrooms,' *Sociology of Education.*

HALE, J.E. (1982) *Black Children: Their Roots, Culture and Learning Styles,* Provo, UT: Brigham Young University Press.

HARVEY, D.G. and SLATIN, G.T. (1975) 'The relationship between child's SES and teacher expectations: A text of the middle-class bias hypothesis', *Social Forces,* **54**, pp. 140–59.

HURST, C. (1979) *The Anatomy of Social Inequality,* St Louis: C. V. Mosby.

JACKSON, G. and COSCA, C. (1974) 'The inequality of educational opportunity in the Southwest: An observational study of ethnically mixed classrooms', *American Educational Research Journal,* **11**, pp. 219–29.

JOHNSON, D.W. and JOHNSON, R. (1984) 'Classroom learning structure and attitudes toward handicapped students in mainstream settings: A theoretical model and research evidence', in JONES, R.L. (Ed.) *Attitudes and Attitude Change in Special Education: Theory and Practice,* Reston, VA: Council for Exceptional Children, (pp. 118–142).

JOHNSON, D.W., JOHNSON, R. and MARUYAMA, G. (1983) 'Interdependence and interpersonal attraction among heterogeneous and homogeneous individuals: A theoretical formulation and meta-analysis of the research', *Review of Educational Research,* **53**, pp. 5–54.

JORDAN, C. (1985) 'Translating culture: From ethnographic information to educational program', *Anthropology and Education Quarterly,* **16**, pp. 105–23.

KAGAN, S. and MADSEN, M.M.C. (1971) 'Cooperation and competition of Mexican, Mexican-American, and Anglo-American children of two ages under four instructional sets', *Developmental Psychology,* **5**, pp. 32–9.

KUNJUFU, J. (1985) *Countering the Conspiracy to Destroy Black Boys,* Chicago: African American Images.

KUNJUFU, J. (1986) *Countering the Conspiracy to Destroy Black Boys (Vol. II),* Chicago: African American Images.

MCDERMOTT, R.P. (1977) 'Social relations as contexts for learning in schools', *Harvard Educational Review,* **47**, pp. 198–213.

METCALF, G.R. (1983) *From Little Rock to Boston,* Westport, CT: Greenwood Press.

MICHIGAN DEPARTMENT OF EDUCATION (1971) *The Treatment of Minorities in American History Textbooks,* Lansing, MI: Author.

NEA SPECIAL STUDY COMMITTEE (1987 a) *Report of the American Indian/Alaska Native Concerns,* Washington, DC: National Education Association.

NEA SPECIAL STUDY COMMITTEE (1987 b) *Report of the Asians and Pacific Islanders Concerns,* Washington, DC: National Education Association.

NEA SPECIAL STUDY COMMITTEE (1987 c) *Report of the Black Concerns,* Washington, DC: National Education Association.

NEA SPECIAL STUDY COMMITTEE (1987 d) *Report of the Hispanic Concerns,* Washington, DC: National Education Association.

New York Times, 4 January 1987, 28F.

New York Times, 14 July 1987, 10y.

PARKAY, F.W. (1983) *White Teachers, Black School,* New York: Praeger.

PAYNE, C.M. (1984) *Getting What We Ask For: The Ambiguity of Success and Failure in Urban Education,* Westport, CT: Greenwood Press.

PHILLIPS, S.U. (1983) *The Invisible Culture,* New York: Longman.

PUGH, L.G. (1974) Teacher attitudes and expectations associated with race and social class, Paper presented at the annual meeting of the American Educational Research Association. (ERIC Document Reproduction Service No. ED 094 018)

RAMIREZ, M. and CASTANEDA, A. (1974) *Cultural Democracy, Bicognitive Development, and Education,* New York: Academic Press.

RIST, R.C. (1970) 'Student social class and teacher expectations: The self-fulfilling prophecy in ghetto education', *Harvard Educational Review,* **40**, pp. 411–51.

RIST, R.C. (1978) *The Invisible Children,* Cambridge, MA: Harvard University Press.

SCOTT, K. (1981) 'Whatever happened to Dick and Jane? Sexism in Texas re-examined', *Peabody Journal of Education,* **58**, pp. 135–40.

SECADA, W. (1987) Empirical models of educational equity. Paper presented at the Annual meeting of the American Educational Research Association, Washington, DC.

SHADE, B.J. (1982) 'Afro-American cognitive style: A variable in school success?' *Review of Educational Research,* **52**, pp. 219–44.

SHARAN, S. (1980) 'Cooperative learning in small groups: Recent methods and effects on achievements, attitudes, and ethnic relations, *Review of Educational Research,* **50**, pp. 241–71.

SLEETER, C.E. (1987 a) *Doing Multicultural Education Across the Grade Level and Subject Areas: A Case Study of Wisconsin,* (forthcoming)

SLEETER, C.E. (forthcoming) 'Preservice coursework and field experience in multicultural education: Impact on teacher behavior relations'.

Time, 6 April 1987, p. 57.

TURNER, B.S. (1986) *Equality*, Sussex, England: Ellis Horwood Limited.

Webster's New Collegiate Dictionary, (1977) Springfield, MA: Merriam.

WILSON, J. (1966) *Equity,* London: Hutchinson.

WILLIAMS, F. and WHITEHEAD, J.L. (1971) 'Language in the classroom: Studies of the Pygmalion effect', *English Record,* **21**, pp. 108–13.

Wisconsin Week, 13 May 1987, p. 3.

Dilemmas of Equity in Art Education: Ideologies of Individualism and Cultural Capital

Kerry Freedman

An examination of art education discourse illustrates that fundamental assumptions of equity are contained within what we consider common sense decisions about curriculum. Represented in the selection and arrangement of knowledge for schooling are beliefs about the rights and desires of people and their 'lot' in life. Reform in art education has generally been considered a just response to existing social tensions concerning who should have access to what knowledge and who is to adopt which values. However, conflicting educational practices have emerged from beliefs about social justice. Practices initiated to promote equity have reproduced social inequalities.

The assumptions of equity and conflicts of practice have historically been hidden in an enabling discourse of reform concerning at least two arrangements of art education. First, curriculum has been organized around ideologies of individualism which presume that children should prepare for productive, well-adjusted lives by making art in school. To focus upon individual production gives the appearance of addressing and solving problems of equity; as will be discussed, however, the stress on individualism has obscured forms of socialization which maintain an acceptance of social differentiation.

Second, curriculum has focused upon the development of a common culture. Looking at and talking about certain works of art has been to develop an appreciation for the 'great accomplishments of man'. The focus in public schooling, which emerged near the turn of the century, has been to raise moral and aesthetic standards and promote social mobility by providing an education in elite cultural knowledge for common people.

However, what has been considered equitable for the general public has promoted the interests of particular groups. Social tensions in the assumptions about individualism and a common culture give focus to the example of art education as a representation of the complex and profound issues of equity bound within curriculum.

The Production of Art and the Individual

Curriculum is designed in relation to theories of childhood, intelligence and competence. The theories are not neutral. They maintain certain beliefs about the relation of individuals to society which have emerged through a particular cultural history. In the United States, there has been a focus on 'the individual' as the manifestation of human rights and possibilities. The theoretical conceptions of childhood, intelligence and competence have been defined and applied in relation to this notion of individualism.

Art curriculum has been shaped by individualism through national agendas and common beliefs about what is just in at least three ways. First, mandatory public school art was originally to provide people of low social and economic status with marketable skills. Second, certain people have been thought special or innately gifted. There has been a search for talent in children so that inborn potential could be nurtured for superior achievement and leadership, regardless of social position at birth. Third, there has been a desire to have children express an inner quality of 'self' to therapeutically overcome socially imposed pathologies. The production of art has been thought to enable independence and self-realization.

These conceptions of individualism, while representing variations in practice, maintain certain common assumptions. The focus on individuals is believed to resolve larger problems of class, race and gender. It concentrates attention on individual differences, removing social differentiation from scrutiny, and placing responsibility on particular people rather than social structures. It carries the assumption, for example, that individuals are good or bad citizens who develop personal qualities in isolation from the social body they live within.

Historically, the instrumental character of individualism as a framework for art education contains certain political and economic premises which pose problems for equitable practice. The individualism has taken forms which have fulfilled industrial purposes, promoted only certain types of merit and defined what constitutes mentally healthy expression. To understand these issues of equity, the emergence of art education as a curriculum of technical skill development will be considered first. Then, implications of ideas about innate artistic ability and conceptions of self-expression in school will be discussed.

Responsible Individuals and the Development of Technical Skills

Art education in the nineteenth century reflected a general belief that character development improved the life of individuals. Art was to discipline the mind through a technical training which focused upon the perfection of drawing and design skills. With practice and the force of will, students were to develop skills which would equitably promote success through work and moral discipline.

Vocational training as social reproduction

A historical discussion of equity in art education must include at least two provincial nineteenth century roots. The first is the private art lessons in drawing and needlework which were to prepare the daughters of the affluent for marriage. The girls were trained as wives and mothers to provide beauty and refinement for their family. Girls designed and stitched floral patterns that would decorate objects for the home. The art education was enobling as well as functional. It was to provide a moral education for those believed to be the keepers of high aspirations and standards of morality (Efland, 1985; Freedman, 1987 a).

By the turn of the century, public girls schools had adopted and elaborated the private program to include training for labor outside the home. The public schools were for less affluent girls than those who had private lessons and were not thought to need vocational skills. The principal of the Washington Irving High School in New York stated,

> The school is an institution that attempts to provide for the young women residing in the lower part of Manhattan Island, every kind of educational and vocational training that experience and investigation suggest as a proper public service. Every one of the two thousand girls in the school must receive training in drawing as an essential feature in the education of a cultivated woman. (Quoted in Carter, 1908, p. 205)

A second root of art education was a common school drawing training to prepare lower class and immigrant boys for industrial work (Freedman, 1987 a; Freedman and Popkewitz, 1988). Before 1870,

American industrialists hired designers trained in Europe. In 1870, leading Massachusetts industrialists obtained a state industrial drawing requirement for common school students. The drawing education was to supply industry with qualified designers, while at the same time providing common school children with marketable skills.

As well as a technical training, the drawing program was a moral education. It was modeled after the industrial work place and was to effectively instill in students certain work habits and values which were sought by corporate management. Design skills were taught as separate from the finished product (as was production in the factories) and developed by meticulously copying simple adult drawings. Through the copying, students were to learn discipline, uniformity, efficiency and other values considered vital to work, home and society, but assumed deficient in poor and immigrant children.

These early forms of art education illustrate dilemmas in the conceptions of equity in public schooling. To prepare girls to become good wives and mothers may not appear to be unjust, but the education reproduced narrowly defined class and gender roles. The mandatory public school training in a technical skill may not seem unfair, but it assumed a division of labor in which particular people were destined to do certain types of work.

There was a strain in education between the role of social reproduction and national ideals of social mobility. To raise one's status was believed a question of having competitive skills and the character to do well. Social mobility for women was through the development of homemaking skills which would enable them to make a good marriage. For male workers, competition in the marketplace was thought to reward those who were deserving. Individuals who took responsibility and displayed diligence would have a fair chance to do well.

To promote social mobility was also to establish structures in which mobility would occur, thus introducing forms of control. Early art education, while apparently providing for the social mobility of individuals, reproduced existing social relations by providing students with only certain types of knowledge. The assumptions of mobility contained a hierarchical structure of forms of labor for different social groups.

A shift in rhetoric from social reproduction to social mobility

Near the turn of the century, overt discussions of social differentiation became muted as a new conception of equity and labor training through schooling emerged (Spring, 1986). There was concern about the unfair treatment of certain social groups and a belief that equitable schooling should be something more than skilled labor training for the poor. The free market became thought of as inefficient and was no longer trusted to reward those most deserving. An emphasis was placed on testing and measurement to produce a more equitable education that selected public school students for particular forms of work (Kliebard, 1986; Krug, 1969).

The change in discourse was tied to new middle class interests which had become prevalent in the schools. Despite egalitarian rhetoric, middle class parents and professionals directed curriculum and instruction toward economic success (Katz, 1987). Most valued was a public school that would prepare middle class students for a higher education. A liberal and specialized training was expected to efficiently and fairly facilitate social mobility.

In this context, a new form of art training developed in the schools. A demand for separate specialized technical drawing courses and manual training for those who would not attend high school remained, but a general art education was created that broadened to include handicrafts and other activities not previously taught in school as vocational skills (Haney, 1908). The children who were considered future managers were to benefit from industrial drawing activities by developing manual dexterity and visual acuity. All public school students were to develop a love of beauty and refinement through drawing the fanciful images and arabesques previously typical of girls' training. The art education was to have practical value for all children and improve the quality of labor and production.

> Indeed, there is not a teacher, a silversmith, a printer, a milliner, a dress-maker, a machinist, a plumber, a paper-hanger, a builder, an engineer, a saleswoman, an embroiderer, a shipping clerk, an electrician, a real estate salesman, a contractor, that would not find value in increasing his potency in his vocation. (*Mississippi Elementary School Curriculum*, 1926, p. 54, quoted in Kern, 1985)

The focus upon the development of art skills as helpful to the vocations of public school students was prevalent through the 1930s and 1940s and has remained a part of curriculum. In contemporary secondary schools where art is an elective, students who are unsuccessful in school and not expected to attend college, are placed into commercial art and industrial design courses.[1] This emphasis in curriculum has produced contradictions in its implications for equity. Technical training, while considered equitable because it promotes the development of marketable skills, also reproduces social stratification.

The Inborn State of Individuals: Equity and the Notion of Talent

Near the turn of the century, education was influenced by particular perspectives on the possibilities of human nature. What was understood as natural in children was shaped by theories of intelligence, eugenics and the interests of a growing middle class. The new definitions of children's performance capabilities had subtle but important implications for equity in schooling.

To understand the assumptions of inborn potential in art education, we must consider the prevalent beliefs about individual differences. The beliefs were framed by a science of biological selection. Social stratification was conceptualized as a result of variance in the intellectual possibilities of different races, classes and genders. Eugenics was concerned with racial improvement through hereditary selection. Eugenicists maintained and legitimated existing power arrangements through the selective use of empirical data and statistical analyses at least through 1920 (Gould, 1981).[2]

Vital to the eugenics movement was an interest in the study of hereditary genius. Eugenicists claimed that genius was passed on through the blood of Northern European men; women, Blacks and other 'races' who were immigrants and poor were not to be diagnosed with genius, except in relation to their own kind. Biographical reports of renowned historical men, especially artists, and their families were used to support the genetic theory (for example, Galton, 1869). There was an assumption that men of genius would be able to rise above a birth of low socioeconomic status and achieve success.

Although readers were given the impression that these studies were biological, the factors used to distinguish genius were social and cultural. The criteria for genius included an outstanding professional reputation which required a desire for prominence and, typically, an education available only to the affluent (Constable, 1905). The only professional group that consistently supported the theory that men could rise above a life of poverty to achieve notoriety were artists, who were thought to actually benefit from the hardships of being poor (Constable, 1905). Studies also linked genius to insanity which was thought to be accompanied by physical abnormalities and immorality. Greater genius meant greater mental and physical unsoundness (Lombroso, 1891; Nesbit, 1900).

The scientific study of human possibilities included a biological and psychological study of children. G. Stanley Hall, a leading proponent of child study, was an evolutionist (Curti, 1959). Hall thought that the natural 'needs' and potentials of children would be discovered through scientific study and fulfilled, in part, through schooling. However, because he believed that the genetic differences of children would determine their outcomes in life, schooling could only be useful if it were individualized because institutional standardization would retard the natural growth of those born to be successful. For Hall, education was to help make the best reach their full hereditary potential; 'dull' children were not to be the primary concern of schooling. Social class, race and gender were thought the outward representation of genetically determined intellectual ceilings. Education was to provide the greatest opportunity for bright boys, who came from the middle class (Hall, 1907). According to Hall, girls were to be prepared for their greatest destiny: motherhood.

Child study was to identify the 'natural' elements of artistic development which were interpreted as measures of intelligence. It was assumed that all normal children drew objects and represented space in particular ways during certain times of growth. The growth of an average child was considered a matter of linear adjustment to certain adult standards of artistic skill. However, the artistic abilities of children were no longer to be conceptualized as technical skills learned through disciplined practice, but rather as stages through which children passed naturally.

The normative interpretation of children's art emerged as part of an ideology of failure and success in children. A child whose development seemed slow or stayed was assumed to have some genetic disfunction or racial inadequacy. Some children appeared to go through the stages faster or reach stages that others could not attain. In contrast to the belief that students excelled through hard work, which was integral to early common school practices, children were taught that some excelled because they had been born meritorious.

The positive deviations in student performance were considered illustrations of genius. However, the idea of genius in children was problematic. Galton's nineteenth-century notion required an age of fifty years (time enough to gain reputation) and was found in one in a million men. Children who were able to go beyond the definitions of normal development, in contrast, were relatively more common. While not all these children would become adult geniuses, all were to have special treatment in school.

By the first decades of the century, art education literature had shifted from discussions of genius to a new notion of talent in children; talent was believed hereditary, but different from genius and found most often among the middle class. A talented child was thought better than his peers, but unlike men of genius, not odd. Talented children were not believed to be insane or to have abnormalities that would reflect negatively upon the family. On the contrary, children with talent maintained values promoted by the middle class in school. To be talented was to be morally good and well-adjusted. Talent meant individuality, psychological strength and an ability to lead.

In part, a search for talent in school emerged because the qualities of a talented child (exceptional skills, middle class values and leadership capabilities) were thought analogous to money. Talent was something you either had or you didn't; it was finite and could be wasted. Children diagnosed as talented would become financially successful if directed in a special way. To give certain children extra attention was considered equitable, not only because it allowed those born to be great to become so, but because it was an efficient means to improve society. Because a prosperous society was assumed to be made up of successful individuals, unnurtured talent became a public concern. Early in the century, state courses of study and federal reports (for example, Course of Study in Art, Idaho, 1915, quoted in Kern, 1985; Farnum, 1926) articulated a belief that the public had a responsibility to specially educate talented children.

Although the search for talent was originally left to the discretion of teachers, they were later considered inadequately trained for making these determinations fairly and efficiently (Farnum, 1926; Carroll, 1940; Hollingworth, 1942). The discrimination of talent was objectified and tested. It was assumed that appraisal through testing would reveal natural merit.

However, the discrimination of artistic talent was framed by culturally specific aesthetic norms. As mentioned above, in the early part of the century, talent in art was determined by the ability of a child to draw more lifelike pictures than some example of averaged behavior. Talent was defined by conformity to a certain aesthetic standard. While lifelike representation is still assumed to indicate artistic ability, characterizations of talent now include divergent thinking, which has emerged as part of an avant-garde aesthetic, a new set of middle class values and a reconceptualization of creativity since the cold war.

The conceptualization of talent in children gave a new focus to equity which still has currency in education. There is a rhetorical insistence upon each individual reaching their greatest potential which is conceived of as something within a person that is 'waiting' to be discovered. Potential is considered biological but is defined in cultural terms and by social possibilities. The 'inborn' state of an individual is bound by the conceptual horizons of scientists and educators. The definitions of talent, while appearing to enable and promote individual interests, have resulted from larger interests in society and have focused curriculum upon children's social and economic inequalities.

A curriculum was developed to make equal the chances of being unequal. It was to provide an efficient method of social mobility, but actually provided means to maintain wealth, status and power differentiation (Entwistle, 1978).

Special but Equal: A Focus on the Self

A third focus of individualism which has framed issues of equity is psychotherapy. Early in the century, the overtly moral quality of art education shifted toward an interest in providing children with a psychologically healthy upbringing. Educators began speaking of art as a means of therapeutic self-expression. Public school children were to have the opportunity for healthy personality development through school art activities.

The therapeutic curriculum emerged with a general redefinition of public affairs as psychological relationships. What had previously been understood as the ethics of behavior was transformed by a discourse of mental fitness. The character, or will of individuals to gain reputation, became conceptualized as traits of personality (Susman, 1984).

The therapeutic production of art was central to progressive private schools during the first decades of the century, and shortly after, gained currency in the public schools. A premise of this perspective was that children were naturally healthy and society was pathological. The process of making art was conceived of as a remedy for the illness imposed on children by society. Curriculum was the organization of activities to provide an avenue for children's free self-expression which was stifled in the world outside school (or outside of art class). Art education was to keep children childlike rather than to prepare them for adult life.

By the 1940s and 1950s, school art was to therapeutically maintain a democratic personality considered vital in a world thought to devisively impose unhealthy, undemocratic principles on weak individuals (Freedman, 1987 b). During and after the Second World War, political tendencies were described as personality traits and mental states (for example, Adorno, Frenkel-Brunswick, Levinson and Sanford, 1950). There was a concern that fascism was a result of and propagated an authoritarian personality. Educators addressed the possibility that children could develop authoritarian tendencies as a result of certain schooling techniques. An equitable curriculum was one that promoted self-expression and awakened an assumed dormant independence in each child (Lowenfeld, 1949).

The assumptions of equity in the therapeutic art contained conflicting dynamics. A primary purpose was narcissistic. It focused upon developing in children confidence in their own actions; they were to consider their own thoughts and beliefs superior while respecting the differences of others as equal to their own. At the same time, children were not to have differences. All children were to display the same personality traits in their art. A particular artistic style was thought to represent the self-expression of children. For example, certain qualities of line and uses of color were assumed to indicate a healthy personality (for example, Lowenfeld, 1949). Children's art was not to be evaluated qualitatively. It was either not expressive (if it did not have the appropriate stylistic characteristics) or, it was expressive and relative in quality.

A curriculum to develop a democratic personality represents a current conflict of equity in schooling. To talk of expression through art gives the illusion of a politically neutral health maintenance, but the notion of expression involves certain social impositions which may not be equitable. While the focus of curriculum is the individual, the manner of expression is defined by experts. It has been argued that, while promoting narcissism, education has produced individuals that are easily socially controlled by instilling faith in certain white, middle class values through a professional expertise of psychology (Lasch, 1979). While curriculum has been designed to make children believe that each is special and important, the students are to respect the authority of professionals who determine what is important within them through a psychology developed in relation to 'normal' behavior and shaped by a particular political milieu.

To summarize, assumptions of what is just are contained in curriculum. Ideologies of individualism involve an assumption that equity is achieved through developing skills, talent or personality which are cast in various forms of responsibility, heredity, and socially induced pathology. However, 'the individual' has been like a mythical hero. It has not represented particular people in real situations. Rather, it has been a socially constructed ideal which has reflected dominant cultural and political beliefs and been applied by experts in ways that appear equitable but maintain the interests of particular social groups.

Ownership, Appreciation and an Equitable Distribution of Culture

Art education, at one level, is believed inherently elite because it draws upon traditions of Western European fine art. Curriculum has involved looking at and talking about masterpieces that represent a lofty and seemingly noble form of culture. A stated purpose of art education has been to make high culture accessible to all through the study of fine art objects.

The conceptions of fine art and high culture are tied to the values and economic status of a dominant social group. Historically, fine art has been included in the definition of the life of a cultivated person with refined sensibilities and a high socioeconomic status. For centuries, the wealthy have both given financial support to the fine art community, and been influential in determining its content and management. The history of fine art has also been a history of gender power arrangements (Nochlin, 1971; Parker and Pollock, 1981). Although an appreciation of fine art has been included in the definition of a refined lady, male artistic production, interpretation and analysis has promoted ideological representations of womanhood and denied quality in women's art.

When art became a subject of public schooling in the late 1800s, private philanthropy controlled the distribution of European high culture to the American population. New wealthy industrialists had become the benefactors of art through purchases made during visits to Europe. Collections were built on the recommendations of art historians who functioned as investment counselors. The philanthropists made their private collections available to the public through the building and financing of museums.

The philanthropic patronage was to develop and support institutions which would make immigrants and the less affluent more cultured, and therefore civilized. The culture of a few was presented as the best culture to produce enlightened citizens and promote a just and moral society. The concern about civility was tied to evolutionary theories and the emerging anthropological studies of 'primitive' societies and races. There was a belief in the civilized nature of those who had gained worldly success and supported American economic and cultural values. Fine art represented the highest form of human production in morality and skill. The development of cultivated taste by the public was to be an indication of national progress.

These noble aspirations coexisted with certain functional imperatives of schooling in relation to social, political and economic arrangements. School art was to equitably distribute cultural capital. While museums maintained and managed the private collections of philanthropic industrialists, they were not educational institutions and were not obligatory. Philanthropic foundations and museums provided schools with traveling shows of art objects and supplemented art education through the production of lantern slides and reproductions of masterpieces available through the development of new technologies. Art education was to promote a respect for those who possessed high culture by focusing attention upon a certain conception of taste. What appeared to serve and enrich also legitimated existing social relations.

Art was distinguished from other forms of production. There was a notion of aesthetics that assumed an inherent value to certain works of art. It represented the object as separate from the context in which it was produced. Certain works of art were thought to have this inherent quality which made them universally appreciated throughout time. To be educated in art meant to be able to appreciate this inherent quality.

A tension exists between the exclusiveness of fine art appreciation and ownership and an equitable distribution of cultural knowledge in American society. Early in the century, developing a common appreciation of high culture through schooling was considered an equitable and democratic education. The tension remains in the categories of high culture and education which are maintained by new social, political and economic agendas.

Recently, as part of the general educational reform movement, there has been a renewed call for a curriculum which focuses upon the study of particular fine art objects and values. A perspective of the reform maintains the belief that an appropriate aesthetic experience is based on an appreciation of certain master works of art which have an inherent, timeless and universal value agreed upon by experts (Smith, 1986). The focus is upon the technical and formal qualities of art objects. An illusion is promoted that there is professional consensus about the value of a work of art and that history will appropriately filter out the less than great. The focus on excellence in curriculum does not make clear that there is continual debate even on those objects the general public are told are masterpieces. It is not made apparent that art rejected in its time has often later been revered, or art valued in its time, is later rejected.

The social purposes and contexts of the art are not considered in this notion of excellence. When considered at all, the work of other cultures is critiqued, not in relation to the context in which it was produced, but in relation to the values represented by the curriculum. From this perspective, children should not encounter contemporary art or art of newer media because they do not have a professionally agreed upon standard of excellence; they have not been 'tested' over time.

The curriculum, which is to give public school children access to high culture, is not necessarily equitable. Rather than improving the quality of social life, the perspective tends to reproduce that by which particular groups maintain power through school processes (Bourdieu, 1984). It does not consider the cultural diversities of art or that appropriate tastes and sensitivities may be found outside this conception of excellence.

The notion of excellence maintains the interests and beliefs of certain social groups as reality for all.

Conclusions

A historical study of art education reveals a focus on the individual which contains assumptions of equity. The conceptions of individualism have been administered through the production of art. The individual has been defined as responsible for achieving his or her greatest potential through an education that enables, but the boundaries of potential have been determined by larger interests than those of the individuals to be served.

Art education has also been concerned with the formation of a common culture. The notion of culture has historically excluded certain groups in its understanding of social production, but assumed that all groups should be enculturated. The perspective has involved an appreciation of art above other forms of production, but trivialized artistic work by presenting it as if it were produced outside of social life. The culturally specific qualities of art, which are tied to the values and traditions of social, political and economic power arrangements, have been presented as universal and timeless. By representing aesthetic value as culturally neutral, curriculum has focused away from the socially constructed character of what is valued as culture. The conception of excellence in a perspective of the current reform denies the importance of the sociohistorical location of production, valuation and management. Assertions of superiority of a particular view of culture on the basis of a claim of expertise or noble values hides the social quality of art knowledge and presents the illusion that a hierarchy of knowledge is fixed and agreed upon.

Notes

1 These students are also counseled into art courses in relation to other conflicting beliefs concerning equity in school. At one level, it is assumed that students cannot fail to produce art if they participate in an art class. On another level, it is believed that if a student does fail an art course, it is unimportant. In this sense, art is considered innocuous; to keep unsuccessful students in such courses will not hurt them because they do not need to spend the time in college preparation courses. Further, making art is thought to be a therapeutic aid, particularly for students who have 'adjustment' problems. To keep these students in art studio classrooms is believed to help manage other courses that appear to require more discipline and attentiveness.

2 For a more thorough discussion of eugenics, see Steven Seldon's chapter in this volume which shows that these ideas, while rejected as legitimate by the

scientific community, remained in influential educational texts much after 1920.

References

ADORNO, T. W., FRENKEL-BRUNSWICK, E., LEVINSON, D. J. and SANFORD, N. (1950) *The Authoritarian Personality,* New York: Harper.

BOURDIEU, P. (1984) *Distinction: A Social Critique of the Judgment of Taste,* Cambridge: Harvard University Press. Trans. by R. Nice.

CARROLL, H. A. (1940) *Genius in the Making,* New York: McGraw-Hill.

CARTER, C. M. (1908) 'Art education in the high schools', in HANEY, J. P. (Ed.) *Art Education in the Public Schools of the United States,* New York: American Art Annual.

CONSTABLE, F. C. (1905) *Poverty and Hereditary Genius: A Criticism of Mr Galton's Theory of Hereditary Genius,* London: Arthur C. Fifield.

CURTI, M. (1959) *The Social Ideas of American Educators,* Paterson, NJ: Pageant Books.

ENTWISTLE, H. (1978) *Class, Culture and Education,* London: Methuen.

EFLAND, A. (1985) 'Art and education for women in 19th century Boston', *Studies in Art Education,* **26,** 3, pp. 133–140.

FARNUM, R. B. (1926) *Art Education in the United States,* Bureau of Education Bulletin, No. 38, 1925. Washington, DC: Government Printing Office.

FREEDMAN, K. (1987 a) 'Art education as social production: Culture, society and politics in thc formation of curriculum', in POPKEWITZ, T. S. (Ed.) *The Formation of School Subjects: The Struggle for Creating an American Institution,* Lewes: Falmer Press.

FREEDMAN, K. (1987 b) 'Art education and changing political agendas: An analysis of curriculum concerns of the 1940s and 1950s', *Studies in Art Education,* **29,** 1, pp. 17–29.

FREEDMAN, K. and POPKEWITZ, T.S. (1988). Art education and social interests in the development of schooling: Ideological origins of curriculum theory. *Journal of Curriculum Studies,* **20,** 5, pp. 387–406.

GALTON, F. (1869) *Hereditary Genius*, New York: Macmillan.

GOULD, S.J. (1981) *The Mismeasure of Man*, New York: W.W. Norton.

HALL, G.S. (1907) 'Education: A lifelong development', *Chautauquan,* **47,** pp. 150–6.

HANEY, J.P. (Ed.) (1908) *Art Education in the Public Schools of the United States*, New York: American Art Annual.

HOLLINGWORTH, L.S. (1942) *Children Above 180 IQ: Origin and Development*, Yonkers-on-Hudson, NY: World Book.

KATZ, M.A. (1987) *Reconstructing American Education*, Cambridge: Harvard University Press.

KERN, E. J. (1985, November) The purposes of art education in the United States from 1870 to 1980. The History of Art Education Conference, State College, PA.

KLIEBARD, H.M. (1986) *The Struggle for the American Curriculum, 1893–1958*, Boston: Routledge and Kegan Paul.

KRUG, E.A. (1969) *The Shaping of the American High School, 1880–1920*, Madison: University of Wisconsin Press.
LASCH, C. (1979) *The Culture of Narcissism*, New York: Warner Books.
LOMBROSO, C. (1891) *The Man of Genius*, London: W. Scott.
LOWENFELD, V. (1949) *Creative and Mental Growth: A Textbook on Art Education*, New York: Macmillan.
NESBIT, J.F. (1900) *The Insanity of Genius and the General Inequality of Human Faculty Physiologically Considered*, London: Grant Richards.
NOCHLIN, L. (1971) 'Why are there no great women artists?' in GORNICK, V. and MORAN, B. *Women in Sexist Society: Studies in Power and Powerlessness*, New York: Basic Books.
PARKER, R. and POLLACK, G. (1981) *Old Mistresses: Women, Art and Ideology*, New York: Pantheon.
SMITH, R.A. (1986) *Excellence in Art Education: Ideas and Initiatives*, Reston, VA: National Art Education Association.
SPRING, J. (1986) *The American School 1642–1985*, New York: Longman.
SUSMAN, W.I. (1984) *Culture as History: The Transformation of American Society in the Twentieth Century*, New York: Pantheon Books.

The Use of Biology to Legitimate Inequality: The Eugenics Movement Within the High School Biology Textbook, 1914–1949

Steven Selden

Introduction

A number of contemporary analysts of the school curriculum have made a rather provocative proposal regarding the course of study of the public school. They have claimed that the curriculum represents a selective tradition[1]; that it represents *some* of what could be told of a particular subject. Contrary to the general belief that schooling aids in the democratization of society, these critics go on to argue that the selection supports the interests of society's most powerful members and interests. For example, as one current critic points out, despite Howard Zinn's (1980) eloquent rendering of vanquished Indian life, Columbus' discovery of America is still generally told to America's school children from the perspective of the European victor, thereby ignoring both Native American history and consciousness.[2]

This chapter reviews forty high school biology textbooks published during the years 1914–1949 and searches for something akin to this idea of a selective tradition in their content. It asks whether these texts presented a particular social vision of human development and used a selection of biological knowledge to legitimate that vision. In many ways, this chapter is an attempt to empirically validate the presence of selective traditions in the school curriculum and its findings indicate that the answers to the above questions are overwhelmingly in the affirmative.

The tradition was eugenics. It was the study of human improvement through programs of differential breeding and it was an integral piece of intellectual structure that saw society as necessarily hierarchical and unequal.[3] But this was not a new idea. Feudal social systems, for example, were surely hierarchical and unequal. Yet arguments for their efficacy were made in theological, not scientific, terms. Eugenics, however, presented itself as legitimate biological science and its supporters argued that genes, not God, demanded social differentiation. While many may view this mainline eugenics as an early form of scientific racism, it is sufficient today to recognize that it was science that served to legitimate these policies on human betterment and human differences, not theology or sociology. The point here is that it would be wrong not to recognize that such views on varying human worth *preceded* their legitimization by science. They were views, unencumbered by scientific formulae, that were well represented in the popular geographies used in the late nineteenth century and early twentieth century classrooms. Here one can easily find a selective tradition at work.

Racial Differentiation and the Geographies

For the authors of many of the early geographies, the issues of human races and their differences were issues of importance. By tying these differences to attainment, whether individual or national, the texts served to describe and legitimize existing social and political arrangements. For example, the *Natural Complete Geography* (Redway and Hinman, 1912), divided the world's people into three unequal racial groups: white, yellow, and black. Written with an Anglo audience in mind, the volume placed the Caucasian at the top of the racial pyramid.

> The home of the white or 'Caucasian' race is Europe, Southwestern Asia, and Northern Africa . . . This race includes nearly half the people of the world, and is the most civilized of all the races. The principal division of this race is the *Mediterranean* type, to which we belong. (Redway and Hinman, 1912, p. 12)

The text further divided the Mediterranean group into Semites and Aryans and the authors note that the Aryan people are rapidly increasing in number and appear destined for international conquest. 'In recent times', they explain, 'thousands of them have left Europe to find homes for themselves . . . and these new settlers have practically taken possession of North and South America and of Australia, and [they] are rapidly taking possession of Africa' (p. 27). This was manifest destiny with a racial engine.

To the readers of this geography, the message was straightforward; race and civilization were linked together. The lesser of the world's peoples included, 'the yellow race . . . about as numerous as . . . the white race . . . but not so highly civilized', and, 'the black race . . . the least civilized of all races' (p. 28). Yet there was room for improvement. In the section on human progress, the readers are reassuringly told that,

> The greater part of the Mediterranean type, and especially its great Aryan branch, have continued to improve, and are still making inventions and discoveries; and these people form the enlightened nations of today. (Redway and Hinman, 1912, p. 28)

This linking of race, civilization, and progress could also be found in *Morton's Advanced Geography* (Morton, 1901), published just after this century's turning. Having identified five racial groups which included the Caucasian, Mongolian, Malayan, Indian, and Negro, the text noted that human progress depended upon the achievement of civilization by them all. Yet, as with the Redway and Hinman text, all had not succeeded. As Morton explains,

> There are people in the world who live in caves or other rude dwellings, wear little clothing, eat roots, insects, and other strange food, and are very ignorant and degraded in their habits. These people we call *savages*. The Indian, Negro, and Malayan races include many savages. (Morton, 1901, p. 33)

Yet a second level of racial worth was attained by some members of these races. Morton reports that these people, 'make pottery, . . . know something of the use of metals, . . . till the soil to a limited extent, and raise domestic animals' (p. 33). More advanced than their racial fellows, they are given the more prestigious title of *barbarians*.

There was another level of racial achievement in Morton's view and she explains, 'There are also people who can read and write, who build cities and manufacture useful articles, yet who have many customs which are degrading'. 'These people', she points out, 'are called *half-civilized*'. Neither all savages nor all barbarians, she instructs that 'many of the Mongolians are half-civilized' (p. 33).

Lastly, Morton identifies the most highly valued group in her racial calculus. Having 'churches, schools, and colleges, railroads, electric lights, telegraphs, telephones and newspapers, . . .' these people are identified as 'civilized' (p. 33). With the assistance of a photograph depicting a horseless carriage, bicycles, and bustles, Morton concludes, 'the greater part of the Caucasian race is civilized' (p. 33). It was not unusual for the geographies of the turn of the century to present their young readers with this model of a hierarchically ordered world based upon a hierarchy of races. It was a socio-racial model that did not entirely disappear from the curriculum as the century developed.

Social Differentiation in a 1930s Reader: Race and Contradiction

For example, when Clara and Edna Baker chose stories for their fifth grade reader, *Making America*, in 1937, they included, 'King Cotton's Big Time', from Rose B. Knox's, *The Boys and Sally Down on a Plantation* (1930). The chapter depicts a day of cotton picking on a southern farm in early September. As with the social world of the geographies, the plantation is hierarchically organized in terms of race. In the story, Sally and her brother, Van, have come to visit the plantation owned by their Uncle Louis. The readers are instructed that the plantation, located in Alabama, has been in Sally's family since the days of her grandfather. The author describes black employees as 'servants' and it is they who manifest the only cheating and stealing behavior in the story. The story goes on to depict Blacks in a stereotypical fashion as fun-loving, well-adapted to menial labor, and naturally musical. For example, when Sally joins black cotton pickers in the fields, she finds it a chore less than to her liking. '. . . Everybody except Sally was having a pleasant enough time [working all day in the hot sun]. [The Negroes] liked the fun of being together in the fields. They were trained for this work; so it did not seem hard to them' (Baker and Baker, 1937, pp. 154–5). The texts continue to express this moral numbness about advantage and disadvantage as other economic realities are described. For example, even though Blacks are described in texts and pictures as poor, in tattered clothing and without shoes, this is not presented as a cause for moral concern on the reader's part. Blacks could, after all, trade their labor for high wages in a system of economic relations which is presented as both highly motivating and just. As the author points out, 'they made such high wages that neither the burning sun of September, nor the raw, chilly days of late fall could keep them out of the fields' (p. 156). This is a remarkably naive interpretation of the labor of people at the economy's margins. But it does not seem unreasonable to note that an acceptance of this view by the Anglo readers of the story would serve to ease any concerns they may have had about the structural nature of economic disadvantage in the rural economy. Such concerns are negated as the story continues with Sally and the Blacks in the fields together:

> After a while, they began to sing and Sally sang along with them. The music was so pleasant it made them forget that they were

> hot and tired. Hannah led. Her high clear voice floated out over the wide cotton fields. 'Swing low, sweet chariot!' she trilled. 'Coming for to carry me home', chanted all the others. (Knox, 1930, in Baker and Baker, 1937, p. 156)

Whether the chariot would arrive and ease their toil is not clear, but the author is less than critical as to the effects of the cotton gin and steam engine on existing human relations. For it is clear, if not so stated, that when Eli Whitney's gin made cotton 'king' (as in the story's title) it also created a class of serfs and a class of machine owners. That these classes are racially segregated is not presented as a problem by the author. As the story ends, it appears that technology will continue to have differential effects upon these two groups. As Uncle Louis, excitedly, tells Sally,

> 'We have machine tools now which plant cotton and cultivate cotton, and they are getting better every year. Some day we'll have one that picks cotton, just see if we don't!' 'Why Uncle Louis!' Sally exclaimed, 'I almost believe it will be "King Machine" next.' 'Maybe you're right', he said. (p. 171)

In this brief example, we can see how the curriculum of the school can reflect narrow class and race interests while scrupulously avoiding questions of the possible transformation of the relations of capital and labor. Not only does the content of the story serve the interests of the machine owners, but anticipated mechanical progress only promises to increase and rationalize existing socioeconomic differences.

Yet the story's evidence is contradictory. It could be argued that the social order depicted was merely an accident of history and that the social location of the various races could easily change. After all, even the geographies seemed to suggest that some could move from being savages to barbarians. The point here is that social change was possible for Blacks in the story as well. If race was not seen as destiny then even Uncle Louis' 'servants' might take or gain control of the steam driven cotton gin and thereby change their status. That is, access to the means of production, in this case, the cotton gin, might just as easily predict social location as would race. In this interpretation, race *would not* be equal to destiny and social location could change regardless of ethnicity. It is here that one can see the geographies and readers as carriers of a rather contradictory message; a message that could threaten entrenched class benefits. If the selective tradition hypothesis were to hold, then a stronger warrant for the maintenance of existing social arrangements would have to be presented in the curriculum. This, of course, was one of the major interests of the Popular Eugenics Movement and it was from its interpretation of biology that such a warrant was to come. Yet if the movement was to be successful, it would have to influence the curriculum of the school; it would have to exert influence upon the textbook. In this case, the biology textbook must have been seen as a prime target.

Eugenics in the Biology Textbook: An Overview

In the thirty-five years between 1914 and 1949, numerous high school biology textbooks were published in the United States. Of these many volumes, forty have found their way into the archives at the National Institute of Education in Washington, DC. The following analysis is made of these forty textbooks. Three major questions are addressed to the volumes: 1) Was eugenics included in the biology textbooks as legitimate science? 2) If yes, what was the nature of the evidence offered in eugenics' support? 3) What social policies, if any, were recommended by the volumes?

The answers to the above questions are rather startling, given the limited knowledge we have of the impact of the eugenics movement on classroom life. For example, in response to the question of whether eugenics was presented in the textbooks as legitimate science, the answer is overwhelmingly, yes. Of the 40 volumes considered (Figure 1), thirty-seven included eugenics in their discussions of legitimate biology (Figure 2). This represents 92.5 per cent of the volumes considered. Only three volumes, or 7.5 per cent of the texts reviewed, either rejected eugenics or did not include it. This is truly a remarkable penetration of a movement

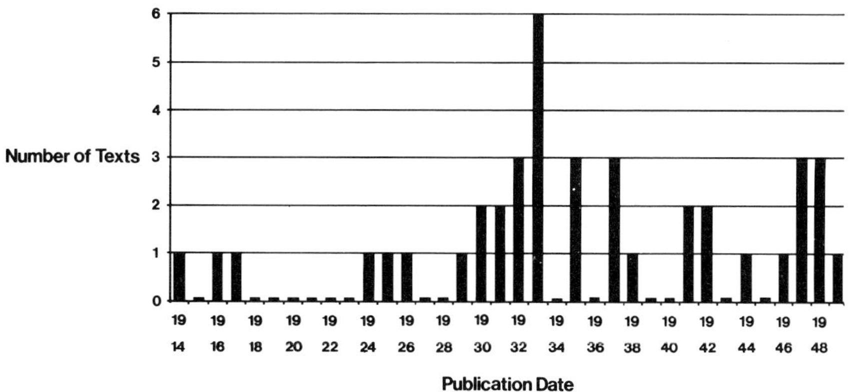

Figure 1. Texts reviewed from NIE archive, 1914–1949 (N = 40).

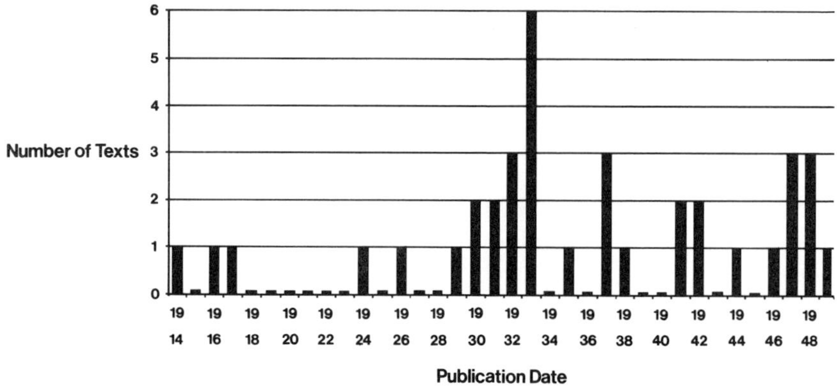

Figure 2. Texts including eugenics as legitimate content, 1914–1949 (N = 37/40 or 92.5%)

that receives virtually no coverage in most contemporary reviews of both the history and sociology of the school curriculum. Given the limited knowledge that the contemporary educator has of the eugenics movement, these data can be seen as comprising part of the null curriculum of the educational professional.

What of the evidence offered in support of eugenics? The typical volume in this study presented its readers with human pedigree or family trait analyses. These took the form of pedigree charts depicting the presence and absence of particular traits across generations in a family. The volumes often took a rather extreme Mendelian single-trait interpretation of human qualities (such as intelligence) and then argued that these traits 'ran' in families. These pedigree studies became the evidence for eugenics as a science. They were studies of contrasting types. 'Superior' families and their worthy traits were presented in comparison to 'inferior' families and their socially destructive hereditary qualities. Over two-thirds of the volumes considered in this study included such comparative family analyses (see Figures 3 and 4). The volumes went on to argue that these findings were a cause for alarm. Superior families such as the Bachs, Darwins, and Edwards, were being threatened by inferiors such as the Kallikaks, Pineys, and the Jukes.

Indeed, these last three families became representative of a national anxiety about what was to become known as a 'rising tide of feeble-mindedness' in the American body politic. Perhaps the most famous of these families was the fictional Kallikaks whose legacy of degeneration and debauchery was documented in Henry H. Goddard's (1912) famous volume, *The Kallikak Family: A Study in the Heredity of Feeble-mindedness.*

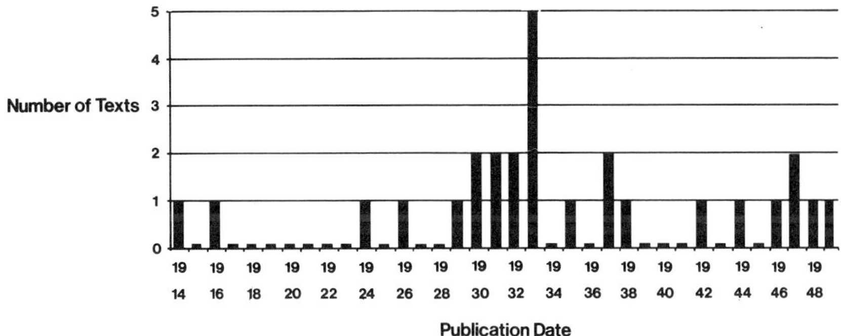

Figure 3. Texts including studies of 'superior' families, 1914–1949 (N = 27/40 or 67.5%).

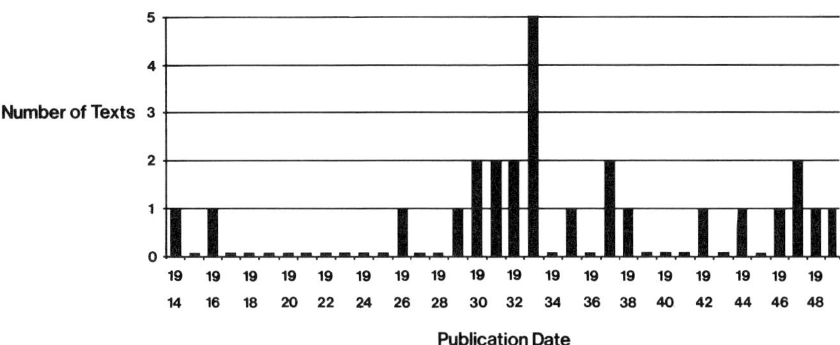

Figure 4. Texts including studies of 'inferior' families, 1914–1949 (N = 27/40 or 67.5%).

The text was complete with pedigree charts depicting the supposed hereditary nature of feeble-mindedness and with photographs exemplifying the degenerate characters themselves in black and white.

The pedigree charts give the reader the strong impression that not only was feeble-mindedness caused by one's biological inheritance rather than by the influence of environment, but so too were the afflictions of alcoholism, sexual immorality, insanity, deafness and criminality (pp. 33–5) biologically inherited traits. Yet as we shall see in this chapter, despite increasing knowledge in the early 1920s depicting the complexity of the hereditary transmission of, say, traits in the fruit fly *drosophila* and the consequent recognition that pedigree charts such as Goddard's could not be taken as compelling evidence for the hereditary transmission of human social traits, that these insights from the field of biology had little effect upon the public school textbook.

It is interesting to note that a contemporary analysis of the photographs themselves suggests that they were, in fact, retouched. They were altered. As Stephen Jay Gould, James Wallace and I have found, the photos depicting Martin Kallikak's degenerated offspring were made to appear even more odious by the darkening of hairlines and the lowering of brows. While we have no indication that Goddard himself was involved in this bit of chicanery, the national anxiety about feeble-mindedness must surely have been fueled through a visually unsophisticated public's acceptance of the Kallikak family's biological threat (Gould, 1981, pp. 171–4).

From these allegedly scientific studies of family types came specific social policy recommendations. Of the many policies open to the eugenically minded biologist, *selective breeding* was one of the most popular. Such a policy had two faces: the first, positive eugenics, suggested breeding 'best' with 'best'; the second, negative eugenics, demanded a restriction on the procreation of 'inferior types'. The data in this regard are striking. Over three-quarters of the volumes that favorably considered eugenics supported positive eugenics (Figure 5) while nearly one-half recommended negative eugenics (Figure 6). Eugenics had significantly penetrated the high school curriculum. But even in its time, there were serious problems with the data offered and the methods used to support eugenical policies.[4]

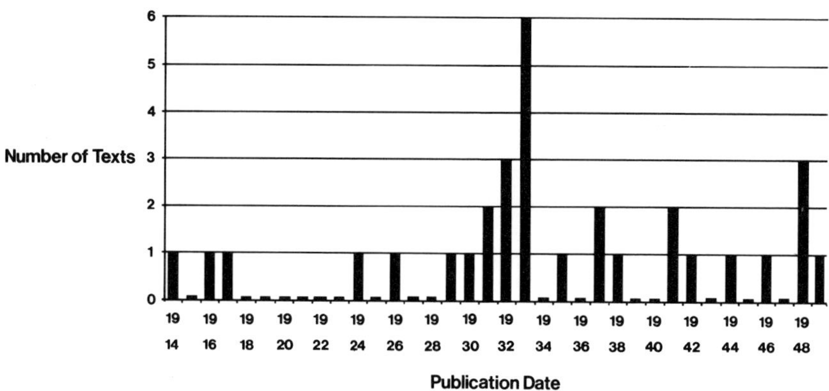

Figure 5. Texts supporting programs of positive eugenics, 1914–1949 (N = 31/40 or 77.5%)

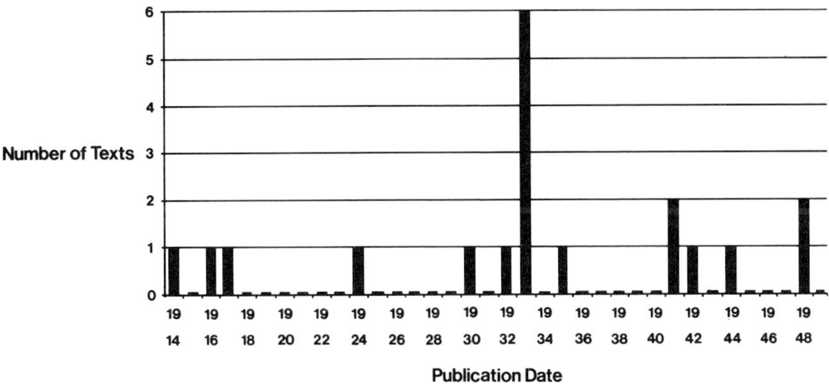

Figure 6. Texts supporting programs of negative eugenics, 1914–1949 (N = 19/40 or 47.5%).

Academics today view science as both content and method and it is interesting to consider the methods used by eugenicists to argue for these programs of selective breeding for they were problematic in many ways. Their approach was to use proxies as warrants. That is, they would either substitute the family to which an individual belonged for his/her hereditary worth or they would substitute an individual's social performance for his/her genetic value. This represented very weak empirical evidence given the points the eugenicists wanted to make. Despite arguments based on differences in genetic value, the studies in question offered no compelling genetic evidence to support their policies.

Further, there were two or more possible explanations for the continuing success of members of, say, the Roosevelt family, as described in their pedigree charts. One was genetic; another was environmental. That the early eugenicists saw this ambiguous data as clearly supporting the importance of heredity over environment should give us pause. The commitment to hereditarianism on the part of these individuals, and on the part of the textbooks in question, reflects something more than just science; it also reflects social attitudes and the maintenance of particular social arrangements.

While surely not racist as in the case of geographies, the science texts under consideration served to legitimate a social order just as hierarchical and just as determinate as that presented by those late nineteenth century volumes. In the case of the twentieth century texts, it was the laws of biology that made demands upon society rather than race. But the net effect was to be quite similar. After all, in a class and race biased order, recommendations to breed from the 'best' would be, as Daniel Kevles (1985) notes, 'freighted with class bias' (p. 176).

Yet we need to recognize that biological knowledge *can* make demands upon us and inform social policy. I am not arguing otherwise. If the scientific facts are warranted, then they demand our attention. Contemporary examples include our increased understanding of the genetic basis of both Tay-Sachs and Huntington's Disease. The knowledge that one is a carrier of such genetic abnormalities suggests potential avenues for individual choice.[5] However, in the case of the textbooks under review, and their suggested social policies, such analogous information was neither presented nor available.

For those who argue today that eugenics was essentially rejected by geneticists and the educational community after the 1920s, and that the findings of studies such as the *Kallikaks* were seriously flawed in their day, the data from this text analysis present troubling and disconfirming evidence. While it is certainly true that geneticists had rejected models of single-trait inheritance for complex human qualities (not to mention those of the *Drosophila*) by the late 1920s, it appears that their rejection had little effect upon the textbooks in question. Whether as a consequence of what one might call 'dissemination lag', or by intention, the books did not keep up with scientific progress. They did not mirror then current developments in human genetics. But they clearly reflected a series of status quo-oriented social views.

An understanding of the way in which these biology texts linked science and social policy can perhaps best be seen by turning to a close analysis of the volumes themselves. We would do well to let them speak, to let them articulate their vision of eugenic's place in the curriculum and in the broader social order. To that end, I have selected nine biology texts written between 1914 and 1948 for consideration.

The first five volumes were written by George William Hunter (1914, 1926, 1931, 1941; Hunter and Whitman, 1935) and were published between 1914 and 1941 by the American Book Company. They have been included as an example of the way in which an author and publisher could maintain a continuing commitment to eugenics, essentially without rejection, for a period of twenty-seven years. Despite the changes that took place in genetics during this period, Hunter and American Book were able to maintain a continuous commitment to eugenics as legitimate science. This lengthy publication record further suggests that the books must have sold well to schools. The point here is that this is not an example of random events; the books should not be judged as out of step with their times. They were not aberrations from a generally liberal and progressive movement. They were part of what it meant to be progressive.

The author was not an extremist who published one book, never to be heard from again. To the contrary, his view appeared to have been generally accepted by the educational community over time. It was a view that essentially argued that there was no way to overcome one's genetic destiny. As Allan Chase (1977) notes, this message was available at the post-secondary level as well. 'This concept [of the destiny of biology] was taught to, and accepted unquestioningly by, generations of college-educated Americans, and to be cited by them for many years thereafter in their political words and deeds. It was . . . one of the major segments of American conventional wisdom' (p. 153). And this conventional wisdom, on the overarching importance of heredity as explained by eugenics, was also presented in the remaining four volumes to be analyzed. Authored by James Peabody (Peabody and Hunt, 1924), John Ritchie (1941), Charles Dull (Dull *et al.*, 1942), and University of Wisconsin biologist, Michael F. Guyer (1948), they aided in shaping a consciousness that can be found in public discourse to this day. Once again, the central question is that of the presence of eugenics in these volumes. Let us consider the texts directly.

Eugenics in the Classroom: The Biology Texts Reviewed

Eugenics appears in Hunter's first volume, *A Civic Biology: Presented in Problems* (1914), in the chapter 'Heredity and Variation'. Not exclusively a hereditarian, Hunter notes that human betterment requires personal hygiene, an improved environment, and the selection of healthy mates. In Hunter's terms, eugenics meant 'freedom from certain germ diseases which might be handed down to [one's] offspring'. The list included tuberculosis, epilepsy, and feeblemindedness; a compendium of afflictions that Hunter viewed as, 'not only unfair, but criminal, to hand down to posterity' (p. 261). Citing the studies of the Jukes and Kallikaks, he warned his readers that,

> Hundreds of families such as those described above exist today, spreading disease, immorality, and crime to all parts of this country . . . they not only do harm to others by corrupting, stealing, or spreading disease, but they are actually protected and cared for by the state out of public money. Largely for them the poorhouse and the asylum exist. They take from society but they give nothing. *They are true parasites.* (Hunter, 1914, p. 263) [Emphasis added]

This belief that negative social traits ran in families and were generally impervious to environmental influence was typical of the texts under consideration. Typical as well was the anxiety expressed about a society in seeming moral collapse. One can empathize with the author's fears even while recognizing the futility of his prescriptions.

Virtually every text that cited the Jukes and Kallikaks countered with a description of superior family types. So too with Hunter's (1914) work. He cites Elizabeth Tuttle, matriarch of the Edwards family and he concludes that members of her family can 'trace the characters which enabled them to occupy the positions of culture and learning they held back to Elizabeth Tuttle'. In the popular parlance of the day, Hunter observes that, 'blood tells' (p. 264).

The chapter ends with a call for euthenics, a program of environmental reform, as well as eugenics, and with references to the work of the industrial efficiency expert, William H. Tolman. It is not surprising that *A Civic Biology* supported social efficiency as a worthy social ideal, for in the social efficiency movement, eugenics always found a comfortable home.

By 1926, Hunter's *New Civic Biology* (1926) would cite Clarence Kingsley's *Seven Cardinal Principles Report* (a classic social efficiency document) and would clearly link social efficiency and civic biology. There were other changes evident from the earlier volume as well. For example, the discussion of euthenics which accounted for twenty-four pages in the 1914 text, now accounted for only *one* page. There had also been a change in the discussion of eugenics. The 1926 edition added a section on choosing a vocation to the general discussion of inherited traits. Here again one can see the utility of eugenics to social efficiency educators. A careful identification of an individual's inherited traits, the text strongly implies, would allow for a rational social order in which one's social location would be determined by one's biology. As Hunter (1926) reminds his readers, 'blood does tell!' (p. 401) and that while 'life is made up of our social inheritance or what we *learn* through our *environment* . . . No one becomes great unless he or she has a nervous system of superior capacity' (p. 403, emphasis in original).

As with the 1914 edition, the reports of the infamous Jukes and Kallikaks and the desirable Edwards' families are presented as empirical evidence for the science of eugenics. It was a science, as noted above, that would inform the text's tenth grade reader on issues of vocational choice and marriage partners. 'Two applications of this [eugenic] knowledge stand out for us as high school students', Hunter instructed,

> One is the choice of a mate, the other is the choice of a vocation. As to the first, no better advice can be given than the old adage,

> 'Look before you leap'. If this advice were followed, there would be fewer unhappy marriages and divorces. Remember that marriage should mean love, respect, and companionship for life. The heredity of a husband or a wife counts for much in making this possible. (Hunter, 1926, p. 401)

Having thus identified the importance of heredity in human relations, Hunter takes the discussion to its logical conclusion. 'Even though you are in high school, it's only fair to yourselves that you should remember the responsibility that marriage brings. You should be parents. Will you choose to have children well born? Or will you send them into the world with an inheritance that will handicap them for life?' (p. 401). It becomes important for those of us reading Hunter's words sixty years after they were written to realize that he could know nothing of amniocentesis or genetic screening. Hunter's analysis was of the phenotype, that is, of the individual. It masqueraded as a genotypic analysis and it was then presented as a basis for social policy. Once again, one can know today that certain single gene abnormalities will destine a fetus to a constrained postpartum existence. In 1926, studies of the Kallikaks and the Jukes supplied none of the necessary information for making such predictions. Social efficiency may accrue economic advantage to those who practice it, but that is to say nothing about genetics. One wonders if Hunter's proposals were not shaped as much by his views of economic imperatives as by his understanding of biology. Indeed, this is a legitimate question to pose today as we enter the beginning of a biotechnological revolution in human genetics.

Hunter's third text, *Problems in Biology* (1931), does not include euthenics in its index, but as with the 1914 and 1926 volumes, general personal, family and community hygiene are well covered. Keeping abreast of changes in biology, Hunter (1931) noted that 'this mechanism of heredity is not as simple as it seems' (p. 628) and he moderates earlier observations. Repeating the litany of the Jukes, Kallikaks, and Edwards family histories he notes that while blood is still important, that 'chromosomes tell the story' (p. 639). And in a discussion of chromosomes and genes, he notes that 'it is clear the experiments which will attempt to separate and make new characters appear in the offspring will be extremely difficult, to say the least' (p. 628). Further, controlling the quality of offspring, a major concern of eugenicists was now recognized as having limited scientific support. Hunter goes so far as to quote H.S. Jennings of Johns Hopkins University who noted that 'these characteristics that are predictable are extremely few', and Hunter reflects 'we are finding out that our problems of breeding are not as easy as we had first hoped' (p. 629). Yet, despite these caveats, Hunter's general discussion of phenotypic improvement did not significantly change. Characters still ran in families, sons were like fathers, and wise choices in marriage and vocation were still driven by the imperative of biology.

Hunter's fourth volume, *Science in our World of Progress*, was designed for the then emerging Junior High School. Its focus was upon an integration of science subject matter 'written from the pupil viewpoint', and such an integration took place in the text's discussion of eugenics (Hunter and Whitman, 1935, p. viii). While judging environmental reform as useful ('through personal hygiene and improvement of the environment, a healthier and stronger race has been produced') the authors offer recommendations for hereditary manipulation. 'If we study . . . certain well-known families in this country who have become a burden to society', they warn, 'we find that breeding in man . . . must be taken into account' (p. 483). Once again, the families in question are the infamous Jukes and Kallikaks and the authors warn of simplistic environmental excuses for their crime and degradation. 'It is not the environment that always causes crime', they explain to their ninth grade readers, 'anymore than it is environment which always conditions an individual's life' (p. 483). Placing the cause of crime on inherited feeblemindedness, Hunter and Whitman warn of its threat and recommend programs of segregation and sterilization if society is to progress.

Indeed, the authors were even able to identify exemplary models for such action. Hunter and Whitman (1935) pointed to 'Germany [as having] laws which allow such persons to be sterilized or rendered incapable of reproduction' (p. 484). A more complete analysis of these laws, at that time, would have revealed more of their political and racial motivation, but the authors included little of such background. Rather, they again put forth the Edwards and Roosevelt families, 'which show that blood will tell, or rather to put it more scientifically, that chromosomes will tell the story' (p. 486). And the story that Hunter and Whitman heard was the story, 'that if the race is to be improved, we must improve the stock . . . ' and 'the science of improving the human race by better heredity is known as *eugenics*' (p. 486, emphasis in original). Once again, except for a few single gene defects, the authors could have known little specifically about the genetic basis for human improvement. That they could have known much about the political uses of eugenics is another issue. The most gentle observation that one can make on this latter question is to assume a rather uncritical naivete on the authors' part about international politics and the social uses of genetics. It does not make them culpable for the misuse of science, but surely it makes them less than a best choice for authoring texts for adolescents.

Having favorably cited policies of sterilization, of negative eugenics, in Nazi Germany the authors considered positive eugenic proposals. 'We must do all we can', they told their readers, 'to have persons of the better stock mate and have children'. It was an issue with overtones of international competition. 'If this country is to succeed', they warned, 'we must have brains and ability handed down to the next generation' (Hunter and Whitman, 1935, p. 486). And, of course, there was another example of such a program in existence at that time. It was also in Germany and also in 1935. There, Heinrich Himmler had established just such a program within the SS. Called *Lebensborn* – the Well of Life – its 'ultimate goal', was 'to form a racially superior stock from which Germany's future leaders would come' (Dawodwicz, 1975, p. 74). Today's readers should be careful not to overinterpret these similarities. Similar programs need not necessarily have similar motivations. But it should also be clear to today's reader that eugenics did not disappear from American education after the economic collapse of 1929. How the young readers of Hunter's text responded to its social messages is beyond the scope of this chapter, but the messages surely must be seen as part of the intellectual environment in which these young people were to grow up.

Common themes tie these four books together. They include commitments to the instrumental value of biology, to social efficiency in the form of a meliorative approach to social problems, and to a continuing belief in eugenics. Hunter's 1941 text, *Life Science*, presents the final and most straightforward articulation of these themes to be considered in this paper. Subtitled, 'A Social Biology', its final chapter warns the reader that 'social progress depends upon biology'. But Hunter was obviously aware of the biological and social scientists who were arguing for the importance of environmental reform in human betterment as he poses the following rhetorical question to his readers: 'Suppose', he queries his readers, 'that we can change the physical makeup of a plant or animal through some outside agency, is it possible to change our mental inheritance?' (Hunter, 1941, p. 766). In framing the answer, Hunter allows that while environment must be considered, 'the important factor to remember', [is that],

> There is no real evidence that the environment changes the intelligence of people. Those of low-grade intelligence would do little better under the most favorable conditions possible, *while those of superior intelligence will make good* no matter what handicaps they are given. (Hunter, 1941, p. 759) [emphasis in original]

In 1941, Hunter concluded from his understanding of biology that 'heredity was the basis upon which success in life is dependent', and that eugenics, 'the science of being well born, or born well, healthy, and fit in every way', was both a legitimate science and a worthy social policy. And so, eight years after the Nuremberg Laws had been passed in Nazi Germany, William Hunter was able to describe eugenics to his American students as follows: '[Eugenics] means that we should make a real effort to separate those who are socially, physically, and morally fit from those who are not . . . ' But separation was only half of the program recommended. Society, Hunter instructed, should '*allow only the fit to hand down their traits to their offspring*' (p. 760, emphasis added). This was a rather extreme proposal for an American textbook in the 1940s and it was warranted in an interesting way. Rather than arguing either that biology required programs of positive eugenics or that positive eugenics was an issue of moral correctness, Hunter placed the issue in the domain of simple public opinion that was not favorable to eugenics but it was open to manipulation. 'Of course, such a proceeding as that is impossible with the present standards of society', Hunter noted, 'but when we realize what has occurred through the breeding of bad stocks, we are shocked and alarmed' (p. 760). We may today read the word-mastery test that Hunter included in this volume as a subtle way of influencing that public opinion. The following sentences, with the right answers italicized, are from that test.

> To make matters worse, the feebleminded are breeding much faster than the *mentally* fit. To meet this situation, it is necessary to have some *physical* control, thus preventing this kind of person from breeding. Two methods, one *segregation* into separate institutions for males and females, the other *sterilization* or prevention of breeding are possible practices. A third is by practicing *eugenics* by having only those of good physical constitutions and *mental* ability marry and have children. (Hunter, 1941, p. 767)

By 1941, the notion that the inheritance of mental ability was a simple matter of breeding best with best and that human intellectual performance was primarily a matter of inherited qualities, regardless of social context, was surely outside of the mainstream of biological thought. Yet this was quite clearly Hunter's position as he readily agreed with Princeton's Conklin, that 'wooden legs are not inherited, but wooden heads are' (Hunter, 1941, p. 772). And in the case of world war rapidly approaching on the horizon, Hunter argued that in the case of war, 'a good biologist would . . . [send] the mentally unfit to be killed off and [keep] the biologically fit at home to continue the race' (p. 770). We find that after twenty-seven years of making biology available to high school students, George William Hunter was not pleased with what he had learned from his discipline. Yet it is important to recognize that what he learned appears more a reflection of his social views than of the findings of biology. By the 1940s, mainstream biologists recognized the importance of nature *and* nurture in human development; they had rejected extreme hereditarianism, and they were wary of simplistic explanations of the expression of the most complex of human attributes, intelligence. Their restraint, however, appears to have significantly influenced neither Hunter nor many of his counterparts who authored biology texts during this period.

Indeed, a review of other texts in the NIE archive suggests that Hunter's views were not atypical. For example, Peabody and Hunt's volume, *Biology and Human Welfare* (1924), considers 'the intimate relation of biological science to human welfare' (p. iv), with a chapter titled, 'How Success in Life is Won', introduces the study of eugenics. The chapter combines aphorisms and moral imperatives for hard work (regardless of biological heritage) with the traditional litany of eugenics. 'Like produces like', the authors remind their readers, and just as it is 'race horses [that] are descended from other race horses, it is blood that tells, whether in race horses or human beings' (p. 542). A rather ambivalent nature and nurture message then follows. 'Improved environment and training may better the generation already born', so work hard, the author instructs, but 'improved blood will better every generation to come, so marry and breed well' (p. 543). As with the Hunter texts, the reader is shortly thereafter introduced to the Kallikak and Edwards families. Of the latter's descendants, Peabody and Hunt find 'that they may be proud that such blood flows in [their] veins, for it is probably true that no other family has contributed more to our national welfare than [that of Jonathan Edwards]' (p. 547). Here we have an example of democracy with a particularly 'biological' twist. As we shall see, it is a twist that is taken by many of the textbooks in this study; it is a twist that permits biology (in the eyes of the texts' authors) to prefigure the proposed political and economic relations of the volume's readers. To succeed, the texts appear to suggest, is not so much dependent upon knowledge of the nation's political constitution, but upon the individual's biological one.

But not all problems are of the Edwards' constitutional makeup. What of those less worthy individuals and their families often referred to in the text? Peabody and Hunt (1924) offer a response. A Dr Hart of the Russell Sage Foundation had 'assure[d the authors] that a few generations only would be required to eliminate from human society the feebleminded and *socially diseased* . . . through a program of institutionalization and segregation' (p. 546, emphasis added). The message is clear for those of poor ancestry. 'Certain it is', the authors conclude, 'that every right-minded individual should avoid marrying into a family in which there is ancestral feeblemindedness and who . . . cannot furnish physical and mental health certificates signed by reliable physicians' (p. 546). For those who wondered as to the source of such recommendations, the authors were quick to identify 'a great movement . . . known as Eugenics', which instructs that, 'any permanent improvement of the human race can only come as a result of better heritage' (p. 548).

Having thus underlined the primary importance of inheritance in human betterment, the authors might well have foreseen a complaint in the part of their high school readers. 'Why', these students might have wondered, 'should we bother to work so hard if so much of our future is dependent upon our unchangeable biological inheritance?' Anticipating this potentially nihilistic response, Peabody and Hunt were ready with an answer that ties biology and class together in a way that leads to social stasis. 'Certainly', they remind their readers, 'enough has been said to show the tremendous consequences that come from good and bad heritage'. But such findings do not have a direct relationship to the readers since, 'most of us . . . belong to the great middle class in which heritage is neither exceptionally good nor strikingly bad. For this reason, in order to win success, each one of us must do all in his power to make . . . environment and response could for all that they are worth' (p. 548). And it is here that the authors underscore the importance of education in this competition; interestingly enough, it is an education that is less a cognitive and critical endeavor than one of good habit formation. Comparing the Edwards and Jukes families this time, Peabody and Hunt (1924) instruct their readers that 'education is something more than going to school for a few weeks each year, is more than knowing how to read and write. It has to do with character, with industry, and with patriotism' (p. 549).

It would be difficult for the adolescent readers of *Biology in Human Welfare* not to see their futures based upon this discussion of biology, education, and class. For the descendants of the Edwards' class, the future holds continued promise for contributions to the 'national welfare' (p. 547). For the offspring of the Jukes or Kallikaks, on the other hand, a life of institutionalization where they would be 'prevented from transmitting to other generations their physical, mental, and moral weaknesses' awaits (p. 546). For the middle class reader, a reader of evident middling heritage, a life of hard work and perseverance will lead to equally modest ends. 'If he keeps faithfully busy', Peabody and Hunt repeat, 'each hour of the day, he may safely leave the final result to itself. He can with perfect certainty count on waking up some fine morning to find himself one of the competent ones of his generation in whatever pursuit he may have singled out' (p. 552). Based on this analysis of the constraints of one's biological heritage, a person could apparently look forward to one of three trajectories for his future: excellence, competence, or institutionalization.

When the World Book Company published John Woodside Ritchie's, *Biology in Human Affairs* in 1941, it reflected the burgeoning knowledge in the biological sciences and was over 1000 pages in length. As with many of the texts considered in this study, it considered biology as a source of socially instrumental data. In an early example of what was to become known as the Life Adjustment approach to curriculum planning, Ritchie advised his readers that biology 'more than any other science . . . teaches us to understand ourselves. This helps us to see ourselves as we are, to perceive what we can and cannot do and to concentrate on what we can change and improve' (p. 31). Ritchie further believed that objective judgments could be made of his readers' abilities and that they were evaluations that one ignored at the risk of considerable personal dissatisfaction. 'We do not fight against gravity, because it is no use', he explained, and 'we are resigned to the succession of the seasons because we know we cannot stop them' (p. 31). As with this knowledge of the physical sciences, Ritchie implied that an understanding of the biological bases for our abilities was available. Accepting this knowledge and its implications would avoid psychological distress. 'When we understand the world and our own abilities, we tend to give up impossible hopes and ambitions and to seek that which is possible for us' (p. 31). And where does the authority lie for such decisions? 'The only wise course', Ritchie counsels, 'is to bow to nature's authority, learn her laws, and live in harmony with her decrees. An understanding of biology', he continues, 'helps us see this and to do the things that nature will approve' (p. 31).

One such law, developed by Sir Francis Galton, father of statistics and eugenics, was that of normal variation. In a most interesting discussion, Ritchie lists individual characteristics that were thought to be distributed on a normal curve. The list included intelligence, artistry, industry, unselfishness, and honesty (Ritchie, 1941, p. 38). The point was to highlight human differences and Ritchie went on to indicate that an improvement in social opportunity would only *exacerbate the differences* between people. 'Those with the best abilities profit most by opportunity and . . . the biologist . . . [appreciates] that the giving of freedom for the development and use of these abilities magnifies these differences' (p. 40). Even assuming that these observations on the inevitability of inequality were true in 1941, it is important to recognize that no specific social order was necessarily implied by human differences. But Ritchie had a social vision; it was a vision of inequalities in innate competence and in social consequences.

To those of his contemporaries who might have argued for a society of equal outcomes, Ritchie indicated that such social policies denied the fixed laws of biology and responded that 'to secure equality of accomplishment in any field of endeavor, "the more efficient must be shackled that they not outrun the less efficient" ' (p. 40). But such a 'shackled society' does not necessarily follow from a study of human differences. One's political or social philosophy makes that link. An understanding of biology, after all, could prepare one for the recognition of human differences and of human possibilities. And this, in turn, could be linked to a political vision of a collective of social equality. The choice to see biology as Ritchie did, as 'prepar[ing people] for living more comprehendingly in the world of natural inequalities that we have until all persons are born alike' (p. 38), is equally a reflection of a personal philosophy and not the implication of the fixed laws of biology.

While it is difficult to imagine any biologist suggesting that all people be born alike, it was not unusual for the authors of the majority of the books under consideration in this study to support programs of selective human breeding. As noted earlier, more than seventy-five per cent of the texts considered, supported eugenic marriage selection and Ritchie's text was among that number. As he instructed his readers, 'the positive part of the program is the arranging of a social order that will allow and encourage those of high abilities and desirable character to marry early and raise large families' (p. 699). Both positive and negative programs of eugenics were recommended for adolescent consideration in 1941. 'As you take your place as . . . citizen[s], you will be called upon to consider one social and political measure after another', he pointed out. The standard recommended for his readers' use in resolving these measures was that of biological determinism. In the political arena where claims for nature and nurture competed, Ritchie seemed to suggest that limited attention be given to environmental reform. ' . . . Scan each measure from the point of view of whether it will in the end give us a citizenry with better or poorer genes', he warned, for 'the welfare of a people in the end is determined by what the people are' (p. 699).

Once again, it is important to recognize that few single gene diseases were identifiable in 1941 and the genetic basis for human social behavior was equally unresolved. As we have noted earlier, there was simply no way for Ritchie to unambiguously identify these 'better' genes. One was limited to phenotypic proxies. His assumption that persons of good character had genes for such behavior that were lacking in those of poor character was without significant empirical warrant. And that remains true to this day.

When Charles Dull, Paul Mann, and Philip Johnson published *Modern Science in Man's Progress* in 1942, they structured their volume around 525 questions and their answers. The last seven questions in their text draw the attention of this paper's analysis. They were as follows:

> 519 Are all persons biologically equal?
> 520 Are there good family lines?
> 521 Who are the Kallikaks and the Jukes?
> 522 What is eugenics?
> 523 To what extent is eugenics being used today?
> 524 How much can man really improve himself?
> 525 What is the goal for each individual?
> (Dull *et al.*, 1942, p. 525).

The answers to these questions give the reader a sense of the authors' position on the legitimacy of eugenics. In response to the query about human equality, the text is clear. Equality in the 'eyes of the law' is not the same thing as biological equality. Mirroring the position of many other books in review, the authors make differences into inequality. Given such inequalities, they answer that yes, there are good family lines and yes, inequalities do appear to run in families. Examples here include the Herreshoffs of boat building fame and the musical family, Bach. There are also poor family lines and the authors don't shy away from the litany of disasters associated with the Jukes and Kallikak family trees. They were disasters that readers were to place at biological inheritance's door. The authors note that of the Jukes' family's '1000 descendants . . . the majority were feebleminded and 130 were criminals. Not a single individual had an elementary school education' (p. 565). And their threat was not simply biological. They were also an economic threat; the cost of maintaining these 'ne'er-do-wells' was known. 'Up to 1877', Dull, Mann, and Johnson tabulate, 'this family cost the state of New York more than $1,250,000'. No one seems to have dared to estimate the amount since that time, yet we as taxpayers pay such bills. 'What', they ask, rhetorically, 'can we do about it?' (p. 565). The answer comes in the texts' next lines as the authors introduce the work of Britain's Francis Galton 'who felt so keenly about . . . [human improvement] that he lectured and wrote on the subject . . . [and] coined the word eugenics . . . which might be shortened to the phrase "improvement of human heredity" ' (p. 566). Yet despite tighter immigration laws and the requirement by many states of health certificates for those planning marriages, the authors wanted stronger eugenic measures to be instituted. As they conclude, 'the civilized world today knows more biological truth than it is willing to practice' (p. 568).

Grudgingly accepting the public's apparent unwillingness to practice eugenics to a degree that would please them, Dull *et al.* (1942) apply the notion of human variety to a vision of an efficient corporate society. In a society that generates a variety of work settings, 'there must be a variety of different kinds of individuals to meet these different needs. We need', they continue, 'heavy draft horses as well as fast racers; beef cattle as well as good dairy cows; crab apples as well as McIntosh apples' (p. 568). Having shown these differences in the plant and animal world, the authors move directly to human applications. They are applications that reflect a naive mutuality between individuals in a perfectly rational social order. 'Among humans', they explain, 'great leaders gather devoted followers, worthwhile musicians play to keen listeners, good athletes are applauded by enthusiastic sports fans, and conscientious teachers have cooperative pupils' (p. 568). The point being made here should be underlined; people were differently endowed as leaders or followers, athletes or fans, players or listeners, operators or cooperators. Maximize your natural abilities, the authors recommended, and *find your place* in the existing and just social order.

But eugenics was but half a program; in the end it is euthenics, 'the environmental training of education' (p. 568) that would assist in both of these tasks. It is interesting to see how Dull, Mann, and Johnson dealt with eugenics and euthenics and the question of vocational placement in 1942. They viewed eugenics as a legitimate science and even if they were not able to completely apply it to humankind in breeding programs (due to uninformed social resistance) it did form the basis for legitimating differences in social location and social rewards. When combined with a program of euthenics, eugenics was able to present its social utility to educators. It could aid in shaping vocational programs by offering a biological basis for existing economic and social relations. As has been noted elsewhere in this chapter, it was in the context of education for social efficiency that eugenics has always found itself most valued.

The first biology text considered in this review was published before the First World War. In it we found a view of eugenics as legitimate science and as an appropriate method for human betterment. In the last volume evaluated, we will inquire whether the monumental changes that took place in biology in the following thirty-eight years influenced the content of the biology textbook when the topic under consideration was eugenics. We turn now to that last volume, *Animal Biology*.

Animal Biology was published in 1948 by the well-known University of Wisconsin biologist, Michael F. Guyer, and eugenics was introduced early in its first chapter as 'a subject upon which the very perpetuation of our civilization depends' (p. 14).

In the context of a progressive concern for the nation's natural resources (forests, pollution, food inspection, vaccination, quarantine, hunting and fishing restrictions) Guyer recommended the husbanding of the genetic resources of the people. Animal and plant breeders, the reader was told, can predict and control future generations and the same is true for humankind. 'In his various strains of plants and animals . . . [the geneticist] can often combine desirable characters and eliminate undesirable ones. And it is now known that human structures and aptitudes, whether they make for man's weal or woe, are subject to the same laws' (p. 15). They were laws that one resisted at one's peril; they mandated action. 'In brief', Guyer concludes, 'such definite advances in our knowledge of the processes of human heredity are being made that we can no longer refuse to take up the social duties which the known facts thrust upon us' (p. 15). It would take Guyer over 500 pages to return again to eugenics. While constrained by the recognition of advances in biology that identified the complexity of human traits such as intelligence Guyer was still able to make many of the traditional eugenicist's points: ability still ran in families; inborn inequalities would not be equalized by training; nature is more important than nurture in human performance; and, maximizing hereditary differences through education was a reasonable social policy (pp. 552–4). All of these recommendations, and a remaining four, were based upon a corporate use of eugenics. The eugenicist, Guyer explained, is interested in programs of differential birthrates. He 'stresses the desirability of producing more individuals who are endowed by heredity with good physical and mental attributes, and fewer who are constitutionally inferior . . . He maintains that the question of breed — of natural endowments of its citizens — is of fundamental importance to a nation' (p. 552).

This importance came, in part, from Guyer's anxiety about the genetic composition of the nation and his vision of differential genetic worth. The similarity between Guyer's observations and those of the earliest biology text in this review are striking and warrant a closer analysis. 'Certain hereditary types', he explained, 'are more valuable to society and the race than others, and in many family strains, the seeds of derangement and disability have become so firmly established that they menace the remainder of the population' (p. 555). In a paragraph that reduces democracy to biology, Guyer warns that 'a successful democracy can, in last analysis, spring only from good blood' (p. 556).

And the less worthy members of society represent a clear and present danger to the nation's future. Speaking in terms reminiscent of those of the racist Madison Grant (1916), Guyer warned in 1948 that

> It is a disconcerting fact . . . to learn that at present, the less able fourth of our population is producing approximately one-half of the next generation. The greatest danger to any democracy is that its abler members and less prolific types shall be swamped by the overproduction of inferior strains. This has apparently been the fate of past civilizations — why not America? (Guyer, 1948, p. 556)

In responding to his own question, Guyer sounded refrains from the eugenicists of an earlier era. We must, he demanded, 'take our own evolution in hand and deal with our four chief menaces'. These menaces included the dysgenic effects of 'war', of 'unwise charity which fosters the production of unfit strains', of 'the immigration of individuals with inferior mentality and ability', and of the relative infertility of our 'superior stocks' (p. 556). In terms strikingly similar to those of Franklin Bobbitt (1909) of almost four decades earlier, Guyer lamented that natural selection was no longer operating naturally; 'inferior stocks are not only holding their own', he warned, 'but some are increasing faster than good stocks' (p. 557). In a text obviously written for just those good stocks, Michael Guyer recommended a program of applied eugenics. 'Unless we can institute an intelligent personal selection', he concluded, in tones more melancholy than scientific, 'in place of the natural selection which we are thwarting, the prospect for our nation — for civilization as a whole, indeed — is far from encouraging' (p. 567).

Conclusion

We may now ask what can be learned from this extensive rendering of four decades of biology texts from the NIE archive. Initially, we can see that eugenics was included as legitimate content in biology textbooks published during a period of time spanning the First and Second World Wars. We can also see that specific social policies supported by the eugenics movement were reflected in the texts. For example, programs of differential birthrates were recommended by a significant majority of the books in question. The nature of the support and the logic of the argument made is also of importance to us today. Surprisingly, the argument for human breeding was *infrequently* made in genetic terms. Very few of the textbooks reviewed talked of genes or chromosomes. Even when these terms were presented, there was no indication of how either had achieved their differential effects. For a great many of the texts in question, the scientific data supporting eugenic marriages were studies in family lines or types with the Kallikaks and Edwards families regularly exemplified. One needs to remember, even discounting the altered photographs in Goddard's *Kallikak* study, that these family pedigrees could not separate out nature and nurture. They could not make a powerful empirically warranted argument for the importance of heredity over environment in human performance. The point here is not to suggest that heredity plays no role. On the contrary, as human beings we are a realization of the dialectical relationship between nature and nurture. Our genetic make-up represents our potential. However, in the work of the authors considered in this review, one's biology spoke to limits; *one was determined by one's genes*. We know today, and the authors were professionally responsible for having known after the early 1920s, that such a view is empirically invalidated in all but the most constrained examples. After all, one could suggest that Bach's musical achievements were more directly related to the presence of a harpsichord in his house than to any genetic predisposition on his part to the fugue. Yet it does appear that the hereditarian attitudes of the majority of the texts' authors kept them from considering these interpretations as well as from seriously reflecting on changes that were taking place in biology and that were contradictory to the eugenicists' program.

In conclusion, it appears that at least in the case of the discussions of eugenics, the forty biology books analyzed in this study presented more a reflection of social attitudes and political theories than a rendering of scientific data. The authors' commitment to a hierarchical and corporate social order in which individuals could be rationally placed based upon their alleged hereditary worth preceded and informed their discussions of eugenics. Science served as neither critique of the world as it was known nor as they wished it to be. Their greatest error, from a pedagogical standpoint, was their use of biology textbooks as vehicles for their social policy prescriptions. As we know today, mainline eugenics wasn't good science, and theirs was not good pedagogy. Today, one expects that when social issues are raised in textbooks, they are raised as issues to be confronted, as problems to be solved. They are problems that require the best scientific and ethical evidence available for their solution. Clearly the biology texts considered in this review did not meet that standard when considering the question of human improvement through breeding. Rather than evidence for problem solving, they supplied an answer from a broad array of possibilities. In many ways, these texts exemplified the desire to use schools as instruments for acculturation or socialization but not for education. While eugenics is probably at a low point in acceptance today, the desire to use the schools for socialization is not. Indeed, such socialization pressures appear on the rise today (Selden, in press). In such a context, it will still be the school's responsibility to speak truth to power. It is a challenge worth meeting.

Notes

1 For an excellent discussion of the 19th century textbook as a transmitter of selected cultural values, see Elson (1964).
2 For a most provocative analysis of the contemporary history textbook, see Anyon (1979).
3 For a broader discussion of the links between eugenics and American education, see Selden (1983, 1985, 1987).
4 A complete listing of the volumes, authors, and page references supporting these data are available from the author, c/o EDPA, College of Education, University of Maryland, College Park, MD 20742.
5 As we move towards the end of the twentieth century, substantive discussions of human genetics can even be found on the pages of the popular press. For an interesting discussion of the ethical problems presented by our increased knowledge in this area, see Blakeslee (1987).

References

ANYON, J. (1979) 'Ideology and the United States history textbook', *Harvard Educational Review,* **49,** 3, pp. 361–86.

BAKER, C. B. and BAKER, E. D. (1937) *The Curriculum Readers. V: Making America*, Indianapolis: Bobbs-Merrill Company.

BLAKESLEE, S. (1987) 'Genetic discoveries raise painful questions', *New York Times*, 21 April.

BOBBITT, F. (1909) 'Practical eugenics', *Pedagogical Seminary,* **26,** pp. 385–94.

CHASE, A. (1977) *The Legacy of Malthus: The Social Costs of the New Scientific Racism*, New York: Alfred A. Knopf.

DAWODWICZ, L. S. (1975) *The War Against the Jews, 1933–1945*, New York: Holt, Rinehart and Winston.

DULL, C. E., MANN, P. B. and JOHNSON, P. G. (1942) *Modern Science in Man's Progress, 3*, New York: Henry Holt and Company.

ELSON, R. M. (1964) *Guardians of Tradition: American School Books of the Nineteenth Century*, Lincoln, NE: University of Nebraska Press.

GODDARD, H. H. (1912) *The Kallikak Family: A Study in the Heredity of Feeble-mindedness*, New York: The MacMillan Company.

GOULD, S. J. (1981) *The Mismeasure of Man*, New York: W. W. Norton.

GRANT, M. (1916) *The Passing of the Great Race*, New York: Charles Scribner's Sons.

GUYER, M. F. (1948) *Animal Biology*, New York: Harper and Brothers.

HUNTER, G. W. (1914) *A Civic Biology: Presented in Problems*, New York: American Book Company.

HUNTER, G. W. (1926) *New Civic Biology: Presented in Problems*, New York: American Book Company.

HUNTER, G. W. (1931) *Problems in Biology*, New York: American Book Company.

HUNTER, G. W. (1941) *Life Science: A Social Biology*, New York: American Book Company.

HUNTER, G. W. and WHITMAN, W. G. (1935) *Science in Our World of Progress*, New York: American Book Company.

KEVLES, D. J. (1985) *In the Name of Eugenics: Genetics and the Uses of Human Heredity*. New York: Alfred A. Knopf.

KNOX, R. B. (1930) *The Boys and Sally Down on a Plantation*, New York: Doubleday Doran and Company, Incorporated.

MORTON, E. H. (1901) *Morton's Advanced Geography*, Philadelphia: Butler, Sheldon and Company.

PEABODY, J. E. and HUNT, A. E. (1924) *Biology and Human Welfare*, New York: The MacMillan Company.

REDWAY, J. W. and HINMAN, R. (1912) *Natural Complete Geography: Kentucky Series*, New York: American Book Company.

RITCHIE, J. W. (1941) *Biology in Human Affairs*, New York: World Book Company.

SELDEN, S. (1983) 'Biological determinism and the ideological roots of student classification', *Journal of Education,* **164,** 2, pp. 171–91.

SELDEN, S. (1985) 'Education policy and biological science: Genetics, eugenics, and the college textbook, c. 1881–1931', *Teachers College Record,* **87,** 1, pp. 35–52.

SELDEN, S. (1986) 'Character education and the triumph of technique', *Issues in Education*, Vol. IV, No. 3, Winter, pp. 301–12.

SELDEN, S. (1987) 'Confronting social attitudes in textbooks: The response and responsibility of educators', in MOLNAR, A. (Ed.) *Social Issues and Education: Challenge and Responsibility*, Alexandria, VA: Association for Supervision and Curriculum Development, pp. 31–46.

ZINN, H. (1980) *A People's History of the United States*, New York: Harper Colophon Books.

Gender, Equity and Mathematics

Elizabeth Fennema and Margaret R. Meyer

Everyone should learn mathematics! There should be equity in mathematics education! Such statements have been accepted as truth in most democracies for many years. However, even though most educators agree at the overt level with such statements, when those statements are examined for their meaning and implications, it is evident that equity in mathematics is difficult to understand and it is even more difficult to determine whether or not it exists. The purpose of this chapter is to examine gender differences in mathematics in relationship to three different interpretations that can be placed on the term mathematics equity.

Equity as Equal Opportunity to Learn Mathematics

In many countries, including the United States, it is assumed that there is equal opportunity for males and females to learn mathematics. Girls and boys in elementary school are not segregated when it is time to learn mathematics; teachers usually teach the entire class at one time and do not make conscious decisions about teaching boys and girls differently or identically. As children move up the educational ladder, a somewhat different pattern appears. Learners are either placed in different tracks as is done in Australia and England, or are allowed to elect mathematics as an optional subject as in the United States. In the US, neither boys nor girls are legally or even consciously prevented from electing mathematics courses, nor is the decision made overtly by sex about tracking students. In fact, many believe that providing equal opportunity to elect mathematics and not tracking by sex ensures that equity in mathematics is achieved. However, when data are examined about who actually elects to take advanced mathematics courses in secondary schools, it is clear that there are differences in the election of such courses with males electing to take such courses more often than do females (see Armstrong, 1985, for a complete discussion). After secondary school is finished, the differentiation between the numbers of females and males studying mathematics or preparing for mathematics related careers is even more dramatic.

Equity as Equal Educational Outcomes

When important outcomes of mathematics education are examined, it is clear that equality of opportunity to take mathematics is not sufficient to achieve equality in outcomes of mathematics education. Two types of outcomes will be considered here: the learning of mathematics and attitudes about mathematics.

The Learning of Mathematics

Girls and boys apparently enter elementary school with about the same mathematical knowledge. Few, if any, gender differences in ability to count are found (Callahan and Clements, 1984). By late first-grade, some differences in favor of boys in solving word problems are seen (Fennema, Peterson and Carpenter, 1987). Starting in late elementary school and increasing throughout high school, larger differences between girls and boys on mathematical tasks are apparent. The best source of empirical data which confirms these differences is the Third Mathematics Assessment of the National Assessment of Educational Progress (NAEP III).

NAEP measured performance of a large stratified random sample of learners, age 9, 13, and 17. These students were tested on mathematical items of increasing cognitive complexity. In Table 1 are shown the mean percentage of items answered correctly by females and males at the three ages. As can be seen, at younger ages females perform better than do males at the lowest cognitive level. However, as the items become more complex and at older age levels, this advantage disappears. This is accentuated when the performance of 17-year-old girls and boys, who have taken the same mathematics courses, are compared (Table 2). Boys performed significantly better than did girls. The difference was greater when the items got more complex. These data, collected in 1982, are basically the same as data from an earlier assessment reported in 1978.

Another study which has received much publicity and which deserves

Table 1 Mean Performance for males and females by exercise type: NAEP III*

	Age 9	Age 13	Age 17
Knowledge			
Male	67.4	73.8	75.9
Female	69.3	73.8	73.9
Skills			
Male	50.2	57.0	61.1
Female	51.1	58.1	58.9
Understanding			
Male	41.0	60.8	63.1
Female	41.4	60.2	60.0
Applications			
Male	40.0	46.1	44.6
Female	39.2	45.1	40.2

*From National Assessment of Educational Progress (1983). The Third National Mathematics Assessment: Results, Trends, and Issues. Report No. 13-MA-01. Education Commission of the States, Denver, Colorado.

Table 2 Performance levels of male and female 17-year olds by highest course taken and exercise type, 1982[a]

Cognitive Level	<Algebra 1	Algebra 1	Geometry	Algebra 2	>Algebra 2
Knowledge					
Males	64.5	71.8*	79.4*	83.4	87.7
Females	62.8	69.1*	75.4*	81.1	87.6
Skills					
Males	45.1	56.3	62.8*	71.2*	77.7
Females	43.8	53.8	58.2*	68.8*	76.8
Understanding					
Males	46.0	57.4*	67.5*	73.2*	80.0
Females	44.0	52.6*	62.2*	69.6*	78.7
Applications					
Males	29.6*	38.9*	45.8*	53.6*	62.9*
Females	27.0*	33.7*	40.1*	48.0*	59.8*

[a]From National Assessment of Educational Progress (1983). The Third National Assessment: Results, Trade, and Issues. Report No. 13-MA-01.
*Male-Female difference is significant at the .05 level.

discussion is the Study of Mathematically Precocious Youth (SMPY) (see Fox and Cohn, 1980, for a complete description). In this study, conducted basically from 1972–9, seventh and eighth grade students who were identified by their teachers or who had scored very high on an achievement test, were tested on the mathematics portion of the Scholastic Aptitude Test, a test commonly given as a college entrance examination. While there are some subtleties in the findings, in general many more boys than girls were identified as being unusually able in what the test developers call mathematical reasoning ability. Fox and Cohn conclude that 'males are more likely than females to perform at a very high level on precollege level tests of mathematical reasoning ability (at least in a voluntary contest situation). Mathematical precocity appears to be not only less visible, but rarer among female adolescents than among males (p. 109).

Some studies report no differences between female and male achievement in mathematics. For example, Smith (1980) reported no gender differences on the New York State Regents High School mathematics examinations in ninth, tenth, and eleventh grade. Senk and Usiskin (1982) reported no gender differences in a large-scale study dealing with geometry.

Another measure of learning is grades given by teachers. Since many elementary schools do not give letter grades to children, data are only available about children in grades 7–12. Grades reflect teachers' assessment of students' performance on what has been covered during instruction. As such, they are a more direct measure of students' learning of the curriculum taught. Girls receive higher grades in mathematics classes than do boys (Stockard and Wood, 1984). Even when only highly precocious girls' and boys' grades are compared, girls receive slightly better grades than do boys (Benbow and Stanley, 1982).

It appears that while sex-related differences are not always found, boys tend to do better on certain types of tasks and girls tend to get better grades. One interpretation of this is that girls learn what is taught somewhat better than do boys, while boys are better able to transfer their learning to untaught high cognitive level situations. (For a complete review of sex-related differences in mathematics achievement, see Fennema, 1984; Stage, Kreinberg, Eccles and Becker, 1985.)

Just what are high cognitive level situations in mathematics? These situations are problems or activities that a child doesn't already know how to do. They require cognitive activity beyond rote recall. For example, consider the exercise in Figure 1.

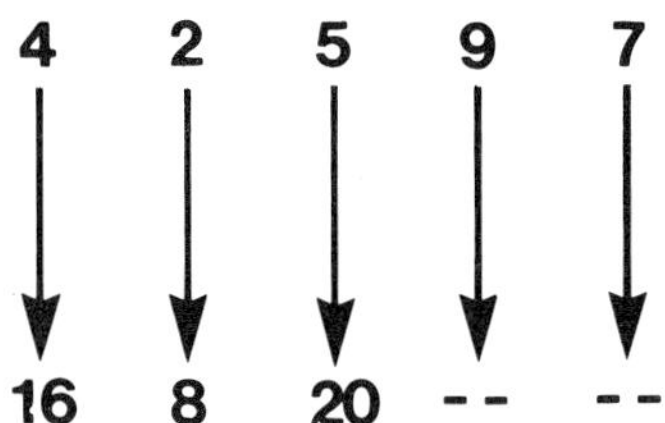

Figure 1. Exercise without taught algorithm.

This is a relatively easy activity for intermediate grade children, but it is one where a procedure for finding the answer is not usually taught. The exercises in Figure 2, which appear to be harder for children, do not usually involve higher level skills, because children are taught procedures or algorithms for finding the answers.

The two second-grade exercises in Figure 3 show the difference

Figure 2. Exercise with taught algorithm

$$\begin{array}{r} 611 \\ -347 \\ \hline \end{array} \qquad 43\overline{)4835}$$

Figure 3. Examples of high and low cognitive level exercise.

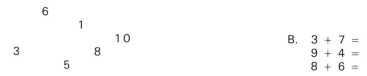

A. USE LINES TO CONNECT THE NUMBERS SO THAT EACH PAIR ADDS UP TO THE SAME NUMBER.

between high and low level cognitive skills. The problem on the left uses addition just as the one on the right does. However, different strategies must be tried for the left one while the right one only requires recall (for most second graders).

The ability to apply mathematics learning to unfamiliar situations is a primary goal of mathematics education. A gender difference in this critical skill is compelling evidence that equity in terms of achievement outcomes has not been achieved.

Attitudes Toward Mathematics

Another important outcome of mathematics education is student attitudes. Attitudes have to do with beliefs about oneself and mathematics. Not only do they influence mathematics learning; development of positive attitudes is an important goal of any educational program. While there are many attitudes, three will be considered here: confidence in learning mathematics, perceived usefulness of mathematics, and attributions of causes of success and failure in mathematics.

Confidence in learning mathematics is related to general self esteem and is a belief that one has the ability to learn new mathematics and to perform well on mathematical tasks. There are many data which indicate that confidence is strongly related to achievement (Fennema and Sherman, 1978) and that females report lower levels of confidence than do males. These differences appear during elementary school and continue throughout secondary school. Females, more than males, doubt their own ability in mathematics (see Reyes, 1984, for a thorough discussion of this). This lower self esteem undoubtedly influences females' achievement in mathematics, their willingness to take advanced mathematics courses in secondary and post secondary school, and their selection of mathematics-related careers.

Perceived usefulness of mathematics is another important attitude. When one believes math is not useful, one will neither exert as much effort to learn nor elect the advanced mathematics courses. Mathematics is a difficult subject and not particularly enjoyable for many learners. Why should one study it if it is of no future use? Females in secondary schools, as a group, indicate that they do not feel they will use mathematics in the future (Armstrong, 1985). Males, as a group, are much more apt to report that mathematics is essential for whatever career they plan. As early as sixth grade, these gender differences appear. If females do not see mathematics-related careers as possibilities, they will also not see mathematics as useful.

Another attitude toward mathematics which is important in understanding gender differences in mathematics is causal attribution. This is a complex set of attitudes which has to do with what one believes causes successes and failures. Typically, causal attributions can be placed in four categories: Ability (I solved the problem because I am smart.); Effort (I tried real hard on the problem.); Task (It was an easy problem.); or Luck/Environment (I was lucky or I got help from the teacher.). These four categories can be placed into a 2 × 2 matrix (Figure 4) with locus of control (internal-external) along one dimension, and stability (stable-unstable) along the other (Weiner, 1974).

One way in which attributions of success or failure influence achievement-oriented behavior is in terms of persistence. In a somewhat simplistic summary, if a student attributes success to an internal, stable dimension (ability), then the student expects success in the future and will continue to strive in that area. If a student attributes success to an unstable or an external cause (for example, the teacher), then the student will not be as confident of success in the future and will be less apt to strive or persist. A somewhat different situation is true of failure attributions. If a student attributes failure to unstable causes such as lack of effort, then the student might work harder the next time and failure

Figure 4. Weiner's attribution classification

	Internal	External
Stable	Ability	Task
Unstable	Effort	Luck/ Environment

could be avoided. With this situation, the tendency to approach or persist at tasks will be encouraged. On the other hand, attribution of failure to a stable cause, such as lack of ability, will lead a student to believe that failure cannot be avoided.

A belief that outcomes cannot be controlled is part of a phenomenon labeled learned helplessness (Seligman and Maier, 1967). Individuals who are 'learned helpless' feel defeated before they begin. Learned helpless students tend to attribute failure to the internal/stable factor of ability, and success to the external factors of task and luck/environment. Their effort is minimal as they do not believe that effort would result in success. And besides, if they failed after extensive effort, their lack of ability would be all the more obvious to others.

If you imagine learned helplessness at one end of a continuum, then mastery orientation is at the other. Individuals who are mastery oriented do not feel they are powerless to succeed. Instead, they see that their success is due to a combination of their ability and consistent effort, and that when they fail, it is a result of insufficient effort. These students are not defeated by setbacks; instead, they try harder.

While we must be careful of overgeneralizing data and concluding that all males behave one way and all females another way, many studies have reported that females and males tend to exhibit different attributional patterns both in mathematics and other achievement areas (Deaux, 1976; Bar-Tal and Frieze, 1977; Wolleat, Pedro, Becker and Fennema, 1980). Males tend to attribute successes to internal causes, and failure to external or unstable causes. Females tend to attribute successes to external or unstable causes and failures to internal causes. In other words, females, more than males, attribute causation in ways that are associated with learned helpless behavior. It has been suggested that this behavior strongly affects achievement (Bar-Tal, 1978).

In summary, there are gender differences in mathematics education outcomes. Boys, more than girls, are able to transfer their learning to solving complex problems, while girls, more than boys, perform better on tasks explicitly taught. Girls, more than boys, report less confidence, exhibit an attributional style which inhibits persistence and other achievement-related behaviors, and perceive mathematics as not very useful. There is not equality in outcomes of mathematics education for females and males.

Equity as Equal Educational Treatment

Another interpretation of equity is equality of educational treatment or equality of mathematical experiences in schools. In particular, the concern here is equal treatment in the mathematics classroom. If equity existed using this interpretation, it would be impossible to detect any differences in the treatment of boys and girls by teachers. While teachers would treat individuals differently, differential treatment of boys and girls as groups would not exist. Girls would be talked to by the teacher as much as would boys. Girls would be asked to solve problems as many times as would boys. Girls and boys would be rewarded in the same way for the same kind of responses. Girls would be scolded as much as would boys. In fact, if one believes that equity in mathematics education means equal treatment within classrooms, there would be no difference in the way that teachers interacted with boys and girls.

There is much evidence that equality of treatment of boys and girls does not exist in most classrooms. Boys interact more with teachers than do girls; girls have many more days in which they do not interact at all with the teacher than do boys. Teachers initiate more contacts with boys than with girls. Boys receive more discipline contacts as well as more praise. Classroom activities are more often chosen to appeal to the boys than to the girls. Teachers respond more frequently to requests for help from boys than from girls and tend to criticize girls more than boys for the academic quality of their work (Fennema and Peterson, 1987). Grieb and Easley (1984) report that teachers allow some boys to exert their independence overtly and refuse to learn specific algorithms.

There are two difficulties associated with efforts to attain equal treatment of girls and boys in classrooms. First of all, differential treatment is often subtle and, as a result, hard to detect much less change. Teachers seldom deliberately treat boys and girls differently. Instead, their behavior is unconscious and, therefore, unexamined.

Another problem involved with equal treatment is inequality of outcomes which can be illustrated with an example. A common drill activity in fourth-grade mathematics classrooms is a game called 'Around the World' in which multiplication (or division) facts are presented to two players. The first player to respond with the correct answer proceeds to the next challenger who is the next person in that row of seats. The object is to win over all challengers and to proceed around the world. On the surface, this would appear to be an innovative way to incorporate drill in a game whose structure ensures equal opportunity for girls and boys to play.

A closer look at this game reveals important differences for girls and boys. First of all, is the game going to be equally appealing to the girls and boys? Numerous observations of the game suggest that the most enthusiastic players of the game are the boys. Indeed, boys are often cheered on by their peers as they meet new challengers. Another potential problem lies in the fact that given equal recall ability by two students, the judgment of correctness usually goes to the player who is most assertive, or the loudest in responding. This person is usually the boy challenger. Finally, one has to look at the educational outcomes. It has been shown that competitive games such as this are associated with achievement gains for boys, but not for girls, (see Peterson and Fennema, 1985, and Fennema and Peterson, 1987, for a complete discussion). To summarize this example, the game, while appearing to represent equality of opportunity and treatment, instead results in inequality of response and outcomes. An activity that is good for one group need not be for another.

What is Equity?

Does equity in mathematics mean that everyone should learn the same thing (equal outcomes) or does it mean that everyone should have equal opportunity to learn? Does it mean that everyone should be treated identically by teachers or does it mean that teachers should systematically vary their teaching to adapt to the way that each individual learns mathematics best? Does it mean that boys and girls should learn in the same classrooms or does it mean that there should be separate classrooms for boys and girls? Does it mean that when boys and girls leave school they should have identical mathematical knowledge and skills?

From the examination of the evidence presented above it is clear that with the possible exception of legal equity in the opportunity to study mathematics, equity does not exist for females in any definition of equity that one wishes to consider. We must conclude that while there is a semblance of equal opportunity to learn mathematics for girls and boys in today's world, this semblance is not enough. Females are not learning and participating in mathematics at the same level as are males. Do females recognize that there is equal opportunity to learn? Females do not have the internal belief systems equivalent to males that support them in learning mathematics. Does the school have a responsibility to respond to these differential belief systems? Is mere legal equality enough or are there other levels of equality that must be enforced if equity in mathematics is to be achieved? Are there less obvious ways in which inequality exists, such as scheduling problems that discourage girls from participating in upper level courses in mathematics?

Enforcing legal equity is obviously a prerequisite to achievement of equity. It is a necessary, but not a sufficient, condition. (See Issacson, 1986 for a complete discussion.) Equity in mathematics will not be achieved until the goals of education are achieved equally by boys and girls. At the end of schooling, there should be no differences in what girls and boys have learned nor should there be any differences in how boys and girls feel about themselves as learners of mathematics. Males and females should be equally willing to pursue mathematics-related careers and should be equally able to learn new mathematics as it would be required.

Equal outcomes is the best definition of equity because knowledge of mathematics and positive feelings about oneself and mathematics increases options. The goal of achieving equivalent outcomes in mathematics education for males and females may require that teachers actually should treat boys and girls somewhat differently. It could be that the most effective teaching for boys is somewhat different than effective teaching for girls. The above example on competition illustrates this concern. However, the question 'Is effective teaching the same for boys and girls?' cannot be answered simply. Fennema and Peterson (1987) suggest that several dimensions of classroom instruction hold promise for decreasing gender-related differences in mathematics. Teachers might place more stress on cooperative mathematics activities and less stress on competitive mathematics activities. Teachers need to increase their interactions with girls on high cognitive level mathematics activities, to expect girls to be able to solve the mathematics problems and then to praise them for doing so. Further, when girls respond incorrectly in mathematics class, the teacher needs to encourage divergent and independent thinking in girls by giving them hints on the mathematics strategy they might use, rather than telling them the answer or the strategy. Perhaps the most important thing that a teacher can do is to expect girls to work independently. Teachers should encourage girls to engage in independent learning behavior and praise them for participating in and performing well on high cognitive level mathematics tasks. The learning of mathematics, particularly acquiring the skills required to perform high level tasks, does not occur quickly or at one point in time. Rather, students develop these skills over a long period of years by participating many times in activities requiring high level thinking. Indeed, a very circular path is required. One learns to do high level tasks by choosing, persisting, and succeeding at high level tasks.

In summary, an examination of mathematics equity using the three interpretations of opportunity to learn, outcomes, and treatment illustrates the complexity of the equity issue. No one interpretation alone is sufficient. The goal of achieving equity of educational outcomes is dependent on equality of opportunity and equality of treatment. Of these, equality of opportunity is a reality and equality of treatment is possible.

That is good news! Teachers can make a difference. They can help reduce gender differences in mathematics achievement. In addition, teachers can also be a positive influence on students' beliefs about mathematics and about themselves as learners of mathematics. Teachers are important change agents, and they, more than anyone else, can help girls to achieve equity in mathematics.

References

ARMSTRONG, J.M. (1985) 'A national assessment of participation and achievement of women in mathematics', in CHIPMAN, S.F., BRUSH, L.R. and WILSON, D.M. (Eds) *Women and Mathematics: Balancing the Equation*, Hillsdale, NJ: Erlbaum, pp. 59–94.

BAR-TAL, D. (1978) 'Attributional analysis of achievement-related behavior', *Review of Educational Research,* **48,** pp. 259–71.

BAR-TAL, D. and FRIEZE, J.H. (1977) 'Achievement motivation for males and females as a determinant of attributions for success and failure', *Sex Roles,* **3,** pp. 301–13.

BENBOW, C.P. and STANLEY, J.C. (1982) 'Consequences in high school and college of sex differences in mathematical reasoning ability: A longitudinal perspective', *American Educational Research Journal,* **19,** 4, pp. 598–622.

CALLAHAN, L.G. and CLEMENTS, D.H. (1984) 'Sex differences in rote-counting ability on entry to first grade: Some observations', *Journal for Research in Mathematics Education,* **15,** 5.

DEAUX, K. (1976) 'Sex: A perspective on the attribution process', in HARVEY, J., ICKES, W. and KIDD, R. (Eds) *New Directions in Attributional Research (Vol. 1)*, Hillsdale, NJ: Lawrence Erlbaum.

FENNEMA, E. (1984) 'Girls, women and mathematics', in FENNEMA, E. and AYER, M.J. (Eds) *Women and Education: Equity or Equality?* Berkeley: McCutchan, pp. 137–64.

FENNEMA, E., PETERSON, P.L. and CARPENTER, T.P. (1987) *Teachers' Beliefs About Girls, Boys and Mathematics*, Manuscript in progress.

FENNEMA, E. and PETERSON, P.L. (1987) 'Effective teaching for girls and boys: The same or different?' in BERLINER, D.C. and ROSENSHINE, B.V. (Eds) *Talks to Teachers*, New York: Random House, pp. 111–25.

FENNEMA, E. and SHERMAN, J. (1978) 'Sex-related differences in mathematics achievement, spatial visualization and affective factors', *American Educational Research Journal,* **14,** pp. 51–71.

FOX, L.H. and COHN, S.J. (1980) 'Sex differences in the development of precocious mathematical talent', in FOX, L.H., BRODY, L. and TOBIN, D. (Eds) *Women and the Mathematical Mystique*, Baltimore: Johns Hopkins University Press, pp. 94–111.

GRIEB, H. and EASLEY, J. (1984) 'A primary school impediment to mathematical equity: Case studies in role-dependent socialization', in STEINCAMP, M. and MAEHR, M.L. (Eds) *Women in Science. Vol. 2: Advances in Motivation and Achievement*, Greenwich, CT: JAI Press, Inc., pp. 317–62.

ISAACSON, Z. (1986) 'Freedom and girls' education: A philosophical discussion with particular reference to mathematics', in BURTON, L. (Ed.), *Girls into Maths Can Go*, London: Holt, Rinehart and Winston, pp. 223–40.

PETERSON, P.L. and FENNEMA, E. (1985) 'Effective teaching, student engagement in classroom activities, and sex-related differences in learning mathematics', *American Educational Research Journal,* **22,** 3, pp. 309–35.

REYES, L.H. (1984) 'Affective variables and mathematics education', *The Elementary School Journal,* **84,** 5, pp. 558–81.

SELIGMAN, M.E.P. and MAIER, S.F. (1967) 'Failure to escape traumatic shock', *Journal of Experimental Psychology,* **74,** pp. 1–9.

SENK, S. and USISKIN, Z. (1982) Geometry proof writing: A new view of sex differences in mathematics ability. Unpublished manuscript, University of Chicago.

SMITH, S. E. (1980) Enrollment and achievement by sex in mathematics and science for five 1978 regents samples. Paper presented at Northeast Educational Research Association Convention, Ellenville, New York.

STAGE, E.K., KREINBERG, N., ECCLES (PARSONS), J. and BECKER, J.R. (1985) 'Women in mathematics, science, and engineering' in KLEIN, S.S. (Ed.) *Handbook for Achieving Sex Equity Through Education*, Baltimore: Johns Hopkins University Press.

STOCKARD, J. and WOOD, J.W. (1984) 'The myth of female underachievement: A re-examination of sex differences in academic underachievement', *American Educational Research Journal,* **21,** 4, pp. 825–38.

WEINER, B. (1974) *Achievement Motivation and Attribution Theory*, Morristown, NJ: General Learning Press.

WOLLEAT, P., PEDRO, J.D., BECKER, A.D. and FENNEMA, E. (1980) 'Sex differences in high school students' causal attributions of performance in mathematics', *Journal for Research in Mathematics Education,* **11,** pp. 356–66.

Equity and Technology in Education: An Applied Researcher Talks to the Theoreticians

Jo Sanders

Among the many things I have learned in ten years of working on sex equity and technology in schools, perhaps the most significant are the things I don't have solid answers for. As an applied researcher – a model program developer, curriculum writer, and author of books for educators – I often read works by my more theoretical colleagues in the hope of finding answers to questions that arise in my work in the schools. I don't find as many answers as I'd like.

I have been primarily concerned with nontraditional occupations and career preparation for girls and women, largely for economic reasons: 'men's' jobs tend to pay much better than 'women's' jobs, women badly need well-paying jobs, and the clear direction of the economy has been in the direction of the technologies rather than the trades. I have therefore spent the last ten years on projects to help women obtain training for nontraditional occupations and, an important precursor, to increase girls' computer participation.

Equity and technology work is an excellent vantage point from which to make observations about the state of sex equity in our schools, focusing as it does on academic courses (computers, science, and math), career exploration and preparation, and employment issues for girls and women. This work has taken me into elementary schools, junior high and middle schools, high schools, and postsecondary community colleges, technical institutes, and vocational/technical schools. I have worked with – and listened to – students (children to adults), classroom teachers, administrators, counselors, recruitment and placement staff, and employers; researchers and analysts, policy developers, and government officials.

This chapter then, is a report from the front lines, from someone who 'translates' theoretical education research into programs and materials that are used in schools for enabling girls and women to lead lives of self-respect and economic self-sufficiency. I'll describe some of the lessons I've learned, the perplexities I have, and the answers I wish theoretical researchers could give me to pass on.

★ ★ ★

A recent incident provides the context for this chapter. A high school history teacher invited me to teach a lesson on women in modern society to his students. After the class I showed him the material I had brought with me on women in the labor force, housework, earnings, women in politics, science, and business, and more. I showed him the figures on women and technology occupations: 7 per cent of engineers, 33 per cent of systems analysts, 8 per cent of physicists and astronomers, 11 per cent of geologists, 35 per cent of science technicians, 4 per cent of airplane pilots. I showed him how men outearned women in every case (US Department of Labor, 1987). He seemed pleased to have all this information, saying he would use it in his classes.

Suddenly, he looked up and exclaimed with great consternation: 'Hold it, I think I'm getting the picture. You're not talking about equality of opportunity. You're talking about equality of results!' It is a profoundly important distinction.

Behind what he said is a conflict at the heart of the historic American ideal of equality of opportunity, our conviction that like Horatio Alger, each of us can rise as high as our talent permits. Recognizing that this ideal was gravely flawed in practice, the civil rights movement of the sixties expressed itself in legislation promising that henceforth all artificial barriers to citizens' accomplishments in public life would be removed, freeing everyone to attain the best education and job she or he was capable of regardless of race, sex, national origin, or disability.

Special education and employment programs for groups at the bottom of the national scale were initially approved as a means of dismantling the artificial barriers of discrimination. After a decade or two of civil rights legislation and special programs, equality of opportunity is now widely perceived to be a reality. Any remaining differences in educational, occupational or economic attainments among individuals or groups are seen by many as due to inborn factors which are unchangeable, their outcomes simply a fact of life. Any further attempts to raise the attainment level of underachieving groups is now given the pejorative term 'social engineering', meaning the artificial enhancement of an undeserving group usually at the expense of a deserving one. This is where the consternation in the teacher's voice came from.

The premise of his analysis is that males and females (in this case) are innately and genetically different in ways that extend far beyond our reproductive system. People believe the premise because there is plenty of 'evidence' for it: in the aggregate, males are interested in computers and females are not, males are good with machines and females are not, the world's great scientists and mathematicians have been male and not female, and so forth. However, the difficulty with the premise of innate inequality is that it is unprovable: we have not nor will we ever observe samples of male and female children grow from birth to maturity without any environmental influences whatsoever.

I freely admit that my assumption that females and males are, in the aggregate, equal in their abilities is just as unprovable. It is precisely the unprovability that makes me assume it. After all, if males and females are unequal at birth and we try to make them equal as adults, all we have done is given ourselves useless trouble. If, however, they are inherently equal at birth and we permit environmental conditions to make them unequal as adults, we have committed a great injustice. We are therefore obliged to assume that equality of results is the norm; special efforts and programs designed to equalize male and female achievement in technology are thus necessary for as long as it takes.

To my mind, equity is what we do to achieve equality of outcomes. The process of equity is quite straightforward: **awareness** of a sex imbalance to the detriment of girls and women, **concern** about it, **action** to correct it, and **results** that eliminate it, thus achieving equality – of educational, occupational, and economic attainments, and therefore equality in self-fulfillment, self-reliance, and the ability to create a decent life for oneself and one's children. It is because these goals are essential that vigorous sex equity efforts in schools are critical. And because technology is the key to our economic future, equity efforts to encourage the full participation of girls and women in technology education and careers simply must be accomplished in our schools.

Nevertheless, equity is often quite difficult to carry out in schools. In this chapter I will describe some of the reasons and will suggest several areas for future inquiry that I hope will be valuable to researchers and scholars who would like to concentrate their efforts in areas most likely to bring about real improvement in women's lives.

The Legacies of History

We are who we have been. Below are some of the ways I have noticed the impact of the past on the present, with results that are not helpful in equalizing the educational and occupational potential of girls and women.

Generational Lag

In my computer equity work, I've spoken with many classroom teachers about the educational and especially the occupational value of computer knowledge and skills for girls. I've discussed the changes in the economy and the labor market and presented figures on the salary and sex differences between jobs that involve computers and those that don't. I've asked them for male/female enrollment breakdowns in elective computer classes and optional computer clubs in their own schools, and they always come up with substantial imbalances. Finally, I offer tested strategies for increasing girls' computer participation (Sanders and Stone, 1986). To my mind, the case is pretty clear.

It may be clear but frequently it's not compelling. Many teachers leave the room aware of the computer gender gap, but fewer of them are concerned about it.

It's natural to gauge the importance of an issue by the role it plays in our own lives. For example, a person who plays the stock market will pay much more attention to the Dow Jones average than someone who has no money to invest. Similarly, 50-year-old teachers have managed to grow up quite well without computers. They learned how to read, write, and do arithmetic without computer-assisted instructional software. They don't need to spend a great deal of time considering the impact of computers on their future careers — they already have careers which don't require computer skill. Their districts may be spending fortunes on computer hardware and software and they may be officially 'encouraged' to learn how to use it all, but they know they will not be fired if they don't. Computers are obviously not a burning personal issue for many classroom teachers.

Their students, however, will live in a society in which technology plays a vastly more pervasive role than it does today. Communications, health care, finances, entertainment, production, consumption — all will be increasingly affected by technology. In ways that we cannot imagine today, tomorrow's adults will need to be technologically literate as citizens and technologically skilled as workers.

If I am correct in my conjecture that teachers who live quite comfortably without computers and other modern technology are the least likely to encourage girls' computer use, does it follow that a substantial introduction of technology into their personal lives would have a positive effect on their motivation to achieve computer equity?

The Comfort of the Familiar

In the course of a project to determine why so few girls were enrolled in a Northeastern city's predominantly male vocational programs, I interviewed a man who had been teaching high school auto mechanics for fifteen years. He was articulate and open as he explained to me why he didn't want girls in his course.

> After all this time in the classroom, many of the skills I've developed are almost automatic. I know how to talk to a guy, what words to use with him and what tone to take. I know how to correct him and when to get firm with him. I can put my hand on his shoulder when I'm looking at what he's doing. It's all very friendly and comfortable. But none of this came naturally when I first started teaching. I remember how awkward and uncertain I was then, and all the mistakes I made in these things. That was the worst part of the job. If I had to teach girls now, I'd have to relearn all that — you can't talk to a girl like you do a boy, you can't touch her the way you can touch a boy. I'll tell you honestly: I don't want girls here because I don't want to feel like a novice teacher again.

Anyone who has ever taught, including me, knows exactly what he means and sympathizes, but his insistence on not having to feel like a novice teacher again helps to keep girls out of his class. Auto mechanics earn a lot more money than secretaries.

It's Old Hat By Now

Title IX was passed in 1972 and took effect a few years later. By the late 1970s, school districts routinely had their teachers attend in-service sessions on sex equity in curriculum, access to programs of study, athletics, counseling, vocational education, and other areas. Title IX reinforced the impact of the 1964 Civil Rights Act, in which Title IV provided federal assistance to support the sex desegregation of public schools and Title VI prohibited discrimination in employment on the basis of sex, covering school employees among others. Since then, the Women's Educational Equity Act in 1974, the Career Education Incentive Act and the Vocational

Education Act in 1976, and the Carl Perkins Vocational Education Act in 1984 were passed, all of which contain sex equity provisions. Thirteen states have passed their own sex equity in education laws as well. During the same period and continuing into the present, the Supreme Court upheld various laws forbidding sex discrimination in education and employment.

By the late 1980s, it would be hard to find an educator who has not been exposed, in all likelihood repeatedly, to the issues and requirements of sex equity in education. What is the response of educators to the sex equity advocate who tells them that nearly twice as many boys than girls take calculus and physics in high school (Malcom, 1984), and that 40 per cent of women are concentrated in ten relatively low-paid occupational fields (Women's Bureau, 1986)? 'It's an old issue, move on to something else!'

New Converts are All Alike

Sex equity in education is a delicate topic. It raises the most personal of issues in each of us: how we feel about ourselves and the opposite sex, our role in the world, how we bring up our children. It is understandable that educators don't exactly welcome upheaval in these areas. However, I and other sex equity advocates may have contributed to the problem of sex bias in the schools years ago when we were new converts to the women's movement.

We were angry because we saw so clearly the myriad ways that schools mirrored and institutionalized sex bias and sex discrimination — the readers that showed little boys exploring and little girls waiting, the math texts that had boys attempting to solve velocity problems and girls attempting to solve recipe problems, the assignment of boys to Industrial Arts and girls to Home Economics, the much higher athletics budgets for boys' teams than girls' teams, and on and on.

In the heyday of schools' attention to the sex equity issue in the mid- to late 1970s, many sex equity trainers fell into the new-convert trap: our passion and our anger at the injustices came through clearly to the teachers who were required to attend these in-service sessions. With hindsight, the result was predictable. Since no one likes to be yelled at or blamed for oppressing poor defenseless little girls, teachers who had been neutral about sex equity distanced themselves from it, and teachers who had been actively sexist found in their resentment justification for being so.

Any sex equity trainer working in the schools today must remember that some groups of educators, particularly those attending mandatory sessions, may be angry before the workshop even begins. On the basis of past experience with an accusatory trainer (or because they have a guilty conscience!), they're probably expecting us to call them bigots and point out their faults one by one, even faults committed by textbook publishers or parents or television or Richard Scarry in his sexist children's books. This means that a sizable amount of time must be spent defusing their resentment before we can hope to convey our message.

Sex-Biased Attitudes

While it's nice to say that educators are entitled to all the sexist attitudes they want as long as their behavior with students is sex-fair, in reality attitudes tend to control behavior. Here are some of the ways it happens.

Don't Lift That Stool!

Teachers generally believe that sex bias is overt and easily recognizable – the counselor who says 'A pretty girl like you doesn't need to take calculus', or the industrial engineering instructor who makes a pass at the only woman in the class. Since they rarely, if ever, witness such scenes or even hear about them and they know they haven't done such things themselves, some teachers don't believe sex equity advocates when they say that sex bias occurs all the time.

This is perfectly illustrated by one of my favorite cartoons. (p. 165)

This may be funny, but it's no joke. For the most part, sex bias is in fact the daily accumulation of all the individually trivial references to lady-like behavior and fiddling with one's hair and lifting stools. It is when only boys are computer assistants, and when teachers make more eye contact with boys than girls when referring to technology, and when female teachers exclaim prettily, 'I just have no mechanical sense!'

Only recently a friend told me about just such an incident. Her daughter, a high school senior, had after much hesitation chosen to take advanced physics rather than advanced biology. She came home from the first day of school very upset. 'I'm the only girl in the class, Mom. I hate it! And after class a bunch of the guys and I were walking down the hall when we ran into our physics teacher from last year. He called out, "Well, here's the advanced physics group – and here's the advanced physics groupette!" I don't think I can stick it out, Mom.' I can't believe

Reprinted from *Equal Play* (1984), **V,** 1, p. 9.

the teacher intended to pressure this girl to drop the course, but nevertheless that's what he was doing.

These things happen every day, in every school. We need better ways to make educators aware of the small, undramatic sex-biased interactions that are quite sufficient to keep girls from pursuing, and finally feeling, any interest in technology.

So Far and No Further

The history teacher I mentioned earlier taught at an urban science magnet high school. In earlier conversations to make arrangements for the class I was to teach, he impressed me as someone who was aware of educational and occupational sex inequities and who was committed to alerting his students to this 'real' world.

The lesson I prepared started off with the students' reports on the research projects I had asked the teacher to assign beforehand, figures on the male/female situation in that school. Sure enough: advanced computer science, three girls and eleven boys; senior math team, four girls and twenty-six boys; advanced physics, two girls and seventeen boys. Of the physics and chemistry teachers, two were women and twenty were men. Thus grounded, I went on to discuss similar imbalances in technological occupations nationally. Finally, I presented information relating to women's economic position in the labor market and the trends that make good salaries especially critical for women: the high divorce rate, the mushrooming rate of single-parent families, the inability of most men's salaries to support an entire family.

It all went fine until I pointed out that given these circumstances, it was probably unwise for a girl to plan on being a homemaker. The teacher, who had been nodding supportively up to that moment, interrupted with obvious irritation. 'I don't think you should criticize homemakers. My wife is a homemaker and she's very happy as she is.'

It is not unusual to find people supportive of sex equity only up to the point, which varies from person to person, where it starts to pinch uncomfortably close to home. How can we help them keep the personal from overshadowing the general?

The Limits of Empathy

I find very few outright sexists in the schools, very few people who truly believe girls should be raised to be barefoot and pregnant in the kitchen.

What is far more common is unintended sexism that arises from a failure of empathy — the ability to put yourself in someone else's shoes.

Sexual harassment is a good example, at least for the men. When I talk to groups of vocational educators, I usually bring up sexual harassment because it is always a potential danger in classes that have a solidly male tradition. They have no trouble with the more obvious manifestations — a teacher promising an A if the female student will sleep with him, or outright physical assault. Most sexual harassment, however, consists of much more subtle behavior: leering glances, sexy 'jokes', comments about a woman's clothes or body, or pinups on the wall, which emphasizes a student's or a worker's sex rather than her work.

This was clear in a report by the female graduate students and research staff at MIT's Laboratories for Computer Science and Artificial Intelligence, in which they describe the specifics of the sexual harassment they confronted daily — patronizing behavior, obscenities, unwanted sexual attention, and more — that caused the relatively few women in the labs much pain and stress, and deprived them of the education their male peers received (MIT Computer Science Female Graduate Students and Research Staff, 1983).

It is very hard for most men to realize that the accumulation of small incidents of unwelcome sexual attention can do just as much damage to a woman and to the classroom or work environment as the more physical kind. I have tried for years to figure out a way to simulate sexual harassment in a workshop setting in order to convey to men how much it hurts. I haven't been able to: men are socially conditioned to welcome sexual advances from women. Because men are in control of the interaction and determine how far it will go, a sexual advance holds no threat for them. As a result, a simulation, such as a woman putting her hand on a man's thigh in an inappropriate workshop setting, is likely to derail in one of two ways. Either the man would find the contact pleasurable, obviously defeating the purpose of the exercise, or he would feel foolish, producing anger and not empathy.

Legislation or policy can only address the grosser forms of discrimination but the eradication of sex-biased attitudes, which are expressed in far more subtle ways, requires empathy. We don't know how to do this.

Selective Vision

Another way sex-biased attitudes are often revealed is that they make people see what they want to see. This pattern is very clear in the case of women preparing for nontraditional technical careers at the postsecondary level. I have found that the most common cause by far of female dropouts from these vocational programs is what I call the Introductory Course Problem.

It's the first day of the Aviation Technology 101 course. The instructor, as is his habit formed by years of teaching male students, makes frequent references to technical terms in aerodynamics and mechanics. The lone woman in the class listens hard but seems confused. On the second day, the woman and three men have dropped out. While all four have decided that they won't be able to make it through the term if they can't even understand the first day's material, the instructor is confirmed in his belief that aviation technology is not for women. The male dropouts produce no parallel conclusion.

We need to know more about how sex-biased attitudes, by means of selective vision, produce confirmatory experiences which reinforce the original sex-biased attitudes, and about how to interrupt the cycle.

The Equity Trap

It's obvious to me that since girls are socialized differently from boys, schools that want to equalize girls' and boys' academic behavior have to take sex differences into account. Many educators are now sensitive to sex differences.

This sensitivity, however, can be a big trap, and here is how it works. Let's say you are talking with teachers about girls' computer avoidance – how girls observe that it's mostly men and boys who use computers in school, at home, in the media, in video arcades, and so forth, and how they conclude that computers are a male thing. You talk about the importance of increasing girls' computer participation, for educational and especially occupational reasons.

One of two things can then happen. A teacher will triumphantly tell you that in his or her school they no longer have a computer equity problem: since many girls like to write, the faculty now encourages girls to use the computer for word processing. Or else a teacher will hear you say that an effective computer equity strategy is to use the computer for writing (which many girls really do enjoy), and triumphantly accuse you of sex bias for not suggesting spreadsheets.

One way to get out of the trap is to say that since many girls like to write, it's sensible to use writing initially to establish their interest in computers, but to go on to spreadsheets once that interest is hooked. It's also essential to remember that some girls will initially be far more interested in spreadsheets than word processing. I'm not totally satisfied with this solution, however.

I am told that there is cosmetics software on the market: you select a face shape, then you experiment with lighter or darker lipstick, eye shadow only on the eyelid or up to the eyebrow, and such. I strongly suspect that a lot of computer-avoiding adolescent girls would love to use this software, and presumably a competent teacher could move them on at some point to spreadsheets and programming. Although I do believe that all good teaching starts with where the student is and then moves her on, I admit that I can't stand the idea of using a cosmetics program, as successful as it would be, to get girls interested in computers.

The fundamental trouble is that a sex-biased society teaches girls to have sex-stereotyped interests. When we initially appeal to girls' interests in writing or, heaven forbid, cosmetics — even when the appeal is a ploy to get them eventually to move on to spreadsheets and programming — are we buttressing the very sex-biased attitudes we are trying to eliminate? If so, then we must propose spreadsheets and programming directly, thus bypassing the traditionally female, stereotyped interests. But most girls won't be interested in these traditionally male computer activities, thus buttressing their computer avoidance. Where is the way out of the equity trap?

The Way Schools Operate Hinders Equity

Into this category I place a number of situations which, although they may have nothing to do with sex equity *per se*, nevertheless hinder or prevent equitable treatment of girls and women in school.

Acute Versus Chronic

Sex equity progress is often hindered because equity is only one of many programs, initiatives and concerns that schools would like to address: beef up the library, get more computer hardware, revise the language arts curriculum, expand the health services, create a family life course, get new uniforms for the football team, patch the roof, hire more science teachers, develop a better discipline policy, and on and on. Since most public schools are underfunded in relation to what the state and the parents expect them to accomplish, it is inevitable that the 'squeaky wheel' rule prevails and the most acute or crisis-laden needs are addressed first.

Equity in technology is in a sense a negative issue, an issue about what isn't rather than what is. Since the class is completely enrolled (usually with males) and it has a teacher (usually a male), and especially since girls (who are socialized to believe that technology is something men do) avoid technology courses themselves and thus don't complain about the imbalance, there is no squeaky wheel to be heard. It is hard to perceive such a quiescent and superficially acceptable situation as a problem, especially compared to a roof that leaks and parental complaints about outdated lab equipment.

To exacerbate the difficulty, it takes no effort to maintain the imbalanced enrollments and faculty sex ratio while it may take substantial time, energy, and possibly money to balance them. How do we challenge the *status quo* here?

It Doesn't Always Trickle Down

When I worked with teams of junior high classroom teachers and administrators to develop strategies for encouraging greater computer use by girls, they reasoned that it was necessary for teachers and parents to become familiar with computers first in order to encourage girls to do so. Accordingly they carried out a variety of formal and informal sessions with both groups to teach them how to use computers, stressing the need for special encouragement for girls.

The indirect strategies turned out to have very little effect on girls' computer use, compared with others that targeted girls directly (Sanders, 1987). Upon reflection, I realized that the teachers and parents got sidetracked before their new computer knowledge ever reached girls. In one pattern, the adults became so enamored of the technology for their own word processing or spreadsheet needs that they forgot about encouraging the girls. In another pattern, especially frequent among teachers, adults felt they had to be 'expert' before actually teaching computing to their female (and male) students, and kept delaying until they were ready. Naturally, this can take a very long time.

When sex equity progress depends on increasing teachers' skills or changing their behavior, it often falls into the trap of assuming that the new skills or behavior will be conveyed to the students, which in turn will lead to the desired changes in student behavior, such as higher female enrollment and completion of computer electives. Without built-in plans and schedules for the adult-to-student transmission, the assumption isn't always justified.

Last in Line

The continued employment of people who teach elective courses or programs of study depends on continued enrollment in the courses or programs they teach. The threat of losing one's job because of declining enrollments is one of the most potent motivators I know for faculty members who teach male-intensive science and technology courses to become committed to increasing the enrollment of girls or women.

The converse, unfortunately, is also true. When enrollments are high — when 'the students are hanging from the rafters', as one electronics instructor told me — equity motivation is low. When there is inability or refusal to expand capacity by increasing facilities and/or hiring more instructors, educators can become actively opposed to the recruitment of women because they see it as reducing the number of men's places, the places they see men as having a kind of squatter's right to.

I haven't yet figured out an argument that is compelling enough to override the tendency to retrench equity efforts when male enrollments are high.

The Career Counselor Filter

Even the most conscientious career counselor cannot discuss all 450 or so occupations listed by the US Department of Labor (US Department of Labor, 1986) with a student who is seeking career guidance. Of necessity, counselors must emphasize those that seem most appropriate for the student and bypass the others. Sex stereotyping is an efficient way to reduce the number of career options by half. This tendency may be even more pronounced in high school than at the postsecondary level because the higher counselor-or-student ratio would seem to put a premium on efficiency (or at least speed) in the counseling process.

Sometimes career counselors feel regretfully obliged to present sex-stereotyped options to students because of special circumstances in the students' lives. I have often seen this in programs that serve displaced homemakers (women who have been homemakers for many years but are forced to enter the labor market due to divorce or their husbands' disability or death). Counselors tend to steer a displaced homemaker into vocational programs that are traditionally female, usually clerical, partly because of the large demand for clerical workers but also because counselors see nontraditional programs as too stressful for her at this point in her life. Supporting a family on a clerical salary of $12,000 a year must be even more stressful, but the urgency of a displaced homemaker's needs induces counselors to see only short-term solutions.

Counselors are the presumed experts about careers, so the information they provide tends to be seen as authoritative. When counselors fail to provide a woman with information about technical careers or when they steer her away from these careers out of concern for what they see as her best interests, occupational segregation is maintained.

The consequences of counselors' influence was decisively demonstrated by Lucy Sells (Sells, 1976) when she reported on a survey of high school students admitted to the University of California at Berkeley. Forty-three per cent of the young men and an astounding 92 per cent of the young women had taken so little high school math that they had effectively disqualified themselves from all fields except the humanities, music, social work, guidance and counseling, and elementary education. Sells called mathematics 'the critical filter', a memorable phrase that distills what happens when career counselors fail to encourage (let alone actively discourage) girls from preparing for careers in math, science, and technology.

The Lack of Followthrough and Followup

One of the reasons we often accomplish relatively little from all the time and effort we spend on educational innovation is that provision for followthrough is rarely made. This year's successful school program is displaced by next year's new program: educators don't have enough time to do both of them well and the current one usually has a more insistent constituency. In this way the benefits of the successful program stop with this year's students.

Sometimes good programs are dropped for other reasons as well. A junior high school implemented a highly successful computer equity program one year, doubling the number of girls who regularly came to use the school computers. The teacher who was the driving force behind the effort had a rather experimental turn of mind: the following year she decided to carry out no computer equity strategies at all to see what would happen. What happened was that girls' computer use declined back to its original low level.

Beyond dropping promising programs, the followthrough problem also relates to the fact that children move on through school. Next year's eighth grade treacher may not care as much about Katie's interest in computers as her seventh grade teacher does. When Katie enters ninth grade in the high school building, those teachers may not even be aware that computer equity is an issue. Without active and continued encouragement from all her teachers during the years when traditional sex-role influences are at their most powerful, Katie may well decide to leave the computers to boys after all.

Educational program development grants rarely include funds for longitudinal followup. I am not alone in using control groups to test the effectiveness of a model program rather than comparison over time because of funding constraints. As a result, we know when new programs are effective in the short run but often have no idea whether the effect remains or dissipates in time.

While the lack of followthrough and followup is a pervasive problem for educational research, it is more critical for equity research. Girls constantly receive messages from society – parents, peers, teachers, the media – that technical subjects and careers are more appropriate for males. Without followthrough or continued active encouragement, society's male-only message ceases to be counteracted and many girls are likely to take the path of least resistance. Without followup, we cannot document that this is happening.

Value, Choice and Responsibility

Beyond the legacies of history, sex-biased attitudes, and school operations, I would like to conclude my discussion of equity and technology with several broader issues of value, choice, and responsibility.

The Researcher Determines the Research

In 1986 the National Science Foundation published *Women and Minorities in Science and Engineering*. The various education sections in the book-length report range from 'Precollege Preparation' through 'Postdoctoral Appointments'. In July 1987 a national conference was held on Women in Science and Engineering.[1] All the sessions were devoted to exploring why so few women have careers at the professional level of science and engineering fields.

Technicians – who usually have a one-year postsecondary certificate or a two-year associate's degree – undoubtedly work in science and engineering as well, but very little research focuses on them. It should. Chemical technicians are only 30 per cent female. Among electrical/electronic technicians, 15 per cent are women. There are so few female mechanical engineering technicians that the table shows them as

'–'. On the average, only one out of five science and engineering technicians is a woman (US Department of Labor, 1987).

I wonder if the reason doesn't lie at least in part with researchers themselves. Being highly educated people, perhaps researchers are more interested in research subjects who are most like themselves: people who are preparing for professional careers or who have doctorates or at least master's degrees. Researchers have also been interested in women in the trades: are blue-collar women seen as exotic, their work tasks and environments fascinatingly different from those of people whose tools are mundane books and paper? Are technicians of little interest to researchers because their status is seen as inferior to professional scientists and engineers – the traditionally female subordinate position, making feminist researchers uncomfortable and others unimpressed?

The relative lack of research (or indeed, attention from the women's movement in general) into sub-professional science and engineering fields means that these occupations are less visible, and thus less accessible, to women who cannot spend years in professional preparation and many thousands of dollars for tuition – in other words, to the vast majority of women who are working and earning low salaries as secretaries, dental hygienists, and cosmetologists. It also means that there is less pressure on high schools, community colleges, technical institutes, and vocational/technical schools to make the enrollment and retention of women in male-intensive programs a high priority. The technician level of science and engineering is a new frontier for equity researchers.

Required Versus Optional

Beyond the required introductory course of a few weeks to a year that is usually given in the junior high grades, computer instruction is offered on an optional basis thereafter. Preparation for careers in technology at any level is also elective. The result of all this free choice is that girls take fewer computer courses than boys do (Becker, 1986), repeating the pattern we have seen in math and science.

After twenty years or so of research, we know a great deal about why so many girls drop math and science as soon as these courses are no longer required. Some girls are overtly or subtly discouraged by teachers, counselors, parents, and friends. Many, I suspect, are neither discouraged or encouraged but are allowed to fulfill the societal expectation that math, science, and technology are male endeavors – when the deck is stacked, no effort is required to reach the predictable outcome.

The unbalanced outcome forces us to reconsider the issue of required versus optional courses. We do not allow children to choose between reading and recess because, despite their probable preference for recess, we know that reading skills are essential to all children if they are to function in our society. On the other hand, advanced biology and music composition are courses that develop interests and skills that vary from person to person, and as such are properly elective.

Where should computer study be placed on this spectrum? If we believe that computer ability is essential – occupationally, and in terms of one's ability to understand and participate in the world around us – for a fully functioning adult in the first half of the twenty-first century, then a semester's course in the seventh grade is grossly inadequate. If we believe that most people will be able to get along just fine without any knowledge of computers, then why do we require children to study computers at all?

This fence-straddling is perhaps inevitable, given the newness of computers and the extremely rapid changes technology has made in our lives. At some point, however, we will have to come down on one side or the other of the question. Until then the computer equity issue will remain one of personal philosophy: since boys' society-taught enthusiasm for the computer leads them to take more computer courses, to what extent do we have an obligation to ensure that girls obtain computer knowledge and skills on a par with boys?

Swimming Up Streams

In asking schools to promote educational and occupational equity for girls and women, we are asking them to operate in a manner that runs counter to the sexism that permeates all of society. Parents call their newborn son 'the big guy' and their newborn daughter 'the little doll'. Toy doctor kits show boys on the package; toy nurse kits show girls. Children's books and television programs present boys who have adventures and girls who admire the boys who have adventures. In elementary school kids have women teachers. They read in their textbooks about more men than women and more boys than girls. The authoritative voice-overs in TV commercials are male. The principal is male. Mommy is the parent who reminds the kids to take their lunch money. And this is only the world of *children* – the sexism continues into the adult world, perhaps more subtly but no less powerfully.

This is not to blame anyone. Because society has been sexist, it inevitably leaves us a sexist legacy: adults can only teach children what they know themselves.

The sex equity movement is built on the belief that beyond simple justice, our society can no longer afford sexism (if it ever could). Equity promotes the equal participation of girls and women in studies and jobs because we are unwilling to discard half of our talent pool and because unfulfilled, dissatisfied women benefit no one.

But to accomplish equity – in this case, to encourage girls' interest in and involvement with computers, to encourage girls and women to enter technology careers – schools swim against the current of many streams. For every teacher who insists that girls become knowledgeable about computers, girls are receiving the constant message from television, the print media, families, friends, other teachers, even the video arcades, that computers are really for males. The pull of all these forces, though often passive, is strong. Educators who resist them need a great deal of support, and where is it to be found?

Implications for Future Research

Equity practitioners such as myself use research constantly. It informs the programs and materials we develop for schools, the approaches we take, the things we look out for, sometimes the ammunition we use. Here is some of the research I find myself wishing were available.

First, we need more research about educators. In my experience, the national awareness of the need for equity in the sixties and early seventies, the legislative requirements, and the years of in-service workshops have eliminated most of the really egregious manifestations of sexism. Outright sexist bigotry in schools is no longer socially acceptable. Sexism, however, has not disappeared but merely gone underground. It is not at all unusual to find sex-biased educators who are unaware that their attitudes lead to biased behavior with students, which in turn leads inevitably to sex-discriminatory outcomes.

We need to know more about educators' attitudes, which I realize are difficult to assess accurately. To what extent do sex equity attitudes relate to educators' personal and family lives – whether they have daughters, what their family history is, what their political and social concerns are, even whether they have computers or VCRs at home? What makes one teacher enthusiastic about computers while another becomes wary and still another remains indifferent? Does fear or resentment of technology have an effect on their equity attitudes? To what extent are educators' equity attitudes influenced by those of their peers? their superiors?

We also need to know more about changing sex-biased attitudes. As a simple first step, how much attention is really paid to equity and technology, or any kind of equity, in teacher-training institutions? What is the relation of in-service sessions about equity to actual increases in female enrollment in computer and science courses? Comparing the effects of strong equity policy requirements in a school or district, the provision of equity information to educators, and the development of active empathy in educators, which approach is most effective in the short term? the long term? What are the motivations that are most effective for awakening an active concern about equity and technology?

Next, we need more research on parents. To what extent does the effect on girls of parental support, discouragement, or indifference about technology interests and careers for their daughters vary with the age of the daughter? When parents encourage daughters' computer involvement from a very young age, does the positive influence persist through adolescence despite the male/computer message that intensifies during those years? How important is parents' own computer knowledge for girls' computer participation? Is there a significant difference between the computer knowledge of fathers and mothers in terms of the impact on girls? If fathers are more influential, are girls in single-parent families doubly disadvantaged?

Third, we need more research on schools. Is there a difference in the institutionalization of a computer equity effort or a program to enroll more women in male-intensive technology vocational programs – the followthrough – when leadership is provided by the head of the school versus faculty members? What is the effect of a strong computer *education* (as opposed to computer *equity*) policy in a school district on the computer participation of girls? If the effect is small, what does this say about the need for and effectiveness of a strong district policy specifically on computer *equity*? If a successful computer equity program is carried out in the upper elementary grades and then dropped, how many years are its effects likely to last with girls thereafter? How does this compare with a program at the junior high level, or the high school level? What school environment factors are most effective in making a faculty proactive about equity? All other things being equal, do girls and women receive more information about nontraditional careers in the technologies from counselors who have lower caseloads and therefore more time to spend with each student?

Finally, we need more research on girls themselves. How much effect does career expectation have on adolescent girls' computer use? What about girls who have no specific career ideas at that point? Which specific computer experiences and skills offered to girls in school maximize the likelihood that they will choose technology careers? Do adolescent girls who are positive about and actively involved with computers differ in terms of sex role attitudes from girls who shun computers? We know that girlfriends are highly influential with adolescent girls (Sanders and Stone, 1986), but how much and what kind of influence do boys have on their technology involvement? Does boys' influence on girls' technology involvement vary with age? We know that having a female computer teacher is not, in and of itself, a strong predictor of high computer participation among girls (Sanders and Stone, 1986); is exposure to non-teacher role models — women in technology careers, for example, or women students preparing for technology careers, more effective?

These are just some of the questions whose answers sex equity advocates such as myself would like to have. With them we can do a better job of helping educators to recognize that sex inequity has causes which lie in the past but have present consequences, such as parents who buy computers for their little boys but not for their little girls, or causes which are subtle but have powerful effects, such as teachers who call on boys for interpretive answers but girls for fact answers (Sadker *et al.*, 1982). We can better help educators to refuse to accept the stacked deck, refuse to permit girls and women to say 'no thanks' to technology just because the stereotype leads them to say it. Finally, we can better help educators to insist on nothing less than equity: determined, persistent efforts to overcome the consequences of sex bias, so that every single one of us has a real shot at being superior.

Notes

1 All labor market statistics in this chapter are drawn from US Department of Labor, 1984, Table A-26, 'Usual Weekly Earnings of Employed Wage and Salary Workers Who Usually Work Full-Time, by Detailed (3-Digit Code) Occupation and Sex'.

2 For information on the proceedings of this conference, contact the Office of Opportunities in Science, American Association for the Advancement of Science, 1333 H Street, N.W., Washington DC 20005.

References

BECKER, H. J. (1986) 'Instructional uses of computers: Reports from the 1985 National Survey', Baltimore, MD: Center for Social Organization of Schools, The Johns Hopkins University, Issue No. 2, August.

MALCOM, S. M. (1984) *Equity and Excellence: Compatible Goals*, Washington, DC: American Association for the Advancement of Science.

MIT COMPUTER SCIENCE FEMALE GRADUATE STUDENTS AND RESEARCH STAFF (1983) *Barriers to Equality in Academia: Women in Computer Science at MIT*, Cambridge, MA: Massachusetts Institute of Technology.

SADKER, M. P. and D. M., BAUCHNER, J. and HERGERT, L. (1982) *Promoting Effectiveness in Classroom Instruction*, Andover, MA: The Network.

SANDERS, J. (1987) 'Closing the computer gender gap in school', in *Contributions to the Fourth GASAT Conference* (Girls and Science and Technology). Ann Arbor, MI: pp. 305–16.

SANDERS, J. and STONE, A. (1986) *The Neuter Computer: Computers for Girls and Boys*. New York: Neal-Schuman Publishers. Available from Women's Action Alliance, 370 Lexington Avenue, New York, NY 10017.

SELLS, L. (1976) 'The mathematics filter and the education of women and minorities'. *ERIC Reports*.

US DEPARTMENT OF LABOR Bureau of Labor Statistics (1984), *Tabulations from the Current Population Survey, 1984 annual averages*. Washington, DC: US Government Printing Office.

US DEPARTMENT OF LABOR (1986) *Dictionary of Occupational Titles*, US Government Printing Office.

Women in Science and Engineering. Washington, DC: National Science Foundation, 1986.

WOMEN'S BUREAU, US DEPARTMENT OF LABOR (1986) *Facts on Women Workers*, Washington, DC: US Government Printing Office.

Index

divergent thinking: mathematics 155